DILEMMAS OF TRANSITION:
THE ENVIRONMENT, DEMOCRACY AND
ECONOMIC REFORM IN EAST CENTRAL EUROPE

Of Related Interest

A GREEN DIMENSION FOR THE EUROPEAN COMMUNITY
Political Issues and Processes
edited by David Judge

SUSTAINABLE DEVELOPMENT IN WESTERN EUROPE
Coming to Terms with Agenda 21
edited by Tim O'Riordan and Heather Voisey

RIO: UNRAVELLING THE CONSEQUENCES
edited by Caroline Thomas

NETWORKS FOR WATER POLICY
A Comparative Perspective
edited by H. Bressers, L.J. O'Toole, Jr. and J. Richardson

ECOLOGY AND DEMOCRACY
edited by Freya Mathews

DILEMMAS OF TRANSITION
The Environment, Democracy and Economic Reform in East Central Europe

edited by

SUSAN BAKER
and
PETR JEHLIČKA

FRANK CASS
LONDON • PORTLAND, OR

First published in 1998 in Great Britain by
FRANK CASS PUBLISHERS
Newbury House, 900 Eastern Avenue,
London, IG2 7HH, England

and in the United States of America by
FRANK CASS PUBLISHERS
c/o ISBS
5804 N.E. Hassalo Street
Portland, Oregon 97213-3644

Website: http://www.frankcass.com

British Library Cataloguing in Publication Data

Dilemmas of transition : the environment, democracy and
economic reform in East Central Europe
1. Environmental economics – Europe, Central 2. Democracy –
Europe, Central 3. Post-communism – Europe, Central
4. Europe, Central – Economic conditions
I. Baker, Susan II. Jehlička, Petr
330/9'43'009049

ISBN 0 7146 4764 0 (cloth)
ISBN 0 7146 4310 6 (paper)

Library of Congress Cataloging in Publication Data

Dilemmas of transition : the environment, democracy and economic
reform in East Central Europe / edited by Susan Baker and Petr
Jehlička.
        p.   cm.
    "Special issue of the journal Environmental politics v. 7, no. 1,
1998."
    Includes bibliographical references and index.
    ISBN 0-7146-4764-0 (cloth). – ISBN 0-7146-4310-6 (pbk.)
    1. Environmental policy – Europe, Eastern. 2. Environmental
policy – Europe, Eastern – Cass studies. 3. Europe, Eastern – Economic
policy – 1989– 4. Democracy – Europe, Eastern. 5. European Union
countries – foreign relations – Europe, Eastern. 6. Europe, Eastern–
Foreign relations – European Union countries. I. Baker, Susan.
II. Jehlička, petr. 1965–   .
GE190.E852D55   1998   98-17800
363.7'00947–dc21   CIP

This group of studies first appeared in a Special Issue: 'Dilemmas of Transition: The
Environment, Democracy and Economic Reform in East Central Europe' of
Environmental Politics (ISSN 0964-4016) 7/1 Spring 1998 published by Frank Cass.

Printed in Great Britain by Antony Rowe Ltd., Chippenham, Wiltshire

Contents

Dilemmas of Transition:
The Environment, Democracy and
Economic Reform in East Central Europe –
An Introduction

SUSAN BAKER and PETR JEHLIČKA

The Empirical Focus

This collection of essays* is concerned with the impact of the twin processes of democratisation and marketisation on the environment in a number of countries from the former Soviet bloc. There are three environmental matters which we investigated: how the twin processes of change have effected (1) the physical environment; (2) the expression of environmental interests; and (3) the effectiveness of environmental management policies.

We began with a search for a common term to refer to the countries under study. 'Eastern Europe' was a term once in common use to refer to European countries under Soviet-dominated Communist regimes. However, as Tellegen [*1996*] has pointed out, it now seems odd to refer to the very small part of Europe that lies west of the former Iron Curtain as 'Western Europe' and to use the term 'Eastern Europe' to refer to the immense area between Germany and Asian Russia. We accept Tellegen's point that clearly there is need to differentiate. Furthermore, we believe that the term Eastern Europe is too associated with the period of Soviet rule to be useful for discussion of the processes of change these countries are undergoing in the period of post-Communist transition.

In keeping with the current trend, we have adopted the term East Central Europe (ECE) to refer to the countries under study here. The countries that comprise ECE are Poland, the Czech and Slovak Republics, Hungary, Romania, Bulgaria, the former East Germany, Albania and the former Yugoslavia (now broken into Slovenia, Croatia, Bosnia-Herzegovina, Macedonia and the rump of Yugoslavia, Serbia and Montenegro). The Baltic countries of Estonia, Latvia and Lithuania are excluded from this category, on the grounds that they were part of the USSR itself and had

---

* This volume is divided into two parts. Part I explores the framework within which environmental policy in ECE countries is situated. Part II presents a number of country studies.

consequently rather different post-war histories..

Not all of the countries that we categorise as comprising ECE are, however, covered in this volume. Our choice is limited by our research focus. In particular, it is limited by the existence of a secondary aim for this volume, namely to analyse the involvement of the West, in particular the European Union (EU), in the transformation process in ECE countries. To capture this influence, we have chosen to focus on those ECE countries who are actively involved in seeking membership of the EU and for whom the EU has responded positively, albeit at times cautiously.

First, there are European post-Communist countries in which the process of democratisation, after an initial promising start, has been slowed down or even reversed. The democratic character of Albania and several succession states of the other former Yugoslavia – Serbia and Montenegro, Croatia as well as war-torn Bosnia–Herzegovina – hold few democratic credentials. This renders their effort to join Western European organisations, such as the EU, meaningless unless fundamental changes are made. This does not hold true for Slovenia, but it has been excluded from analysis because of the fragile nature of the political situation in the former Yugoslavia.

This process of elimination left us with a group of six countries – Poland, the Czech Republic, Slovakia, Hungary, Romania and Bulgaria – to be examined. All were independent countries in the post-war period, with the exception of Czechoslovakia which peacefully divided into Slovakia and the Czech Republic. They were all members of the Warsaw Pact and the Council for Mutual Economic Assistance (Comecon). In their post-1989 history they have engaged in a process of political and economic reform, including democratisation and marketisation, albeit with different speeds and priorities. Although the timing within which full membership will be gained differs among them, all six countries are now Associate Members of the European Union, as well as candidates for NATO membership.

While using a collective term to cover the whole area, the editors are aware that very large differences exist among the countries covered by the term ECE. Historically, country experiences differ widely, with Bulgaria, for example, under Ottoman rule while further north the influence of the Habsburg Empire shaped the emergence of today's states. There were also different experiences under Communism, obscured by the fact that during this period the West saw only a uniformity in the region because of its strategic definition of Eastern Europe as the enemy. This masked large differences, not least in term of industrialisation (Waller).* The region is marked by religious diversity, with Roman Catholic Poland, Orthodox Bulgaria and Islamic Albania, as well as linguistic diversity and ethnic

---

* References to contributions in this volume appear within parentheses.

divisions. Yet, despite this diversity, the authors believe that the region has sufficient similarities to justify this comparative project. Countries in this region have a shared experience of Communism and life under Soviet influence, resulting in a centralised state and weak civil society. Since 1989 all have carried out a process of transition to marketisation and democratisation. It is, as Waller and Millard have pointed out, their *shared* Communist experience that justifies the collective use of the term for societies whose histories before the Communist takeover were very varied and whose post-Communist experiences are leading to quite marked divergences [*Waller and Millard, 1992: 164*].

The Transition Process

Having established the empirical boundaries of our focus and agreed terminology, the next step is to elaborate more clearly what was meant by the transition process, and in particular, the twin processes of democratisation and marketisation. It is widely recognised that the process of transition is occurring at different speeds and with different priorities within the ECE countries. This is because of the complexity of issues involved in that transition, including a shift to constitutional democracy, the construction of a market economy, state building and the development of civil society. This is combined with the need to come to terms with the Communist past, through restitution and, at times, retribution. While our main focus in this volume is on the first two of these changes, namely democratisation and marketisation, we have consistently found that account has to be taken of the wider social and political processes of transformation within which democratisation and marketisation are embedded.

A working definition of democracy has proved useful in analysing the findings of the many contributions to this volume. By democratisation we understand a shift from one-party rule to pluralist, multi-party parliamentary systems with democratically elected and accountable government. The process of democratisation requires abandonment of the principle of state centralism in favour of far-reaching deconcentration and decentralisation of political power, which has to be exercised under the rule of law [*Hesse, 1993: iii*]. It also requires the development and nurturing of civil society.

Experiences to date have shown that the process of democratisation within ECE has had its difficulties. In Slovakia, for example, it has been turbulent and the country has recently seen a swing towards anti-reform, anti-democratic politics (Podoba). Bulgaria has shown similar tendencies towards incomplete transformation (Baker and Baumgartl). This is particularly noticeable at the subnational levels, which are important as far as the implementation of environmental policy is concerned. Other countries are experiencing high turnover rates of government. In Poland, for example, frequent changes of government have resulted in a lack of continuity of leadership at the apex (Millard). In all the countries under study here, the development of civil society has also proved difficult, alienating environmental interests from the reform process. This is discussed in greater detail below.

The process of democratisation is intimately linked with economic restructuring. It is fair to say that the stability of the democratisation process is related to the success of economic restructuring in maintaining, and eventually improving, economic well-being. Yet, at the same time, economic reform requires the rejection of the principle of unity between the polity and the economy, in such a way as to allow the emergence of distinct spheres of political and economic life. This means that reforms have to aim at the strengthening of private enterprise, the denationalisation (privatisation) of a large share of the previously state-controlled production and a substantial deregulation and liberalisation of the national economy [*Hesse, 1993: iii*].

In practice, marketisation has to be accompanied by an end to government subsidies, liberalisation of prices and the opening up of the economy to global competition. Effective marketisation, however, also needs appropriate legal and administrative frameworks within which markets can operate, including the establishment of institutions such as a central bank and enacting bankruptcy laws. Marketisation also requires changes of a more cultural nature, particularly changes in business culture, including the introduction of Western-style managerial, financial and business practices.

Marketisation has been characterised by varying degrees of commitment and success. Countries began from very different starting points. In Hungary, for example, some private enterprise was allowed after 1968, which could subsequently act as a base for the construction of the new market economy. Other countries, however, found that the collapse of the old system of central command, and in particular, the collapse of Comecon, left them weak and vulnerable, slowing down and at times even halting the shift to marketisation. Bulgaria is a case in point (Baker and Baumgartl). Marketisation has also proved politically volatile in the face of the economic harshness of the new reform regime and its accompanying social welfare losses. Faced with economic insecurity, crime, the collapse of production, unemployment and poverty, it is not surprising to find a hankering for the security of the old regimes and the rise of Communist successor parties across the region. Under these circumstances resurgent Communists 'pluck a responsive cord' when they blame the reform process and capitalist tools for their problems (Jancar-Webster).

Problems with the policy of privatisation, a key policy component in the marketisation process, mirror these wider difficulties. In Slovakia former state-owned companies have, to a large measure, been privatised into the hands of supporters of the current anti-reform regime. Here the abandonment of the Communist doctrine of the unacceptability of private property coupled with a continuation of the Communist model of industrial development has proved very problematic as far as environmental management is concerned (Podoba). In other cases privatisation has resulted in a property grab by the former *nomenklatura*, which has allowed former managers of firms to purchase state-owned enterprises (Jancar-Webster). This has strengthened the power of the old elites. This in effect weakens the ability of the economic reform process to consolidate the process of democratisation. Furthermore, it actively contributes to undermining democratisation by increasing public scepticism about the reform process itself. Such scepticism keeps public participation in political life low and civil society weak. Here participation continues to be linked with 'dirty politics' especially where 'the threshold between contamination and participation is not fully delineated' (Jancar-Webster).

Similarly, the sale of the more profitable enterprises to foreign interests has left a rump of unsellable, and often highly polluting enterprises, in state hands. These have, at times, been handed to the care of local authorities, who lack either the commitment or the expertise to manage them in an environmentally sustainable way. Furthermore, in the early years of privatisation, attention was not paid to the environmental liabilities inherited from the firm's earlier period under state control (O'Toole and Hanf; Millard). Privatisation has not always been successful, with a rise in bankruptcies as firms face the harshness of the market. In Hungary, for example, this has placed additional strains on the developing institutions of the mixed economy, as well as on the governments that are seeking to stimulate economic success (O'Toole and Hanf).

Thus, while we argue that economic reform and political change may be in the long term mutually reinforcing and, indeed, as we have argued, one may be the prerequisite for the other, in the short term there may be tensions and even outright conflicts between them (O'Toole and Hanf). What O'Toole and Hanf have found for Hungary can be applied to the region as a whole: on the one hand, marketisation is seen as the perquisite for providing the material basis for long-term social welfare and well-being; but, in the short term, privatisation has resulted in high levels of unemployment and decreased production. On the other hand, democratisation has created new political actors and new demands for the development of civil society, and new forms of co-operation and collaboration. But at present the political climate has given rise to centrifugal forces that fragment and undermine effective institutional capacity and separate different sets of actors from each other (O'Toole and Hanf). Our examination of the influence that democratisation and marketisation has had on environmental issues has recognised this wider context of conflict and tensions.

The Impact of the Transition Process on the Environment

Having delineated our empirical focus, agreed terminology and provided some detail as to the complexity of issues involved in the processes of democratisation and marketisation, attention can now turn to a more detailed examination of the environmental dimensions of our research. As was said above, there are three environmental matters which we investigated: how the twin processes of change have effected (1) the physical environment; (2) the expression of environmental interests; and (3) the effectiveness of environmental management policies.

The Physical Environment

To examine the impact of the transition process on the physical environment, contributors briefly examined the environmental legacy of Communist rule and Marxist industrial ideology. In doing so the editors are nevertheless aware that to recount the current environmental problems of ECE solely with reference to the Communist past can be misleading (Waller). This is because the economic and hence environmental impact of Soviet intervention varied considerably across the region. Furthermore, historical factors, in particular those related to the level and nature of economic development before the period of Soviet domination, has also shaped the extent and type of environmental problems currently facing individual ECE countries. Having said this, however, the environmental legacy of Communist rule does provide a convenient backdrop against which current progress in environmental management and pollution amelioration can be measured.

Ascertaining the extent of environmental damage in ECE countries is difficult [*Baker, 1996; Waller and Millard, 1992: 159*]. Despite this difficulty, commentators are agreed that there are great variations in the degree of pollution, with high pollution rates particularly noticeable in Northern Bohemia and south-western Poland. Other areas of high pollution concentration include the Black Sea and the Danube river basin. The pollution problems of these areas are, by now, well documented [*Baker, 1996*]. These environmental problems arise from the mismanagement and misuse of resources (Dragomirescu *et al.*), mismanagement being a feature of both Communist and capitalist development. On a general level the Marxist ideology that underpinned Communist rule emphasised economic growth, industrialisation and technical progress. In this world-view, nature was seen as an obstacle to technical progress, to be overcome through scientific and technical progress. While differing in emphasis, this ideology holds much in common with an Enlightenment approach, which was important in shaping the development of Western capitalism [*Baker, 1996: 139*] and which also resulted in environmental degradation in the West. Communism in Eastern Europe was not the only system to produce environmental degradation and, in this respect, the West shares much in common with its Eastern neighbours.

However, despite this similarity, the countries of ECE share a common legacy that arose as a result of their experience under Communist rule, with its centralised, planned economy. This economy was resource intensive, making highly inefficient use of energy, especially in production. This generated unique problems as far as environmental degradation and, more especially, environmental management was concerned. First, under Communism there was a dogmatic assumption that environmental damage could never be caused by the state, as it has no profit motive [*Baumgartl, 1993: 158*]: environmental damage was a product of capitalism and profit-oriented modes of production. Second, official interpretations of environmental problems were based on the premise that they were mere temporary aberrations, physical phenomena to be dealt with by the tools made available through scientific and technological advancement. They were not seen as arising from inappropriate industrial projects or unsustainable production methods. These beliefs have the combined effect of blinding the authorities to the reality of their own environmental degradation, inhibiting effective and early responses to environmental deterioration [*Baker, 1996: 140*].

In those cases where environmental damage became so severe that the state was forced to intervene, effective response was also hampered by the nature of the Communist planned economy. The system lacked flexibility, requiring top-down, command-driven approaches towards policy, including environmental policy. Furthermore, while environmental legislation was put in place in many of the ECE countries during the period of Communist rule, implementation of this legislation remained weak. A single authority was often both the source of pollution and responsible for its prevention. To add to this, environmental solutions rarely addressed the source of damage, imposing instead a (small) fine on polluters. At the factory level, it was often in a manager's interest to pay such fines, rather than to adhere to pollution-control standards and run the risk of not meeting production quotas [*Baker, 1996: 140*]. Furthermore, during the Communist regime, civil society was weak and the formation of public opinion was ruled out by Party control over the means of communication (Waller). This had the effect of limiting environmental criticism, at least up until the 1980s when the Soviet and indeed Party grip on society began to weaken.

As a consequence of this approach, countries in ECE have been left with a legacy of environmental degradation that now has to be addressed: polluted air and water, inadequately disposed hazardous, including radioactive, waste, contaminated agricultural soil, deforestation, and soil erosion (Dragomirescu *et al.*). But these countries have also been left with other legacies, including their administrative structures and political culture, that add to the difficulties associated with environmental management. These include a centralised, top-down command-driven policy style, with its resultant policy and indeed institutional rigidity, a history of implementation failure and a prioritisation of economic, over environmental, considerations. Centralised planning gave little power to the regional or local level and this is another legacy of Communist rule that has important implications for environmental management: enforcement and monitoring of environmental policy, if it is to be successful, has also to take place at the local level.

Many contributors point to the fact that the end of the Communist regime led to environmental improvements in many of the ECE countries. However, this has, at least in part, been attributed to the fall in production that accompanied the collapse of Communism and the end of Comecon. Studies also point to the overall decline in the use of artificial fertilisers and pesticides (Podoba), which can be attributed less to new environmental consciousness and more to cash shortages and the difficulties with land reform and restitution. However, there have been positive improvements in the quality of the environment, which have arisen directly as a result of new environmental policies put in place after 1989. Podoba points to improvement in waste management following new policy decisions (Podoba). Millard has found similar improvements within Poland, pointing to the setting of new standards and to new investment decisions, in particular in waste management. These drew heavily upon EU requirements. However, she also points out that the transition process has brought with it new environmental stresses, particularly with respect to the growing use of private cars (Millard). All this points to the fact that there is no simple causal relationship between Communist command economies and environmental degradation, on the one hand, and market-driven economic reform and environmental improvement, on the other.

The Expression of Environmental Interests

The Communist regime was not blind to the problems of environmental degradation as evident by the fact that the period of Communist rule saw the introduction of numerous laws aimed at counteracting environmental damage (Waller; O'Toole and Hanf; Dragomirescu *et al.*) and the establishment of official environmental organisations (Waller; Fagin and Jehlička; Jancar-Webster). These state-sponsored organisations were by and large concerned with conservation issues. However, a deeper critique of the underlying causes of environmental degradation was effectively prevented by several measures, including the state monopoly on information gathering and dissemination, restrictions on independent and autonomous activities, and the imposition of limitations on outside contacts, including for the scientific community. These restrictions were buttressed by an adherence to an ideology that saw the solution to environmental problems as laying in better planning and improved management of production activities, that is, greater concentration of power in the hand of the state.

However, visible environmental deterioration in many industrial regions of the former East bloc, in particular the correlation between high levels of pollution and below average life expectancy, was eventually to help weaken the regimes across ECE. Regime inability to redress environmental problems undermined the legitimising claim of Communist rule to be the guarantor of human well-being. This occurred against a backdrop of deepening economic crisis within the region, as seen through increasing difficulties in maintaining acceptable standard of living and economic growth.

The growing concern about the threat to human health through environmental degradation coincided with the period of Gorbachev's *perestroika* and *glasnost*. Although fear of undermining their own regimes led many of the ECE leaders to adopt hostile attitudes to the Soviet Union's new openness, it was nevertheless impossible for them to reject it overtly. Many leaders were forced to pay at least lip-service to these changes. Environmental activists, in contrast, seized upon the opportunities opened up by changes in Soviet policy. In short, the more open climate of perestroika facilitated the growth of environmental protests while at the same time making outright rejection of these protests by the state difficult.

Under these circumstances environmental protest, be it against specific instances of pollution affecting human health or ecologically damaging development projects, was to become a relatively safe outlet for expressions of more general discontent (Jancar-Webster; Fagin and Jehlička; Podoba; Baker and Baumgartl). While the level of government tolerance differed in each country, across the region as a whole protest over environmental issues became linked to a concern for human rights and for liberation (Waller). Environmental protest was itself strengthened by these linkages with wider issues of peace and liberation, as seen, for example, by the support provided by Solidarity in Poland for environmental activism (Millard). With the exception of Romania, environmental groups and activists went on to play an active role in bringing down the Communist regime in all countries under examination in this volume. Their role was a particularly significant one in Bulgaria, Hungary, Poland and the then Czechoslovakia. In Slovakia, for example, the environmental movement played such a prominent role that there is some justification for calling what happened in 1989 the green velvet revolution (Podoba). A similar argument can be made for Bulgaria (Baker and Baumgartl). However, we must be careful to place the role of environmental activism in context.

While environmental protest was important in bringing about an end to the old regime, the collapse of Communism was not, in itself, a victory for the environmental movement: the collapse is best seen as the culmination of a rise in support for a more general movement of liberation, in which issues of peace and protection of the environment featured predominantly (Waller). In ECE environmental concerns themselves provided a focus for social discontent at the right moment in time [*Fisher, 1992*]. Nevertheless, each country had its own mobilising environmental issue, such as air pollution in the town of Ruse in Bulgaria (Baker and Baumgartl). At other times it was the existence of ecological interdependency, such as between Hungary and its neighbours, that contributed to the development of high-visibility and in this case international, conflicts and negotiation (O'Toole and Hanf).

The emerging environmental concern found expression through the growth of various independent organisations, ranging from purely dissident groups suppressed by the regime to groups tolerated by the state, such as the Bulgarian group *Ekoglasnost* (Baker and Baumgartl). These groups contained within them three types of protest: first, that coming from nature conservationists, who focused on the need for effective management of nature reserves and for ecological education, and who saw themselves as apolitical actors; second, there were those, often academics, who advocated broader reform and who believed that improvement in the quality of the environment also required social and political changes; third, there were those for whom environmental groups were merely a vehicle for pursuing the main goal of overthrow of the Communist regime. There was thus an element of opportunism in these protests (Fagin and Jehlička; O'Toole and Hanf). This was to be especially so in countries where environmental interests were not deeply rooted in the value system of the people, such as Romania (Podoba). However, despite this, the growth of the environmental movement was politically very important: because it evolved outside state-sponsored institutions it facilitated the development of civil society (Jancar-Webster).

As a result, many observers expected that the collapse of the old regimes would be followed by a strengthening of the environmental movement and an increasing development of civil society. The fact that environmentalists had earned a great deal of authority in society through the prominent role they played in bringing an end to the old Communist regimes reinforced this expectation. However, what actually happened was a far cry from this: the post-1989 period was to be accompanied by a drop in the popularity of environmental issues generally, a fundamental shift in how environmental concern was expressed, and a loss of electoral support for green political parties.

First, the drop in the popularity of environmental issues has been attributed to the material shock of the transition process. This resulted in a shift of attention to economic issues (Waller; Jancar-Webster; O'Toole and Hanf; Fagin and Jehlička). Others point to 'the victory of the one alternative', that is, the overriding adoption of the Western European economic and political model, evident in the priority given to membership of the EU (Jancar-Webster). In this model economic considerations take precedent over environmental ones. The overriding interest in joining the EU has made the EU the chief arbitrator of development and had the effect of displacing alternative, more environmentally sustainable models from the policy agenda (Kolk and van der Weij). Others point to the growth of new consumerism and social and political instability (Baker and Baumgartl).

Second, the post-1989 period saw a fundamental change in the way in which environmental concerns were expressed. This change occurred against a backdrop of loss of unity among the environmental movement as a whole, which was accompanied by an end to their authority in society (*Podoba*). Splits, mistrust and fragmentation are features of the movement in the immediate transition period (O'Toole and Hanf; Podoba; Waller; Jancar-Webster). In the place of the environmental movement was to emerge a host of new environmental non-governmental organisations (NGOs). Many of these NGOs have a specific, narrow focus, which is often of a localised nature. They differed both in spirit and in influence from the environmental movement that spawned them. The post-1989 period also saw a decline in state-sponsored environmental organisations. In effect, after 1989 the environmental movement shifted from being the mobilising agent for populist protest against the *totalita* of the Communist regime and in its place emerged pragmatic goal-oriented professional organisations (Jancar-Webster; Podoba). Despite their professionalism, however, financial uncertainty continues to plague the new environmental NGOs in the region.

Exactly why this transformation happened has been the subject of much discussion within this volume. Some point to the distrust that existed between environmental groups as a major cause for their subsequent dysfunction. This distrust operated within and between groups, arising from their history of penetration by informers (Jancar-Webster), fear of opportunists (Fagin and Jehlička) and, at times, nationalistic or ethnic biases (Podoba). Yet despite the specificity found within particular countries, all see the movement as having got caught up in the dynamics of the transformation process. In effect, the achievement of liberation from

Communist rule first robbed the environmental issue of its mobilising potential, and changes since then have forced environmentalists to survive in much changed circumstances (Waller).

Many have been highly critical of the change in the way in which environmental concerns are expressed in society. It is seen as having impoverished political discourse in the region (Jancar-Webster). Furthermore, the process of professionalisation has isolated environmental interests from its grass roots, resulting in a loss of local knowledge and local input and making environmental interests politically vulnerable. Environmental groups are now seen as having reduced capacity to operate as mobilising agents in the future: they are increasingly seen by the public as non-representative and as part of the power structure (Jancar-Webster). Lack of effective mechanisms of coordination between NGOs, lack of funds, and the syphoning off of the most experienced leaders into government posts or lucrative private consultancy has also proved problematic (Millard). The fragmentation of environmental interests through the establishment of numerous, and often local, NGOs, has often meant that many ECE countries lack major national environmental organisations. This has proved a disadvantage, for example, in attempts by NGOs to influence national environmental policy making in Poland (Millard). Others point to the tragedy of the exclusion from the political process that has accompanied the changing nature of environmental expression in ECE. In the case of the Czech Republic, for example, professionalism and increased conservatism has not resulted in environmentalists being welcomed in from the cold and greeted as new converts to democratic compromise: on the contrary their influence has waned (Fagin and Jehlička).

However, there are differences across the regions. In some countries, most noticeably in Hungary, despite the fact that the environmental mass movement has given way to less overt and highly fragmented efforts, NGOs have nevertheless begun to participate in public debates surrounding environmental issues. They have, for example, provided input into discussions surrounding new environmental policy considered by parliament in the last couple of years. The government, for its part, is in the early stages of learning how to interact productively and with openness with environmental NGOs (O'Toole and Hanf). However, as a general rule, environmental NGOs do not play a substantial role in the decision-making process of governments within the region [*Tóth Nagy, 1993*].

The changes in how environmental concerns are expressed has been strongly influenced by outside agencies and the international environmental community (Jancar-Webster). An element of tutelage is involved in the relationship between the region's NGOs and international environmental actors (Waller). The significance of this involvement is multifold. On the positive side, it has helped with capacity building, imparted new skills and given some, albeit limited, financial security to the newly emerging NGOs. However, many point to the negative consequences of this influence. It has at times divided domestic environmental groups, between, on the one hand, those professional groups aided by foreign donors, and on the other, the grass-roots groups who have not received funding and who feel increasingly alienated from recent developments. This can have the effect of fragmenting the movement even further. Foreign involvement has also resulted in a financial dependence on outside funding agents (Fagin and Jehlička; Jancar-Webster). One of the major criticisms of this relationship is the role that external influences play in shaping the strategies as well as the priorities of the NGOs (Jancar-Webster). The training of NGOs by outside groups is leading to a focus of attention on conflict-resolution training and decision-making skills. This can distract from the adversarial role that might be appropriate for these NGOs in the current period (Waller). International environmental NGOs, used to negotiating at the highest levels, have evolved a strategy of showing the same undifferentiated concern for business, government and environmental protection which is both unfamiliar and may even by unwise in ECE (Waller). This is especially so in those countries where environmental interests are still excluded from the policy process and often mistrusted by government, as in the Czech Republic (Fagin and Jehlička).

Many of the contributors argue that the changing fortunes of the environmental movement are of wider political significance. In Slovakia, the fate of the movement reflects more general problems within the transformation process. Here there is increased resistance to change and nostalgia for the past in the fact of the uncertainties of the present (Podoba). The fate of environmentalism, in particular its demobilisation and replacement by goal-oriented professional organisations, is ultimately bound up with the fate of the revolutions of 1989. At all levels the potential for radical reform that was embedded in the initial revolutionary period of 1989 was ultimately to be severely constrained. Limitations were placed on the reform process by the freedom offered by the market, the succour held out by foreign aid and advise, and the sectional competition of electoral politics (Waller). Ironically this rang the knell of any aspiration the environmental movement entertained of instituting a society marked by the decentralised cooperation of non-governmental actors dedicated to quality-of-life issues (Waller). Across ECE the discourse of politics is now impoverished (Jancar-Webster) and the development of civil society remains limited (Baker and Baumgartl). The continued weakness of civil society has allowed the democratic deficit of the Communist regime, that is, the inability of citizens to influence the policy-making process, to continue (Fagin and Jehlička).

This in turn reduces the effectiveness of environmental management policies.

Finally, we turn to the loss of support for green political parties in the post-1989 elections. While some environmental groups fared well in the first free elections, by the time the second elections were called, the environment slipped surprisingly abruptly down, and almost off, the political agenda across the region (Waller; Jancar-Webster; Fagin and Jehlička; Baker and Baumgartl). Environmental groups did best when they joined coalitions, such as the Czech Civic Forum or *Ekoglasnost* joining with the Bulgarian Union of Democratic Forces (Jancar-Webster). The erosion of public confidence in political elites, with the subsequent rise in apathy and disillusionment with regard to the development of pluralism (Millard) can in part explain the poor performance of environmentalists in the elections: the election process is in many countries still tainted and therefore neither strongly supported by the citizens nor open to new, environmental, interests.

Nevertheless, while they did not win popular support, national legislatures often had a small number of environmental deputies. However, in the numerous cases where environmentalists accepted environmental briefs in one of the new governments, they found themselves constrained by the harsh economic and political demands of the transition (Waller).

The Effectiveness of Environmental Management Policies

As has been pointed out above, environmental legislation was in existence prior to the collapse of the old Communist regime. In some cases this legislation was updated, as in Poland as recently as 1987 (Millard), indicating a deepening of government concern about environmental degradation. However, it is generally recognised that a large deficit existed with respect to the implementation of this legislation, attributable in part to the priority given, especially at the level of the firm, to production over environmental management. After the collapse of the Communist regimes a new wave of environmental management was begun. This new wave shared much in common with past policy responses, with a similar focus and method to that adopted under Communism: new measures were mostly of a regulatory kind aimed at mitigating air and surface-water pollution. Thus in the initial period there is more of a continuity and less of a rupture with the past. Post-Communist environmental legislation also resembled legislative innovations of the 1970s in the West [*Weale, 1992*].

Contributors speak of the immediate post-1989 period of legislative activity as the enthusiastic period (Fagin and Jehlička) or a period of legislative hyperactivity (Jancar-Webster). Subsequently, as we will see below, this activity was to founder on the rock of implementation (Millard). During this period environmental policy was shaped by a number of factors.

First, the new governments were compelled to tackle the worst of the environmental black spots, especially those that had been the focus of mobilisation in the pre-1989 days. Policy, by and large, aimed at dealing with pollution problems which threatened human health and well-being. There was also need to deal with the environmental pollution left behind by the retreating Soviet army. Thus policy was often imposed by the immediate circumstances (Waller). However, some proactive steps were also taken, especially the passing of legislation to control further pollution (Waller; Jancar-Webster).

Second, external actors played a role in shaping the initial policy responses. The fact that the West had placed priority on dealing with transboundary air and water pollution was particularly important in shaping the environmental responses of the newly emerging governments of ECE. The decision of ECE to harmonise their legislation with that of the EU, as part of the membership requirements, is also of prime importance. Third, policy was shaped by the available resources and, at times, severely constrained by them. Many of the contributors, for example, point to the renewed acceptability of nuclear power during this period (Fagin and Jehlička; Millard), which was influenced by both external economic interests and the constraints under which governments were operating (Baker and Baumgartl). Here we come face to face with the complex political reality of environmental policy-making and the contradictions, paradoxes and conflicts that accompany it. Substituting nuclear for fossil fuel reduces air pollution, but creates waste problems. Other projects to solve airborne pollution by harnessing hydropower, for example in the Danube, give rise to new, transitional, environmental concerns (Waller). These three influences, namely immediate need, external pressure and resource limitations, resulted in a predominantly reactive policy mode which limited any long-term and more sustainable approach towards environmental policy management (Millard; Fagin and Jehlička).

This period of renewed legislative activity has also highlighted a major problem of policy implementation across the region. Some countries, most notably Poland, have begun to take action to deal with their implementation deficit (Millard). However, the key factors contributing to this problem remain. Weak institutional capacity is a major source of this implementation deficit (Kolk and van der Weij; O'Toole and Hanf), but they can also be attributed to the passing of a large amount of new legislation in a short period of time, lack of funding, weak environmental ministries, fragmentation in administrative responsibilities, poor quality of expertise and the syphoning off of the most experienced into more lucrative private-sector posts, corruption, especially at the local level, lack of capacity, again at the local level, conflicting goals, and problems in monitoring. These problems are not exclusive to the environmental policy arena. However, the tensions between the demands of the transition process, in particular economic reform, and environmental management makes the problems associated with dealing with the environmental policy deficit all the more marked.

The emphasis on punishment for violation of regulatory standards rather than the use of other policy tools, adds to these problems (O'Toole and Hanf). However, the use of a wider range of tools is in itself dependent upon the success of other reforms. These include an effective market system, the establishment of a proper regulatory framework and an efficient administrative structure. The use of fiscal tools, for example, is dependent upon the existence of a functioning market economy, while the use of the polluter pays principle is dependent upon a proper regulatory framework to enable identification of the polluter and an effective administrative structure to collect the payment. Similarly, the use of tools such as green equity schemes are only useful in countries with a relatively advanced privatisation process (Kolk and van der Weij). This has not stopped, however, attempts to widen the range of tools available for environmental management, the most noticeable example being Poland (Kolk and van der Weij; Millard).

Under Communist rule there was no development of independent local government with the capacity to exercise autonomous choices regarding environmental issues (O'Toole and Hanf). Since the collapse of Communism the persistence of strong centralism in decision-making impedes local environmental management in a number of ways. First, it blocks local environmental problems from finding their ways to national government (Kolk and van der Weij). It also hinders the development of local expertise and experience with policy enforcement (Kolk and van der Weij; Fagin and Jehlička). There are also other problems. At the local level governments have had to contend with contradictory regulations established by the national level and a daunting number of duties (O'Toole and Hanf). There can also be conflicts of interest between the requirements that local government initiates new businesses, manages the industrial firms that have been placed in their hands as part of the ongoing privatisation process, and protects the environment. In short, much depends upon the effective reform of local government (Fagin and Jehlička). However, it has also been pointed out that in some countries there is an ingrained culture of localism. In Romania this has legitimised accommodations which enabled local authorities to coexist with their communities, even if at the expense of the national interest (Dragomirescu et al.).

Reform at the subnational level is bound up with wider reform, particularly within public administration. This is particularly important within ECE because in situations of political and economic instability, public administration gains in importance. Reform of the public administration is therefore part of, and at the same time will contribute to, the ultimate shape of the outcome of the transition process. It is both the object and the chief agent of reform [*Hesse, 1993: iv*]. This means that successive transition will have to see a redefinition of the role of public administration in society, and of its relations with politics, the economy and civil society [*Hesse, 1993: iv*]. The transition process involves a strengthening of democratic control over state administration and an increase in its accountability to democratically elected bodies. It also involves a deconcentration and decentralisation of the bureaucratic apparatus, bringing public administration strictly under the rule of law and guaranteeing the legality of administrative acts [*Hesse, 1993: iii*]. In short, there will need to be a change in the organisation of governance, which has, to date, proved a difficult undertaking. Despite all of the difficulties facing ECE countries at the level of policy implementation, there have been some positive developments as far as the administration of environmental policy is concerned. Most importantly, there has been a depoliticisation of enforcement and an altering of the relationship between the regulated and the regulator, in part due to privatisation (O'Toole and Hanf).

The Role of the EU

This volume examines the role of the EU because of the influence it exercises on environmental policy within ECE. In Poland, for example, the determination to join the EU is *the* central factor influencing the shape of current environmental policy (Millard). Current EU involvement with the region is taking place within the context of more widespread international involvement and is ultimately linked with international politics in the post-cold war period. There is, for example, a pan-European Environment Ministers' conference which was established in 1991 and includes representatives from the US and the former Soviet Union that is also shaping environmental policy in ECE. Its first meeting was held in Dobriš, a second meeting in Lucerne in 1993, and a third in Sofia in 1995.

The Nature of EU Interest

There are a number of reasons why the EU is interested in ensuring the consolidation of democracy and the effective construction of a market economy in ECE countries. These include the desire to ensure political and military stability on its eastern flank and the belief that economic reform opens up trade opportunities for EU industry. This can include an interest in preparing the way for substitution of Russian for Western nuclear reactors (Waller). Besides these general political-economic reasons, the EU has a specific interest in the reform of environmental policy in ECE countries.

This includes a desire to reduce the amount of transboundary pollution it imports and an interest in harmonising pollution-control standards throughout Europe as a whole, in order to avoid trade distortions and unfair competition. Closely related to these interests is the desire to provide an opportunity for European industry to export modern pollution-abatement technologies and environmental management skills to ECE countries. There is also a belief that an improvement in the living and working environment, and hence in health, would demonstrate in a tangible way the benefits of reform and thus help legitimise the transition process in the face of its harsh economic consequences [*Baker, 1996: 149–51*].

While the EU wishes to expand its sphere of interest in the region, it is less certain as to whether this extends to granting full membership of the EU to all ECE countries. For the EU enlargement is fraught with difficulties. In terms of economic development the entire region lags behind the EU, and the EU lacks the financial resources to facilitate cohesion. This is one of the reasons why countries like Ireland, Greece and Spain have been less than enthusiastic about encouraging future enlargement on the eastern front: they fear the increased drain on EU resources will negatively effect their budget allocation. Moreover, further enlargement would cause severe operational difficulties for the EU institutions, leading to renewed calls for institutional reforms. Achieving reform in these areas has already proven difficult. Nevertheless, the positive benefits associated with enlargement are seen as outweighing the negative, at least in so far as certain ECE countries are concerned, in particular, Poland, the Czech Republic and Hungary.

The Nature of ECE Interests

Membership of Western European organisations like the EU is seen in a positive light within ECE, not least because it offers these countries an historical opportunity to leave the Russian sphere of influence [*Crawford, 1996: 316*]. It is also seen as an opportunity to improve living standards by joining a highly-developed, Western economic bloc. EU membership is also seen as helping to consolidate the democratic transition. Preparation for membership also offers a pragmatic advantage to domestic political actors with ECE countries: it allows them to justify unpopular actions, or their unwillingness to meet popular demands, by reference to the conditions and limitations imposed on them by the need to meet EU membership criteria. Nevertheless membership will be costly in terms of meeting environmental and health regulations and standards that are proving difficult for some countries, such as Romania and Bulgaria (Dragomirescu *et al.*; Baker and Baumgartl).

Association Agreements and Achieving Membership

As part of its ongoing involvement in influencing the transition process in ECE countries, the EU signed Association Agreements with Poland, Hungary and the former Czechoslovakia in December 1991. By 1995 Bulgaria, Romania and Slovakia had also become Associate Members through signing similar Agreements. Kolk and van der Weij trace the evolution of this involvement (Kolk and van der Weij). These Agreements were aimed at the gradual elimination of trade barriers and the approximation of national legislation in Associated Countries to that of the EU across a wide range of policy areas, including the environment. As far as the ECE countries were concerned, the expectation was that signing an Association Agreement with the EU would lead to eventual membership of the Union, in particular as it is related to the EU (Kolk and van der Weij).

It has been argued that despite the existence of mechanisms for mutual consultation, the relationship between ECE countries and the EU is marked by 'a substantial element of asymmetry' [*Caddy, 1997: 326*]. High priority is given to membership of the EU by ECE countries, whereas for the EU further enlargement remains a low priority. Furthermore, the decision to accept applications for membership remains the prerogative of the EU [*Caddy, 1997: 327*]. Moreover, it is fair to say that the terms of these Agreements were largely in the interest of the EU, not the ECE countries, as they restricted trade in favour of the EU and it has led to the erection of barriers, both with respect to trade and the entry of ECE country products into the EU as well as inward migration of workers. The terms of the policy dialogue are thus skewed heavily in favour of the EU, leaving little room for consideration of the policy experience of ECE countries and is 'reinforced by the significant discrepancies which exist between the two partners with regard to financial and technological resources as well as cumulative experience of pursuing public policies with a market-based economy' [*Caddy, 1997: 328*]. There has, furthermore, been little public discussion of the wider issues, such as the political and economic conditions that the EU is laying down for Association or about the elements of pluralist democracy that Association and aid are intended to encourage [*Pinder, 1991: 38*].

Despite the asymmetry, preparation for membership continues. The European Council meeting in Copenhagen in June 1993 confirmed the prospect for future membership of the EU for Associated Countries. This was followed, in December 1994, by the European Council meeting in Essen agreeing the broad outlines of a pre-accession strategy with the Associated Countries. This led in 1995 to a White Paper, which set out a general programme of action to be undertaken and identified key measures to be adopted within each sector by each Associate Country [*CEC, 1995a*].

By 1996 Poland, Hungary and the Czech Republic and Slovakia had applied for full membership.

However, marked differences in levels of economic development and in the extent to which the processes of marketisation and democratisation had been consolidated make some of the countries less prepared for and less acceptable to the EU for membership. In July 1997 the EU published its Agenda 2000 plan, which accepted the case for full membership for Poland, the Czech Republic and Hungary [CEC, 1997]. While the door was left open for other countries, their case for full membership remains more fragile (Baker and Baumgartl). Acceptance of some and, at least in the medium term, rejection of others, carries a risk of polarisation within the region, with the likelihood that countries in the former Soviet Union and those ECE countries which are deemed not suitable for membership in the near future lagging behind and even dropping out of the European framework altogether. As a consequence they may fail to be involved any more in initiatives to tackle regional environmental problems (Kolk and van der Weij; Baker and Baumgartl).

Environmental considerations form part of the programme of preparation for membership of the EU. In particular, the Association Agreements involve harmonising the environmental legislation, standards and international agreements of ECE countries with those of the EU. In this context, the pull towards membership has exerted a powerful influence on the policy choices of ECE governments (Waller). As a result of acceptance of the policy of harmonisation, as seen, for example, in the case of the Czech Republic, in no case is current environmental regulation inconsistent with that of the EU (Fagin and Jehlička).

Putting Policy into Practice: PHARE

The PHARE programme (Poland and Hungary: Action for Restructuring the Economy) was initially confined to helping Poland and Hungary deal with the immediate aftermath of the end of the old Communist regime. Since then, PHARE has been extended to include 11 countries of ECE, with the aim of supporting the process of economic restructuring and encouraging the changes necessary to build a market-oriented economy and to promote private enterprises [CEC, 1992: 2]. It was hoped that foreign investment would stimulate this process. However the unstable economic situation, limited creditworthiness and numerous uncertainties made foreign investors reluctant to become involved in the economic regeneration of the region (Kolk and van der Weij). Given this, international aid, including that of the EU, is to a large measure part of the process of making the region safe for this foreign investment (Waller; Kolk and van der Weij).

The connections between democratisation and market reforms were also made explicit and a second, closely related concern, was to help strengthen the newly forming democracies of Eastern Europe [*CEC, 1994: 1*]. Phare is now the main EU vehicle for the provision of technical assistance, training, grant finance, and investment to ECE. It is the largest single grant assistance programme in the region (Kolk and van der Weij).

Some of the initial problems associated with EU aid have been dealt with (Kolk and van der Weij). This included problems associated with a lack of clear targets for action, which after 1991 led the Commission to target a small number of core areas, judged to be key in ensuring the success of the transition process. They include privatisation, the provision of legislative and regulatory frameworks for a market economy, modernisation of banking and financial services, the promotion of small and medium private-sector firms, labour-market policies and policies to strengthen civil society and environmental protection [*Baker, 1996: 153–6*]. However, PHARE has gradually changed its nature, from being a vehicle for the delivery of emergency aid to that of an integration tool, with one of the main areas of activity of the programme now being that of assisting Associated Countries in their efforts to make their legislation compatible with that of the EU [*Caddy, 1997: 322*]. Unfortunately, the focus on legislative harmonisation has diverted attention away from the implementation stage of the policy process.

One of the main problems with PHARE has been the limited absorptive capacity of the host countries, making it difficult for them to make full use of the programmes. In particular, the ill-adapted national administrative structures and lack of experience in managing foreign aid programmes can be pointed out [*CEC, 1995b: 7*]. This differs across the region, as does the extent of aid, the amount contributed by the host country, and how much of the allocated budget is actually spent. There has also been a lack of horizontal coordination (between host and host), with a concentrating on vertical coordination (between host and donor). This lack can be particularly problematic in border areas which often share common ecological features. It can be argued that in these cases, the self-interest òf the donor can clash with the effectiveness of the aid (Kolk and van der Weij). This issue was raised in the preparatory documents for the Sofia Conference.

According to Baker, the position of environmental policy in PHARE is ambiguous. She points to the fact that the Commission has, on the one hand, claimed that environmental policy forms a crucial component of its reform package for ECE countries. On the other hand, it continues to give priority to economic reform, even if these measures being negative environmental consequences [*Baker, 1996: 153*]. There are also cases of concrete contradictions within PHARE, as seen by the Czech example of the PHARE-funded programme to solve air pollution from power stations by using limestone quarried from within a nature protection area, which was itself receiving PHARE funding (Fagin and Jehlička).

Also the fact that environmental funds did not rise above ten per cent during the first five years of the programme is a reflection of the low priority accorded to the environment (Kolk and van der Weij). As well as having an inbuilt bias towards projects of interest to the West (such as transboundary air pollution), this aid has a built-in prejudice towards large projects. This diverts attention away from small-scale projects, which could have a significant environmental effect, help increase local involvement and the use of local expertise (Kolk and van der Weij). Small-scale projects also have the potential to increase energy efficiency and savings. A shift of funding towards small-scale projects has also been sought by both the Czech and Polish ministries of the environment (Fagin and Jehlička).

This uneven relationship between the EU and ECE can increase the likelihood of policy failure as well as add to the implementation deficit, thus making environmental management less effective and efficient. Top-down policy imposition, as opposed to policy exchange, is problematic, not least because it ignores the experience and expertise of ECE countries (for example in nature conservation). It is also problematic because the EU is committed to the promotion of sustainable development, which involves acceptance of the principles of shared responsibility and an openness to bottom-up participation in the policy-making process.

There are a number of other problems associated with the adoption of EU legislation and with the use of EU policy goals and tools by ECE countries. These are particularly evident in the environmental policy arena. First, many of these policy tools, especially those targeted in the EU's Fifth Environmental Action Programme, require functioning and effective market systems, which remain underdeveloped in ECE countries. Second, EU environmental policy evolved as a response to specific environmental policies in Western Europe. Their adoption by ECE countries assumes that they are possible to implement and that, in terms of policy priorities, they are the most appropriate responses to the environmental problems of ECE countries. This assumption is not a priori warranted.

In terms of the actual aid itself, not the conditions under which it is granted, there are also problems. Environmental aid has turned out to be much lower and subject to more complicated conditions than initially expected by the host country. This was confirmed at Lucerne and there is now a shift of responsibility to the recipient countries themselves (Kolk and van der Weij). As a number of contributors have pointed out, the limitations of Western aid became clear at Lucerne (Waller; Baker and Baumgartl).

Despite these problems, we must nevertheless acknowledge that the signing of Associated Agreements with the EU has had a positive impact upon environmental policy in ECE countries – not least because poor environmental protection records may negatively influence the EU's decision on eligibility for membership. This ensures that a certain level of attention to environmental policy is maintained, despite the predominance of other pressing policy issues [*Caddy, 1997*].

Some Preliminary Findings

We recall that the aim of this volume was to examine the impact of the twin processes of democratisation and marketisation on three environmental matters: (1) the physical environment; (2) the expression of environmental concerns; and (3) the effectiveness of environmental management policies. We recall that examination took account of the wider context of international involvement with the transformation process in ECE and, in particular, the role played by the EU in that process.

The Physical Environment

This has found that while the transition process has brought new environmental stresses, there have been some very positive developments with respect to the quality of the physical environment. This is in part due to lower production but this is not the only reason. It is also due to investment in pollution control, improved legislation and renewed efforts at enforcement. The importance of foreign assistance in this clean-up and the adoption of EU legislation have been of prime importance.

The Expression of Environmental Interest

We have found across the region as a whole that the initial upsurge of interest in and mobilisation around environmental issues was not sustained beyond the period of the collapse of Communist rule. The transition process has seen the replacement of the environmental movement by increasingly professional environmental NGOs, who operate at a distance from the grass roots and at times even from each other (Jancar-Webster). Although, we should point out, history has shown that the fact that there may be periods of latency in which mass mobilisation is slight or absent, and only the organisations are visible, does not *ipso facto* signify the death of the environmental movement [*Rootes, 1997*].

Yet despite the declining fortunes of the environmental movement, the process of democratisation has positively altered the context within which environmental policy is developed and executed. In many ECE countries there is now a more open political processes, political competition, a significant reduction in the role of the state in the management of key industrial sectors, and the beginnings of the establishment of independent local government (O'Toole and Hanf). There are nevertheless marked differences across the region, as, for example, between Hungary and Bulgaria, and continuous problems relating to institutional fragmentation, limited capacity and lack of coordination, especially between the local and national levels. These problems serve to remind us of the gap between the procedural changes that have occurred under democratisation and the substantive changes that are still needed. In particular, there is need for the development of civil society and a renewed participation and faith in the political process and a reduction in state centralisation.

Marketisation has been less beneficial to the environment. The policy of marketisation has served to legitimise a continuation of the belief that economic considerations must take precedent over environmental matters. Except in the limited case of Hungary, ECE countries show little evidence of shifting towards a more sustainable development model, one where the environment and economic cease to be seen in terms of trade-offs but as mutually reinforcing. Indeed in some cases there has been downright hostility to the concept of sustainable development (Fagin and Jehlička).

The Effectiveness of Environmental Management Policies

In terms of environmental management the transition process has resulted in a period of renewed legislative activity. The reliance upon the regulatory approach provides a continuity with the past as does the fact that effective environmental management continues to be plagued by resource problems. Administrative deficiencies are made worse by local incapacity, often reinforced by corruption. However, given the complex relationship between the reform process and environmental policy the problems of implementation and policy effectiveness can not merely be resolved through improving institutional capacity. Improved environmental policy effectiveness is ultimately linked to efforts to democratise society and facilitate the growth of civil society.

The Influence of the EU

The EU has played a major role in shaping the transformation process in ECE. This influence has not been a democratic one and many contributors have pointed out that the involvement of the EU has displaced the centrality afforded to domestic concerns on the policy agenda, replacing it with those environmental problems most pressing for the EU, for example problems relating to transboundary air pollution.

Nevertheless, it is fair to say that since 1989 the funding programmes of the EU and the transfer of technological and management skills that form part of those programmes, have made an impact on the state of the environment of ECE countries. Whatever the motives of the EU are, this can only but be of benefit to the citizens of the region (Dragomirescu et al.).

Furthermore, the involvement of the EU is part of a process that has so far enabled a change of regime to take place in the region without major social turbulence (Waller). Yet, this conclusion needs to be qualified, not least because of the fate of the ideas and hopes that shaped the mass mobilisation leading to the collapse of Communism (Waller; Fagin and Jehlička; Jancar-Webster). Then there was a spirit of liberation that contained aspirations of popular participation that went beyond the norms of Western Europe's liberal democracies. These aspirations have not been realised.

In conclusion, the transition process has brought both positive and negative consequences for the state of the physical environment, for the manner in which environmental concerns are expressed and dealt with within society and through the political process, and for the management of environmental policy. On balance, however, it is fair to say that environmental policy has but a tenuous position on the policy agenda of ECE countries. Political and economic instability and external pressures have displaced environmental considerations from centre stage. This has meant a failure on behalf of ECE countries to realise a more far-reaching and ultimately more rewarding approach towards the management of transition, one where economic reform and democratisation can feed into the construction of a new sustainable model of economic and social development.

REFERENCES

Baker, S. (1996), 'The Scope for East–West Co-operation', in A. Blowers and Pieter Glasbergen (eds.), *Environmental Policy in an International Context, Vol.3*, London: Arnold, pp.135–65.

Baumgartl, Bernd (1993), 'Environmental Protest as a Vehicle for Transition: The Case of Ekoglasnost in Bulgaria', in Anna Vari and Pal Tamas (eds.), *Environment and Democratic Transition: Policy and Politics in Central and Eastern Europe*, Dordrecht: Kluwer Academic Publishers, pp.157–75.

Caddy, J. (1997), 'Harmonisation and Asymmetry: Environmental Policy Co-ordination Between the European Union and Central Europe', *Journal of European Public Policy*, Vol.4, No.3, pp.318–36.

CEC (Commission of the European Communities) (1992), *The PHARE Indicative Programme*, 1/673/92-EN, Brussels: European Commission.

CEC (1994), *What is Phare? A European Union Initiative for Economic Integration with Central and Eastern European Countries*, Brussels: European Commission.

CEC (1995a), *White Paper on the Preparation of the Associated Countries of Central and Eastern Europe for Integration into the Internal Market of the Union*, COM(95)163 final, Luxembourg: Office for Official Publications of the European Union.

CEC (1995b), *infoPHARE. No. 8*, Brussels: European Commission.

CEC (1997), *Commission Opinion on Bulgaria's Application for Membership of the European Union*, COM(97)2008 final, Luxembourg: Office for Official Publications of the European Communities.

Crawford, K. (1996), *East Central European Politics Today*, Manchester: Manchester University Press.

Fisher, D. (1992), 'The Environmental Movement in Central and Eastern Europe: Its Emergence and Role in the Political Changes of 1989', in D. Fisher, C. Davis, A. Juras and V. Pavlovic (eds.), *Civil Society and the Environment in Central and Eastern Europe*, London: Ecological Studies Institute, pp.182–97.

Hesse, Joachim Jens (1993), 'Introduction', *Public Administration*, Vol.71, No.1, pp.iii–vi.

Pinder, J. (1991), *The European Community and Eastern Europe*, London: Royal Institute of International Affairs.

Rootes, Christopher A. (1997), 'Environmental Movements and Green Parties in Western and Eastern Europe', in Michael Redclift and Graham Woodgate (eds.), *International Handbook of Environmental Sociology*, Cheltenham: Edward Elgar, pp.319–48.

Tellegen, E. (1996), 'Environmental Conflicts in Transforming Economies: Central and Eastern Europe', in P. Sloep and A. Blowers (eds.), *Environmental Policy in an International Context, Vol.2*, London: Arnold, pp.67–96.

Toonen, T. (1993), 'Analysing Institutional Change and Administrative Transformation: A Comparative View', *Public Administration*, Vol.71, No.1, pp.151–68.

Tóth Nagy, M. (1993), 'Observations on the Relationship between NGOs and Governments in Central and East European Countries', in P. Hardi, A. Juras and M. Tóth Nagy (eds.), *New Horizons? Possibilities for Cooperation between Environmental NGOs and Governments in Central and East Europe*, Budapest: Regional Environmental Center for Central and Eastern Europe, pp.17–22.

Waller, Michael and Frances Millard (1992), 'Environmental Politics in Eastern Europe', *Environmental Politics*, Vol.1, No.2, pp.159–85.

Weale, W. (1992), *The New Politics of Pollution*, Manchester and New York: Manchester University Press.

PART I:

ENVIRONMENTAL POLICY AND THE TRANSITION PROCESS IN CENTRAL AND EASTERN EUROPE

Geopolitics and the Environment in Eastern Europe

MICHAEL WALLER

The causes of the severe pollution that has affected parts of Eastern Europe lie in the production methods and the political authoritarianism of the Communist period, but the relationship between most of the region and Western Europe in developmental terms has to be taken into account. On either count the geopolitics of Eastern Europe was an important historical factor before 1989, and it has remained one since then, but with influences from the East being replaced by influences from the West. The change of economic and political system brought expertise and techniques capable of making production more sensitive to the protection of the environment, at the same time making the region safe for the inward foreign investment that it needed. But aid, expertise and advice brought an element of tutelage which has influenced the evolution of the environmental movement in the region, substituting itself for grass-roots activism and weakening environmental groups in relation to their governments.

The crisis of awareness that resources are finite and that humankind is destroying the world that it inhabits spread from the United States in the 1960s into a Europe whose diverse economies were at very different stages of industrial and technological development. Exaggerating these differences and imposing a particular pattern on them was the political division of Europe consequent on the onset of the cold war. This had a profound effect on the economies of individual countries, particularly those lying within the Soviet sphere of influence, in some cases – the German Democratic Republic (GDR) and Czechoslovakia – impeding the technological development of an industrialised economy, in others promoting industrialisation at a rhythm that transformed the urban/rural balance and created acute generational differences. Part of the heritage of the Communist years was a severe degradation of the environment in the region.

In what follows a brief account will be given of the factors that led to that degradation, and of the linking of concern for the environment to the broader movement of dissent against Communist rule in Eastern Europe. This will be followed by an examination of the important change that took place in the politics of the environment in the region when the Communist regimes fell. Finally, the impact of international factors on the process of marketisation and democratisation as concerns the environment will be analysed.

Whilst the environmental damage done to Eastern Europe can be attributed in large part to the region's Communist past, it is of the first importance in any analysis of Eastern European politics to take into account the deeper history of the region and of its individual countries in relation to the overall pattern of industrialisation in Europe. The authoritarian uniformity of Communist rule was viewed in Western Europe largely in current strategic terms. It defined the enemy. This distracted attention from the fact that the enemy was, taken as a whole and with significant exceptions, poorer and developing, in contrast to a Western Europe which, taken again as a whole, was developed and richer. It ignored also the quite marked differences in economic development within the region, and differences in the extent to which a given nation identified with the Soviet Union and its developmental problems. There was a great deal to distinguish Czechoslovakia, an industrial leader already in the inter-war years, Western Christian in its cultural and Habsburg in its political traditions, from agrarian and Orthodox Bulgaria with its folk memories of Russian aid in liberating the nation from the Turk in 1878. Czechoslovakia's advanced stage of economic development contrasted also with the position in neighbouring Poland, where the pall of smoke that hung over Cracow was the result of the post-war construction of the vast Nowa Huta steelworks, the workforce of which had to a great extent been recently recruited from the Polish countryside [*Lane and Kolankiewicz, 1973*].

To recount the current environmental problems of Eastern Europe solely with reference to the Communist past can therefore be misleading, since the diversity in the region that has been increasingly evident since 1989 derives from historical factors with a strong developmental content. It is true that without the intervention of Communism, there was nothing to prevent Prague from solving its problems of air pollution at about the same time as Manchester did. But the circumstances of Prague in Czechoslovakia were exceptional. Other countries of the region were still developing industrially during the Communist period, and the Communist leaderships were assigning what, in the circumstances, appeared to be appropriate priorities. The industrial development of the region could have been environmentally cleaner, and with Western investment and without Soviet intervention it no doubt would have been. But Western investment was working no great marvels in Bulgaria or Romania before Communism came along, and the economic impact of Soviet intervention varied considerably across the region.

Admittedly, it is difficult in the circumstances to tell whether the local leaderships were in fact following policies autonomously chosen, because of the extent of Soviet influence. In a later section we shall see how this situation has now been reversed: the choices open to the new governments are restricted by influences coming from the West. The point is to register the historical predicament of dependence of the region – and also the variety of its incidence and of the opportunities for escaping it. It is too simple to say – as is broadly true – that the populations of the region are more content with their present circumstances than they were with the old, and far too simple to assume that liberation from Soviet domination means complete autonomy. Nowhere is this more clear than in the environmental realm, where external influences, however benevolent, have had a significant impact on the policy options of the new governments, and on the development of autonomous participatory structures.

One effect of the removal of Communist uniformity and of the cold war is that the connotation of the term 'Eastern Europe' is now unclear, and its future value clearly in doubt. It will be retained in what follows to connote all non-Soviet countries that were members of the Soviet bloc during the Communist period – that is, Poland, the GDR, Czechoslovakia, Hungary, Bulgaria and Romania.

Influence from the East: The Communist Years

The environmental problems that the new regimes of Eastern Europe inherited from the Communist past have now been thoroughly documented in the literature [*Carter and Turnock, 1993; French, 1990; IIEC, 1991; Kabala, 1991; Kramer, 1983; Russell, 1990; World Resources Institute, 1992; ZumBrunnen, 1990*]. They affected the quality of all three of the air, the land and the water. Most striking in its impact was airborne pollution, affecting in particular the 'black triangle' formed by the south-east of the GDR, northern Bohemia and Polish Silesia. Not only the burning of lignite, which is high in sulphur content, but its mining through opencast methods, were environmentally extremely damaging and were given pride of place in external comment on the region's environmental problems. Prodigal use of pesticides in agriculture affected both land and water in the countryside throughout the region. Equally widely distributed was a deficiency in sewage treatment, the case of Warsaw, which discharged sewage directly into the Vistula (and still does), being a particularly striking and often quoted example.

There were a number of celebrated black spots, perhaps foremost among them being Copsa Mica in Romania, where the Carbosin plant spread a fine black dust produced in the processing of rubber over the whole town, and where the neighbouring Sometra plant emitted no fewer than 21 toxic substances, including zinc, cadmium and lead. Such cases acquired a particular prominence in the early 1980s as the peace movement of those years linked Western activists with Eastern dissidents. Often presented without any basis for comparison with pollution outside the region, and with a cavalier disregard for differentiation within the region, the accounts given by the publicists of those years were unfortunately largely accurate. They were corroborated by authenticated reports from occasional experts within the region who made a significant contribution to elevating the environmental issue to pride of place, though always behind that of human rights, in the symbolism of the dissidents' struggle with the ruling parties. This occurred as Gorbachev's policies of *perestroika* and *glasnost* in the Soviet Union began to undermine the power of those parties.

The literature has also dealt with those aspects of communist rule that were most to blame for the environmental damage [*Manser, 1993; Waller and Millard, 1992*]. First, political priorities working through the system of central command planning in the economy imposed an emphasis on quantitative indicators of production that took no account of environmental – or indeed any other – costs. The energy consumed per unit of production was universally very high in the region, and although legislation was passed to protect against the greatest damage to the environment, the laws were not adequately enforced, and managers knew that a failure to produce would count more heavily against them than an act of pollution. Secondly, whilst expert opinion circulated relatively freely except in certain value-laden spheres, the party exercised a control over the means of communication that ruled out the formation of public opinion, and a more general control that made it impossible to organise for political ends.

In such circumstances, public protest over environmental problems could only be muted. As noted, some experts working in the environmental field were prepared to present evidence in ways that did involve some risk to themselves. Interestingly, they were joined, in the case of some countries, by members of organisations that were actually sponsored by the ruling parties, including the very official peace committees and the parties' youth organisations. But most important of all was the adoption of the environmental issue by the major dissenting groups in the northern tier of countries – Poland, Czechoslovakia, the GDR (where the Evangelical churches functioned as the spearhead of a significant pacifist and environmental movement) and Hungary. Bulgaria was not affected until 1988, and Romania not at all [*Waller, 1989*].

Of particular interest, in view of the way in which things turned out, was the movement of protest in Hungary directed against the projected double damming of the Danube at Gabčíkovo in Slovakia and at Nagymáros in

Hungary itself. The activities of the Danube Circle, formed to contest the project, involved petitions and protest marches which mobilised thousands of supporters in the face of police harassment. There were strong nationalist overtones in that protest, concerning the awkward relations that have obtained between Hungary and the Slovaks in history and concerning also the particular attachment that Hungarians have towards the stretch of the Danube Bend where the Nagymáros dam was to be built [*Manser, 1993: 140–42; Waller, 1992*]. These historical points of reference had, of course, a contemporary relevance as dissent against the ruling party, and through it against Soviet domination, built up during the 1980s. Not only in Hungary, but in Poland and Czechoslovakia too, protest over environmental issues was linked to an overriding concern for human rights, which in the circumstances meant a concern for liberation. The fall of the Berlin Wall was not, in itself, a victory for any environmental movement. But it was the culmination of a rise in support in those four countries for a more general movement of liberation in which the issues of peace and protection of the environment featured prominently.

Thus even a brief examination of the early responses to environmental problems is sufficient to indicate their dependence on the circumstances of the time and, by the same token, the uncertainty of their future. The future was to prove as problematic as the past had been glorious, and the greening of Eastern Europe was not destined to outlive the system that it had done so much to discredit.

It remains to point out that, despite these features of Communist rule which led to a failure to check, and even a tendency to augment, a degradation of the environment, the Communist regimes were not blind to the need to provide technological, and indeed political, solutions to an industrial problem. For the first, they conformed to the almost universal policy of seeking to eliminate smoke by splitting atoms. Except in the cases of Poland and Romania, the latter of which used Canadian Candu reactors in its nuclear facility at Cernavodă, all the countries of the region used, or were planning to use, reactors made in the Soviet Union. The first generation of these were 400 megawatt reactors of the Voronezh VVR model, but a second generation of 1,000 megawatt reactors was being installed at the moment of the change of regime. It might be noted in passing that the disaster at Chernobyl caused no check in this programme: the countries of the Council for Mutual Economic Assistance confirmed at the beginning of 1987 its plans in this domain that were made before the accident occurred.

As for political measures, the Communist regimes compensated for their refusal to tolerate autonomous organisation for political ends by providing their own, controlled, forms of organisation. It cost them nothing to create societies for the protection of nature, and this they did throughout the region.

But the activities of these societies could never be allowed to interfere with governmental priorities and, whilst it would be quite misleading to suggest that they did not contribute to an awareness of at least a part of the range of environmental problems, their main political function was to serve as a shield behind which the ruling party could hide.

On the Cusp: The Change of Regime

All the Communist regimes of Eastern Europe fell in the one year of 1989. Everywhere a political monopoly in the hands of the ruling party gave way to competitive politics, and a start was made, rather fitfully, in replacing the system of central command planning by the market. The Western economic advisers who thereupon offered the benefit of their skills to the new governments of the region were not wrong in assuming that the task on which they embarked with such enthusiasm was a common one. The political steps that the new regimes took to transform monopoly into choice and voice were, likewise, common to all the regimes, and included notably laws establishing freedom of the press and of association, and an electoral law. Figure 1 presents a diagram of a generally-shared periodisation of the change of regimes reduced, for heuristic purposes, to a skeletal form.

FIGURE 1

GENERALLY SHARED PERIODISATION OF THE CHANGE OF REGIME

X Fall of the Communist regime
a Helsinki Accords
b Gorbachev comes to power
c First fully free elections

The foregoing has concerned the period from the Helsinki Accords up to the fall of the Communist regimes, given here as a convenient marker in the process of change which draws its chief relevance from the use that dissenters in the region made of the Accords. Now, however, it is the period immediately following the fall of the regimes that concerns us (X–c). It was a period packed with events as the social, political and economic system of each of these countries underwent profound change. It was marked by the universal prevalence of a sense of liberation, and a crude polarisation between Communism on the one hand and the aggregated forces for change on the other formed the basis for all aspects of the political competition that the new order ushered in. As concerns the politics of the environment, a number of developments merit attention.

First, the prospect of electoral success, which the prominence of the environmental issue in the movements of dissent prior to 1989 seemed to hold out to the green parties that formed to fight the elections, proved illusory. The electorate throughout the region made clear where its priorities lay as the material shock of the economic transition became evident, and the environmental issue slipped surprisingly abruptly down, and almost off, the political agenda. In circumstances where party profiles were necessarily indistinct, the green parties were at times even suspected of harbouring recycled Communists [*Jehlička and Kostelecký, 1992: 75*]. Only in Bulgaria did an environmental movement enter a parliament in any strength, and even there *Ekoglasnost* and the Green Party were part of the anti-Communist coalition of the Union for Democratic Forces. They were, moreover, to split, and when Filip Dimitrov assumed the mantle of premier in 1991 as leader of the UDF, it was as a member of a splinter of the Green Party incongruously named the Conservative Ecological Party, whose commitment to environmental goals was not conspicuous (for the developments in the transition period see Waller and Millard [*1992*]).

Secondly, in the numerous cases where convinced and convincing environmentalists cashed their role as a dissident before 1989 by accepting the environmental brief in one of the new governments they found themselves constrained by the economic policies that the transition was seen as involving, by government and people alike. A prominent case was that of the geographer Vavroušek who, in a Czechoslovak government led by the archmarketeer Václav Klaus, could find expression for his informed commitment only in devoting his energies to the international politics of the environment. The atrophy of the environmental movements of the pre-1989 period are treated further in Barbara Jancar-Webster's contribution to this collection.

Thirdly, the new governments of the region, constrained as they were by the resources available, set about tackling the worst of the environmental blackspots and passing legislation to control further polluting activity. Certain tasks were imposed by immediate circumstances. A case in point was the waste left by the departing Soviet armed forces, the worst of which took the form of spills of fuel oil These were in some cases serious enough to threaten the quality of ground water in the vicinity of the camps that were being vacated. More generally, in 1989 the Polish government marked out 80 particular blackspots for immediate attention, and a further 800 were identified by *voivodships* as the worst local polluters [*Manser, 1993: 72*] although it was clear that the gap between marking them out and dealing with them adequately would be enormous.

Fourthly, however, help was at hand for this task, in the form of aid and technical advice from Western countries which had a number of good reasons for taking part in the clean-up of the region. This international aspect of the environmental politics of Eastern Europe will be addressed below in greater detail, since it is of the greatest analytical importance. International involvement took many forms, some of it short-range and simple in its motivation. For example, although the reactor at Chernobyl was of the RBMK type, it was quite understandable in the circumstances of the time that the German Federal Republic should move as soon as politically possible to take the former GDR's Voronezh nuclear facilities under its wing. Intervention at a longer range, however, was soon involved as the programmes for aid and investment in the region got under way, and the motivations were rather more complex.

A fifth feature of the transition period (X–c in the diagram) concerns the evolution of the dissenting movements which, particularly in the cases of Poland, Czechoslovakia, Hungary and the GDR, had since the late 1970s been articulating a protest that included an appeal for the protection of the environment. As noted, that appeal was in the circumstances part of a broader mobilisation at the heart of which was the issue of human rights, and this in turn evoked the issue of liberation – from Communism and from domination by the Soviet Union. The ideas of those dissenting movements were not, by definition, formed in a debate over government policies, nor could they emerge from a programmatic competition between structured political parties. The opinion leaders who shaped and propagated those ideas as well as they could in circumstances of police harassment were destined to form the first post-Communist governments, but the viability of their ideas in the new circumstances, once liberation had been achieved, was from the moment of regime change questionable. Certain it was that those earlier ideas were swiftly eclipsed by what were seen as the imperatives of the transition to a market economy and an alignment with the Western world.

In the event the new governments inherited a circumscribed power in circumstances over which they had limited control. Constraints imposed by the powerful eastern overlord were replaced by other constraints which, whilst they came from the benign quarter of the countries whose economic and political practices the erstwhile dissenters had envied, worked in a way that was hostile to many of their fundamental ideals. The freedom offered by the market, the succour held out by foreign aid and advice, and the sectional competition of electoral politics, ironically rang the knell of any aspiration the movements entertained of instituting a society in which their message could be translated into the decentralised cooperation of non-governmental actors dedicated to quality-of-life issues. In the case of the Czech Republic (then part of Czechoslovakia), Civic Forum split into a Civic Democratic Union, led by a former finance official who had joined Civic Forum only at the time of the fall of the Communist regime, and a Civic Movement, which became the respository of the ideas of the dissident movement and which was soon to atrophy. In a different but parallel case the Polish Solidarity split into a whole congeries of parties and movements after a similar anguish over the loss of its identity as a movement rallying the nation against a Soviet-sponsored ruling party.

The facts of that period of the transition, between 1989 and the first fully free elections, are now available in the literature [*Batt, 1991; Brown, 1994; Huntington, 1991; Roskin, 1991; Rothschild, 1989*]. In the following section the focus of attention will be on one particularly salient aspect of the transition: its international dimension. For in this realm the more general features of the transition from Communism meet up with specifically environmental features to produce a particularly rich illustration of what the process of change in Eastern Europe has involved.

The International Factor: Aid and Investment

The politics of the environment at any level and in any region throws up complexities that create at times problems of interpretation and judgement. One such problem is the gap between fears and fact, between apprehension and comprehension. It is a gap that in a sense can never be bridged, since what may seem irrational fears to the scientific or technological expert have to be taken as fact by the political analyst, politicians themselves having the task of weighing technological fact against public fears which often contest the technical fact.

A second problem – of greater relevance to the discussion here – is that the politics of the environment is riddled with contradictions, paradoxes, and conflicts of goals. Creating or recreating bridleways robs the dormouse of its habitat. Substituting nuclear fission for fossil fuels as a source of energy produces problems of waste disposal. A variant of this was encountered above with the project to solve the problem of airborne pollution by harnessing the hydraulic power of the Danube.

Such contradictions are everywhere to be found in a world that is finally beginning to take environmental problems seriously. But Eastern Europe since the fall of the Communist regimes has been afflicted by a contradiction arising from the very particular circumstances of the breaking down of the barrier that separated the planned economies of the former Soviet Union and Eastern Europe from the market economies of the West. That barrier was no doubt responsible for many of the environmental problems associated with Communist rule noted above. By the same token, its removal meant that the environmental problems of the region were likely to decrease – as indeed they did, although in the early stages of the transition this was due as much to a simple fall in production as to measures taken to combat pollution [*Manser, 1993: 73–4*]. But it is not the internal battle to limit environmental damage that will provide the chief focus of this section. It concerns rather the problem of assessing the impact of external actors on the internal politics of the Eastern European countries, in a day when the East–West confrontation has been resolved in favour of the West. For, to varying degrees, liberation from Soviet tutelage has spelled dependence on Western financing, and the question has to be raised of the extent to which cleaning up the environment has come to be bound up with taking advantage of opportunities for investment.

The *Zeitgeist* has moved on from a day when any such dependence could be denounced in round terms as exploitation of poorer countries by rich. In the broader scheme of things these countries form part of a North that is well endowed in relation to the South, and they are all bound eventually, in one way or another, to benefit from the influx of foreign finance and expertise that they have experienced, unless some unexpected turn radically changes the present course of events. None the less, any sensitive analysis of the politics of the environment in Eastern Europe at the close of this century is bound to attempt an assessment of the impact of that influx. It can reasonably be claimed that all have gained: foreign providers of funds, regional governments, the inhabitants of the Eastern European countries, and also their Western neighbours who have felt threatened, for example by insecure nuclear installations. It is true also that aid and investment have not been forthcoming in the quantity expected and desired. Moreover, in view of this general gain, questions of motivation may be judged inconsequential. None the less it would be surprising if in a field so prone to conflicting agendas and priorities the environmental aspects of the process of change did not raise important questions about the political impact of international factors in the recent evolution of Eastern Europe. Perspective is hard to achieve, and to arrive at a balanced view, the role of that factor as concerns the environment must be seen in its entirety. Only when that full picture has been sketched in can the significance of the impact of external involvement be adequately presented. The treatment here will begin with a description of the nature and extent of external involvement; it will then consider the stances and policies of the region's new governments; and finally an analysis will be undertaken of the relations between and among three key political actors: the external providers of funds and advice, the regional governments, and local movements and NGOs.

The Scope and Nature of External Involvement

A first area of international interaction is one in which external involvement cannot be claimed to have had any oppressive character. It covers the substantial number of cases of fruitful partnership between regional and external actors. This is illustrated by the Danube Environmental Programme, which was designed to promote the environmental management of the Danube basin and scientific knowledge about it. The Programme involves teams from a number of riparian states, including notably Bulgaria, Romania and Slovakia. Foreign expertise and funding plays an important role at this regional level, though without having a significant impact, in this case, on the internal politics of the Danube countries. The Equipe Cousteau takes part in improving environmental management, whilst funding has been provided from numerous sources including the Global Environmental Facility, the European Bank for Reconstruction and Development (EBRD), USAID and the World Bank

To such cases of regional cooperation should be added the numerous initiatives taken to solve or reduce transboundary problems, which by their nature have usually involved external actors. Examples are the international agreements to clean up the Baltic and the Black Seas, and to protect the river Elbe. Indeed, the Baltic Marine Environmental Protection Commission dates from 1980, though it was not until 1988 that it resolved to reduce the emission of pollutants to 50 per cent of 1987 levels by 1995. In 1990 Czechoslovakia, Denmark, Finland, Germany, Norway, Poland, Sweden, the then Soviet Union and the European Commission signed a declaration confirming the commitment [*World Resources Institute, 1992: 68*]. The Black Sea Environmental Management Programme has been initiated by the Global Environment Facility and other sources of funding on the one hand, and regional governments on the other (in this case Bulgaria, Georgia, Romania, the Russian Federation, Turkey and Ukraine). In the case of the Elbe, a treaty was signed by Germany, Czechoslovakia and the European Commission to protect the river.

Secondly, a good deal of external involvement has been directed towards stimulating the growth of local environmental movements (which tend in the literature and indeed in their self-description to be labelled, often indiscriminately, NGOs). Here history has worked a particular irony, which was hinted at in the previous section. The major dissenting movements of the final years of Communist power were, as noted, both vocal and active in their support of the protection of the environment. But the extent to which this was a matter of rallying all possible support behind general universalising symbols was revealed when the collapse of the Communist regimes saw the environmental issue slip sharply down the political agenda.

The successor governments were neither willing nor indeed able to give environmental considerations a high priority, the achievement of liberation from Communist rule robbed the environmental issue of a good part of its mobilising potential, and such environmental movements as survived had to maintain themselves in being in much changed circumstances.

To their rescue came the foreigner, and the irony of the earlier position of the environmental movements was replaced by a new one. As champions of a cleaner environment, their role and their opportunities were both much enhanced. But as radical dissenters from the kind of society that a growth-oriented economy fosters they could only be perplexed by the manifest links between the agencies that were giving aid to their governments and those that were encouraging their own development as non-governmental organisations.

Of central importance in this support to local movements was the setting up of a Regional Environment Centre (REC) in Budapest. The statement that each issue of the REC's quarterly newsletter *The Bulletin* carried, in its early years, described the organisation as 'an independent, non-advocacy, not-for-profit foundation', and gave as its mission 'to promote co-operation among diverse environmental groups and interests in Central and Eastern Europe; to act as a catalyst for developing solutions to environmental problems in this region; and to promote the development of a civil society'. It was established in 1990 by Hungary, the United States, and the European Commission. Seven further countries later joined these founding sponsors. The beneficiary countries are Albania, Bulgaria, Croatia, the Czech Republic, Hungary, Poland, Romania, Slovakia, Slovenia and the Former Yugoslav Republic of Macedonia. 'In these countries', the mission statement also states, 'the REC primarily supports environmental non-governmental organisations (NGOs), but also co-operates with local authorities, national governments, academic institutions and the private sector'.

The REC offers earmarked grants for industrial problems and energy conservation, and for public participation. It also offers local grants. As an example of the money disbursed, in July–August 1995 a total of ECU 78,453 went to industrial problems and energy conservation, ECU 88,981 to public participation, and US$158,564 to local grants (*REC Bulletin,* Vol.5, No.3, 1995, p.20). These last are often very small. In a list of local grants awarded during another period (April–June 1994), US$122,784 went to 105 projects – an average of US$1,170 each (*REC Bulletin,* Vol.4, No.2, 1994, pp.7–9). The grant was often for a typewriter, a printer, a summer camp, or an event. To receive a grant, the receiving body has to be properly registered as an association.

In funding the work of the REC it is clearly the intention of participating governments to help the Eastern European countries to help themselves by fostering popular involvement. And indeed a reading of any listing of awards in *The Bulletin* reveals a vast array of organisations, large and small, that benefit from the REC's support. Both the personalities involved in the Centre's work – such as the Czech Bedřich Moldán, a veteran of the dissident movement – and the articles that the Bulletin carries make it difficult to see the REC as a stool-pigeon of the participating governments, internal to the region or external to it. The tone of those articles, however, whilst frequently critical, is rarely polemical. Articles in one issue on nuclear power in the region, for example, come out clearly in favour of substituting energy saving for the atom, and are critical of the intention of the regionn's governments almost universally to complete the nuclear programmes that they initiated during the Communist years (Vol.5, No.4). But this is no campaigning, and articles of that kind fit comfortably into a category of contributions – one on ecotourism and one on the motor car follow in later numbers – concerned to raise issues rather than to mobilise around them.

The same lack of distinction between hares and hounds, or gamekeepers and poachers, is illustrated by a further example of external involvement affecting environmental movements and NGOs: the case of the World Wildlife Fund (WWF). The WWF has been very active in Eastern Europe since 1989, putting forward often very imaginative schemes, such as that for converting the wide strip of land that effectively constituted the iron curtain, and which was consequently not a congenial place for human activity of any kind other than the military, into a pollution-free zone. Like the REC, the WWF has devoted attention and money towards fostering local environmental movements and, like the REC, it shows the same undifferentiated concern for business, government and environmental protection. Its involvement takes place through a variety of organisations and associations based in the US and Western Europe, its highly informative *Central and Eastern European Newsletter* being published in Washington DC.

For example, WWF–US conducts most of its work in ECE through the Environment Training Project for Central and Eastern Europe (ETP). ETP is funded by the US Agency for International Development, is directed by the University of Minnesota, and enrols as further partners the Institute for Sustainable Communities and the Centre for Hazardous Materials Research (CHMR) of Pittsburgh. Since the launch of ETP in 1992, WWF-USS's principal role 'has been organising and overseeing conflict resolution skills, training workshops for all of ETP's audiences, developing and managing training courses for NGOs, and promoting development of environmental library and information centre networks', the central goal of ETP being 'to improve the capability of people in ECE to address environmental problems in the context of a competitive market economy' [*Liroff, 1995: 6*]. In another project involving the CHMR the three-year effort aimed 'to identify environmental infrastructure projects ... in which US firms can become involved and will link the need for environmental technology in those projects with goods and services provided by US companies' (*Newsletter,* No.7, 15 Sept. 1992, p.5).

The integrative thrust of such an approach, brought out by the emphasis of conflict resolution in these and other statements, and the element of tutelage that motivations stemming from an expertise in running a competitive market economy promote, is brought out in an article by Randy Kritkausky and Carolyn Schmidt in the WWF's *Newsletter.* Commenting on multimillion dollar development and investment projects that are planned in ECE, the Baltics and the former Soviet Union, they point out that

> these projects are funded by multilateral international organisations such as banks and by Western corporations. Along with Western loans and investments, large foreign consulting companies arrive. In theory consulting companies have much to offer. Their large staffs often include an enormous variety of talented experts. This expertise can greatly enhance technical planning for and implementation of an environmental or developmental project [*Kritkausky and Schmidt, 1995: 9–12*].

However, these very strengths are a problem for the indigenous NGOs, which have established their political presence by offering professional quality expertise.

> Now, quite suddenly, highly paid, professionally staffed, and technically well equipped foreign experts appear on the scene. On the one hand foreign experts and local NGOs have much in common and may have much to gain by co-operating ... On the other hand, different expectations and different goals may lead to disappointments and disagreements [*Kritkausky and Schmidt, 1995: 9–12*].

The authors go on to point out that an emphasis on conflict-resolution training and decision-making skills can distract attention from the adversarial role that might be appropriate to NGOs working in a democratic environment. To which it might be added that the major international NGOs such as WWF themselves do not always show any great awareness of this contradiction. True, the effectiveness of these international NGOs depends upon their steering a discreet course between collusion with governments and a campaigning stance. But they vary in the balance they strike between these poles, and the case of the WWF shows how easy it is in the circumstances of Eastern Europe, where a common goal appears to be generally assumed, for external involvement to confirm those assumptions and to favour those forces that benefit from them.

There is no ambivalence in a third case of foreign involvement – that of loans and other forms of financial aid. When the EBRD was set up in 1990, provisions for environmental protection and sustainable development were incorporated directly into the bank's enabling legislation [*Crockett and Schultz, 1990: 261*]. Other international lending institutions that have extended loans and aid specifically for environmental purposes are the World Bank and the European Investment Bank.

To loans from banks should be added government-to-government aid programmes, with Western European governments contributing both individually and by way of the European Union – the latter through its PHARE and THERMIE programmes. For example, in its Multi-Country Programme for the Environment PHARE made a total of ECU 66 million available in 1995 for initiatives under that programme, broken down as in Table 1.

TABLE 1

PHARE MULTI-COUNTRY INITIATIVES: 1995 (MILLION ECU)

CEEC Cooperation with the European Environmental Agency	7.0
'MARS' and related environmental applications	4.0
Regional Environmental Center (REC)	1.0
Integrated Environment Programme for the Danube River Basin	0.8
Black Sea	0.5
Black Triangle	5.0
Development of Remediation Concepts for Uranium Mining Operations in Central and Eastern Europe	1.0
Regional Environmental Fund for Project Preparation	0.5
Programme Management and Liaison	0.2
Total 1995	20.0

In 1993 the European Community commented on its assistance to Eastern Europe in the energy sector with the words:

The potential for energy saving is enormous and, if realised, significant economic and environmental benefits will accrue to the eastern countries and indeed to the Community as well. It would also allow eastern countries more freedom of choice with regard to their range of future energy options [*IIEC-Europe, 1995: 12*].

But, fourthly, aid has been not only a matter of money. In the nuclear field in particular, but in other spheres too, aid has come in the form of expertise.

The nuclear case is analytically important, in that oversight of that sector in Eastern Europe by external actors has been clearly a matter of external governments protecting the health and survival of their own populations as much as of a Western interest in making the region safe for inward investment, or preparing the way for a substitution of Russian by Western reactors. The Chernobyl disaster of 1986 played an important part in bringing external expertise both to the former Soviet Union and to Eastern Europe, although the reactors in the latter region are of the VVR rather than Chernobyl's RBMK type.

Since 1989, inputs of external expertise involving the physical presence of technical experts have often amounted to supervision, as in the case of the ailing Kozloduy reactors in Bulgaria. In fields outside the nuclear there have been numerous schemes for the exchange of information and for technology transfer. Cases of the former were encountered above, in the activities of the Regional Environment Centre and the WWF. But the list of external bodies that have come forward with offers of expertise is substantial, and includes – simply as examples – the Institute for European Environmental Policy, Friends of the Earth International, the World Environment Centre, Management Sciences for Health, the Environmental Law Institute, The Rockefeller Brothers Fund, the World Conservation Union, the Ecological Studies Institute, and the International Institute for Applied Systems Analysis (*WWF Central and Eastern Europe Newsletter,* 15 January 1991, pp.1–6).

Most of these will be recognised as US-based organisations. But it will be recalled also that the UK's own programme of aid to Eastern Europe, which disbursed £63 million in 1993–94 [*IIEC-Europe, 1995: 9*], is labelled the 'Know How Fund'. The name was well chosen, for both its explicit and its implicit connotations. It registered the fact that the actual sums envisaged for contributing to cleaning up the Eastern European environment were unlikely to be commensurate with the need. But it also reflected the relationship that was seen to exist after 1989 between Western teachers and post-Communist learners. There was indeed much to learn, and the health and possibly the survival of populations was at stake as concerned environmental aid. None the less the new circumstances and the new relationships brought a particular political configuration, to an analysis of which we return below.

Regional Governments in the International Context

The Communist governments had themselves made a point of signing all the major conventions to regulate transboundary environmental problems whilst they were in power, and the new governments were hardly likely to do less, if for no other reason than that foreign aid was likely to be attendant upon a correct comportment in relation to international agreements. But after 1989 a new dimension was added to their international activity when a series of pan-European Environment Ministers' conferences was established in 1991 (which includes in fact representatives of the governments also of the USA, the former Soviet Union and the other G-24 countries). The first such meeting was held in Czechoslovakia in a castle at Dobriš near Prague, the choice of venue owing much to the activity of Vavroušek who, as noted above, was compensating for the limitations on his ability to force radical environmental policies on the Czechoslovak government by bringing his commitment to environmental concerns to bear by concentrating on international environmental diplomacy. A second meeting was held in Lucerne in 1993, and a third in Sofia in 1995.

The limitations of this process became clear at the Lucerne meeting. Much had been expected of that conference, and it did produce a 320-page Environmental Action Plan but, as Bernd Baumgartl comments in his account of the conference:

> Its starting point is precisely the fact 'that unfortunately there is no money available', as Richard Ackermann of the World Bank explained in a press conference. 'We did not try to prescribe what has to be done, but if [and] how it should be done' [*Baumgartl, 1993: 249*].

Talk of 'burden-sharing' made it clear that the countries of the region were expected to fend for themselves to the greatest extent possible, and it is true that much of the optimism that preceded the conference rested on an expectation that new ideas would be underpinned by more substantial aid from external sources. The nuclear issue was prominent in the discussions, nuclear-free Denmark dropping its support for 'a general phase-out of nuclear energy in the long run' put forward by the Austrians and a number of small states [*Baumgartl, 1993: 249*]. The proposal was to become a footnote in the final declaration as a general call for safety and for the adoption of a more radical position in the future.

The Sofia meeting – 'a fight against decline' in the words of a spokesperson for the Environmental Citizens' Organisation [*Silina, 1995: 3*] – confirmed the main message of the Lucerne meeting. Regional governments, but also the region's industry and the consumers, were going to have to bear the brunt of the continuing costs of environmental protection. But discussions on methods of finance going beyond the confines of individual national budgets made some headway, covering mechanisms such as grants, loans (and subsidised loans, enabling an unviable project to borrow money at rates below the prime), environmental equity funds and debt-for-nature swaps, hypothecated environmental funds, and market-based mechanisms such as green taxes and pollution charges (*REC Bulletin,* Vol.5, No.3, pp.11–14).

This series of conferences was designed for discussions at ministerial level, but NGOs also participated. Although their interventions were controlled by stern chairing, radical voices were none the less heard. In view of the stress placed in this study on the strength of external influences, it is worth pointing out that in this case the emphasis on self-reliance, coupled with a very positive and at times radical contribution from the NGOs, suggests that the integrating effect that the injection of external aid and expertise has on political relations in the countries of the region does have limits.

A second important influence on the environmental policies of the new governments of Eastern Europe has been the pull of the European Union, and here the strength of the international factor can be very clearly seen. Once they had inherited the power vacated by the fall of the previously ruling Communist parties, the new governments of the region without exception adopted two immediate policy goals. The first was to abolish the system of central command planning in favour of the market. The second was to take whatever steps might be deemed necessary in order to qualify for ultimate acceptance into the European Community (as it was then styled).

Four years were to pass before the policy of moving closer to the European Community bore fruit. Between 4 October 1993 and 4 October 1996 Hungary, Poland, Romania, Slovakia, the Czech Republic, Slovenia and Bulgaria all signed Association Agreements with the European Union. The EU's decision was not straightforward. When the three Baltic states of Estonia, Latvia and Lithuania were added, the accession of the nine countries that had been either component parts of the Soviet Union or had been members of the Soviet bloc could hardly be contemplated without a deepening of the EU's structures and procedures. There were, moreover, marked differences in the economic level of the Eastern European countries. It was in fact political considerations that determined the decision to open discussions about future membership and to place these countries ahead of Turkey in the queue for entry, though nothing guaranteed that some of them at least would not join Turkey in the inhospitable antechamber to EU membership.

However, in June 1993 in Copenhagen the European Council agreed that all the countries that had signed Association Agreements would be eligible for membership, a decision that was confirmed at a later meeting in Luxembourg. Then six Eastern European countries were invited to send delegates to the EU summit in Essen in December 1994. It was a mark of the seriousness with which the EU viewed the negotiations with Eastern Europe that the brief on the Commission for conducting those negotiations was hotly disputed between Hans van den Broek and Leon Brittan – the former being victorious in that contest. In that same year of 1994 Hungary and Poland officially applied for membership. Slovakia, Romania and Bulgaria followed in 1995, but it was not until 23 January 1996 that the Czech Republic took that step.

On 16 July 1997 the EU's Commission announced its 'Agenda 2000' plan, which accepted the case for full membership for Poland, the Czech Republic, Hungary, Slovenia, Estonia and Cyprus, with final inclusion expected 'around about 2002'. The Commission stressed that the door would remain open for Bulgaria, Romania, Slovakia, Latvia and Lithuania to join at a later stage.

These protracted negotiations went on against the background of the economic policies that were designed to pave the way for integration into the EU, and which included programmes of privatisation and the establishment of market mechanisms. These programmes proceeded at varying paces in the different countries and will no doubt have an effect on the final dates of entry. Environmental considerations necessarily formed a part of those programmes, since rebuilding the economies of the region required attention to an infrastructure which was at many points in a lamentable state. But also the Association Agreements included aligning the environmental policies and international agreements of the various Eastern European countries with those of the EU. This was in part simply to remove some of the more evident risks to health, to reduce transboundary pollution, and to ensure the complementarity of international agreements entered into. It had the further purpose, however, of facilitating the process of entry into the EU, and indeed of hastening the advent of that day. It need hardly be said that this pull towards membership of the European Union has exerted a powerful influence on the policy choices of Eastern European governments.

External Actors, Regional Governments, and Local NGOs

Some analytical conclusions may now be drawn from this account of external involvement in the environmental politics of Eastern Europe.

A first conclusion must be that in the years since 1989 a transfer of funds and expertise has taken place sufficient to make a significant impact on the state of the environment in Eastern Europe. Before any judgements are made about motivations or ultimate comparative profit, this cannot but be of benefit to the populations of the region, and indeed to those of Western neighbours. It is moreover part of a process that has so far enabled a change of regime to take place in the region without major social turbulence. That change of regime has created in all the countries of the region the conditions for establishing an open competitive political system, in which governments can be made accountable to the people through the mechanisms associated with the form of liberal democracy prevalent in Western Europe. What more is there to say?

There are, in fact, considerations that might be held to qualify this conclusion, without necessarily denying its validity. One is a matter of perspective and political choice, and it concerns the fate of the ideas that the forces for change in Eastern Europe, and a part of Western opinion also, held in the heady years leading up to the toppling of Communism. There is no doubt that the spirit of liberation that was abroad in those days contained notions of popular participation that went beyond the norms of Western Europe's liberal democracy. This was evident in the hesitations over adopting a party mode of organisation and in the whole tenor of the discussion in West and East about civil society and what it entailed. Such a strand of thinking would expect to see a sturdy growth of – among others – environmental movements bringing politics down to the locality and giving preferences expressed at the periphery of the political system access to decision making at the centre. This was not to be, and by far the clearest illustration of the defeat of any such notions was provided by what was shortly to become the Czech Republic. The turning point was the election of Václav Klaus as leader of Civic Forum in October 1990, the creation of the Civic Democratic Party from his faction within the Forum, and his assumption of the post of Prime Minister.

Klaus expressed his views on what was involved in the transition in an article in *The Economist*. 'The available evidence suggests that Western Europe does not provide an optimal model for balancing freedom with regulation', he wrote.

> The welfare state, with its generous transfer payments unconnected to achievements undermines the basic work ethic and thus individual responsibility ... It is fair to observe that the Thatcherite (or anti-Keynesian, or liberal) revolution stopped at best half-way in Western Europe, and is yet to be completed. The visible manifestations of Western Europe's failure to reform include a wasteful and socially explosive rate of unemployment – and one which seems, moreover, to respond little to changes in the business cycle. The main cause lies not in an excessive supply of labour, nor in a lack of demand for labour, nor in immigration, nor in a lack of technological progress ... The factor which comes closest to explaining the problem is the excessively high rate of domestic wages relative to workforce productivity [*Klaus, 1994: 45*].

Klaus has made his impatience with environmental movements clear, and nowhere more than in his principled objection to the phrase 'sustainable development' – a matter analysed fully by Brian Slocock in an earlier issue of this journal [*1996*], where Klaus is also cited as saying that

> an unequivocal and conclusive 'polluting trend' – requiring the

artificial stoppage of the industrial process to date and the refining of economic conditions of peoplee's lives based on that process – does not exist … Contamination is a necessary evil which we cannot avoid if we want to have at our disposal the most varies goods and services to enrich and facilitate our lives [*Klaus, 1996: 510*].

The point of quoting these views at length is not necessarily to dispute them, but to suggest that they conflict rather sharply with the dominant views of the leading figures of pre-1989 movements, and that they do not encourage an invigoration of civil society in the form of a vibrant life of social movements in the localities.

Is this not, though, a matter internal to the Czech Republic, with no connection to external involvement in the environmental politics of the region? Again, we can rest the matter there, and add to the environmental benefits that the transition has brought to the region the further conclusion that it has created also a liberal normality. But two further qualifying considerations can be brought. The first – which, it should be said, applies more in other cases than in the Czech – concerns what has been termed the 'dependency triangle' [*Keohane and Nye, 1977; Stadler, 1994*]. In Stadler's words:

> The bargaining-triangle is a possible way of conceptualising political dependence. The actors 'international environment', 'government' and 'interests groups' play different roles in bargains struck over certain policies. Structural and regional power is unequally distributed. We can speak of dependence of the government on the international environment when socio-economic interest groups are either excluded from the triangle and play no part in the bargain, or are included to such a limited extent that the government's policies are mainly shaped by the international environment [*1994: 47–8*].

That is, regional governments can use the conditionalities that external funding bodies attach to their aid to claim that the demands of groups, and of opposition parties, cannot be met. This is particularly salient where substantial demands are involved, as is so often the case with environmental groups. But the dependence and also the mere feeling of impotence can go beyond this funding nexus in cases where external expertise substitutes itself for local, as was seen above to be the case of local NGOs. This is not so say that the dependence or impotence is willed be the external actors. It is a matter of a certain logic that is at work. By the nature of things, political actors cannot put themselves outside their ideology, or else the ideology would not be theirs in the normal sense.

The final consideration brings us back to the starting point of this exposition. The dominance of Western over Eastern Europe is not of recent date, in terms either of a political model or of direct economic relations, although the Communist interlude of Eastern dominance has led many to forget this. As noted, the dominance has been subject to wide variation, with the Czech Lands – now the Czech Republic – as a pole of weak or zero dominance. This consideration brings out the ultimate absurdity of the calculations that banks and other have made of the costs of putting the environment of Eastern Europe to rights, because any such exercise presupposes a standard that flies in the face either of the historical relationship between Western and Eastern Europe, or of present possibilities. It also raises the question of why the West should be so solicitously pumping – admittedly restricted – amounts of aid and investment into a region that did not command this interest before Russia rose to strength. That question is germane to the concerns of this study, but goes beyond it, and must be left for other pens and other times.

*   *   *

This analysis has emphasised the international factor in the impact of marketisation and democratisation in Eastern Europe as concerns the environment. It is an approach that throws into relief the particular geopolitics of the region. The individual countries of Eastern Europe are situated at differing points on the general European continuum that runs from the more advanced to the less advanced areas, although most of them were in a disadvantaged position in relation to a more advanced Western Europe at the time of the imposition of Communist rule. The cold war rendered the gradations of the continuum less visible through the political division of Europe into two blocs, Soviet power imposing a high degree of political uniformity on Eastern Europe, and bringing to the region policy priorities reflecting those of the Soviet Union in its drive for economic development. Those policy priorities, and the production methods chosen to pursue them, bore hard on the environment.

With the fall of Communism the pendulum of influence swung from East to West, the plan giving way to the market throughout the region and public opinion being liberated from its authoritarian straitjacket. The change of economic and political system brought benefits by demonstrably checking waste in energy use, removing or reducing some of the major causes of pollution, making governments accountable to an electorate, and giving environmental movements freedom to operate. It also brought from outside the region expertise and techniques capable of making production more sensitive to the protection of the environment, at the same time rendering the region safe for the foreign investment that it needed. But aid, expertise and advice brought an element of tutelage which has influenced the evolution of the environmental movement in the region, substituting itself to some extent for grass-roots activism and weakening environmental groups in relation to their governments.

REFERENCES

Batt, Judy (1991), *East Central Europe from Reform to Transformation*, London: Pinter/Royal Institute of International Affairs.

Baumgartl, Bernd (1993), '"Burden-sharing" as a Euphemism: Delusion at the Lucerne Conference, April 1993', *Environmental Politics*, Vol.2, No.4, pp.249–52.

Brown, J.F. (1994), *Hopes and Shadows*, Harlow: Longman.

Carter, F.W. and D.Turnock (eds.) (1993), *Environmental Problems in Eastern Europe*, London: Routledge.

Crockett, Tamara Raye and Cynthia B. Schultz (1990), 'Environmental Protection Issues in Eastern Europe', *International Environmental Reporter*, June.

French, Hilary (1990), *Green Revolutions: Environmental Reconstruction in Eastern Europe and the Soviet Union*, Worldwatch Paper 99, Washington, DC: Worldwatch Institute.

Huntington, Samuel (1991), *The Third Wave: Democratization in the Late Twentieth Century*, Norman, OK: University of Oklahoma Press.

IIEC (International Institute for Energy Conservation) (1991), *Energy Efficiency, Developing Nations and Eastern Europe*, Washington, DC: IIEC.

IIEC-Europe (International Institute for Energy Conservation – Europe) (1995), 'Pollution in Eastern Europe', submission to the Environment Committee.

Jehlička, Petr and Tomáš Kostelecký (1992), 'The Development of the Czechoslovak Green Party since the 1990 Election', *Environmental Politics*, Vol.1, No.1, pp.72–94.

Kabala, Stanley (1991), 'The Hazardous Waste Problem in Eastern Europe', *Radio Free Europe/Radio Liberty Report on Eastern Europe*, Vol.2, No.25, pp.27–33.

Keohane, Robert D. and Joseph S. Nye (1977), *Power and Interdependence: World Politics in Transition*, Boston, MA: Little, Brown.

Klaus, Václav (1994), 'So Far, So Good', *The Economist*, 10 Sept., pp.45–6.

Kramer, John M. (1983), 'The Environmental Crisis in Eastern Europe', *Slavic Review*, Vol.42, No.2, pp.212–16.

Kritkausky, Randy and Carolyn Schmidt (1995), 'NGOs and Western Consulting Companies: Forging Productive Relationships', *Word Wildlife Fund Newsletter*, No.11, pp.9–12].

Lane, David and George Kolankiewicz (1973), *Social Groups in Polish Society*, London: Macmillan.

Liroff, Richard A. (1995), 'The Environmental Training Project for Central and Eastern Europe', *World Wildlife Fund Newsletter*, No.11.

Manser, Roger (1993), *The Squandered Dividend*, London: Earthscan.

Roskin, Michael G. (1991), *The Rebirth of Eastern Europe*, 3rd edn., Englewood Cliffs, NJ: Prentice Hall.

Rothschild, Joseph (1989), *Return to Diversity*, Oxford: Oxford University Press.

Russell, Jeremy (1990), *Environmental Issues in Eastern Europe: Setting an Agenda*, London: Royal Institue of International Affairs.

Silina, Mara (1995), 'Looking beyond Sofia', *The REC Bulletin*, Vol.5, No.4, p.3.

Slocock, Brian (1996), 'The Paradox of Environmental Policy in Eastern Europe: The Dynamics of Policy-Making in the Czech Republic', *Environmental Politics*, Vol.5, No.3, pp.501–21.

Stadler, Andreas (1994), 'Problems of Dependent Modernisation in East Central Europe: A Case for Social-Democratic Concern', in Michael Waller, Bruno Coppieters and Kris Deschouwer (eds.), *Social Democracy in a Post-Communist Europe*, London: Frank Cass.

Waller, Michael (1989), 'The Ecology Movement in Eastern Europe', *The Journal of Communist Studies*, Vol.5, No.3, pp.303–28.

Waller, Michael (1992), 'The Dams on the Danube', *Environmental Politics*, Vol.1, No.1, pp.121–7.

Waller, Michael and Frances Millard (1992), 'Environmental Politics in Eastern Europe', *Environmental Politics*, Vol.1, No.2, pp.159–85.

World Resources Institute (with UNEP and UNDP) (1992), *World Resources 1992–1933*, Oxford: Oxford University Press.

ZumBrunnen, Craig (1990), 'The Environmental Challenge in Eastern Europe', *Millenium*, Vol.19, No.3.

Financing Environmental Policy in East Central Europe

ANS KOLK and EWOUT VAN DER WEIJ

The transition in East Central Europe (ECE) created a general optimism which was reflected in a belief that a solution to the environmental problems faced by these countries would be found. There were great expectations regarding the blessings of the market economy, which would diminish state-guided waste and pollution, the political openness which would arise from democratisation, and the positive developments which would result from the inward flow of Western investments and aid funds. Although the demise of central planning and Western funding led to improvements, new problems emerged. Environmental aid has turned out to be much lower and subject to more complicated conditions than initially expected. Moreover, financing and implementing environmental policy in a market context, without a proper regulatory framework, has proved difficult. However, the past few years have also shown some positive experiences with market-oriented instruments as well as a strengthening of institutional capacity. In addition, a more flexible approach towards environmental assistance has been adopted and increasing emphasis has been placed on public participation. In this respect, the process set in motion by the Environmental Action Programme for Central and Eastern Europe (EAP) has been important.

This contribution examines Western financing of East Central Europe (ECE) environmental management policy. It begins by outlining the initial optimism of transition countries concerning the benefits of marketisation and democratisation. In particular, it focuses on the perceived advantages of Western aid for environmental clean-up and management. It then charts the process through which countries realised that Western aid would be limited, requiring in turn greater domestic input into the management of the environment. The analysis then shows how this input had to take the form not only of greater financing of environmental projects but the adoption of new managerial skills by administrators – including privatisation of environmental goals, increased administrative efficiency, wider participation, and more effective coordination. The response to those challenges has been mixed and the article concludes by outlining those areas where need for change still exists. At the same time it points to the need for a donor learning curve, as the biases and limitations inherent in Western aid become evident and the danger involved in constructing an environmental policy around the needs of donors, as opposed to those of the recipient, become apparent.

The Environmental Action Programme for ECE

Concern about the environmental problems of ECE countries grew in many Western countries, especially as much of this pollution was transboundary in nature and thus constituted a direct threat to the environment of Western Europe. At the same time, the end of the cold war resulted in an optimism that a joint approach to the existing problems could be taken. This was expressed in policy terms in the consultation among European Ministers of the Environment under the motto 'Environment for Europe'. The first meeting took place in 1991. The Environmental Action Plan (EAP) was presented at the second conference, held in Lucerne in April 1993, which was the result of extensive discussions and studies in the intervening period. Not only delegates from the European countries but also the World Bank, the Organisation for Economic Co-operation and Development, and the Commission of the European Communities played an important role in setting up the EAP. The EAP and Western aid to the region were evaluated at the follow-up conference in Sofia in October 1995.

In addition to an extensive catalogue of the environmental problems facing transition countries, the EAP contained a list of recommendations [*Environment for Europe, 1994: 77–833*]. 'Win–win' measures, which benefit both the environment and the economy, occupied pride of place. These included a recommendation to abolish subsidies which encourage overuse and waste of fuel and water; developing immediate policies to combat local environmental pollution, partly with an eye to major health problems; the introduction of market-oriented measures to reduce pollution, and a strengthening of legislation and regulation, and the application of realistic environmental standards. The principal targets were those activities which cost relatively little or which could be combined with an increase in economic efficiency. Furthermore, the EAP underlined the need to strengthen local and regional institutions, and to bring about a transfer of knowledge, technology and financial resources.

The Western funds for the environment in ECE, which increased after 1989, were both reactive and proactive: they were aimed at helping to clear up existing pollution, while at the same time applying technologies to reduce emissions and pollution, contributing to a change in the methods of production which led to pollution. Importance was attached to environmental education and the effect which a number of model projects are expected to have. The funds are provided through multilateral channels such as the European Union (EU), the World Bank, and the European Bank for Reconstruction and Development (EBRD), from bilateral aid programmes and sometimes through Western environmental organisations.

The Amount of Funding

The price of tackling the environmental problems in ECE can, at best, only be estimated. It was only recently that the major EU aid programme, PHARE, came up with the estimate that ECU 300 billion is needed in the next 15 years to make substantial improvements to the quality of the environment; this sum corresponds to almost ten per cent of the economic output of the region [*PHARE, 1995: 29*]. Some governments did make different estimates of the sums required for the reduction of the environmental problems in certain sectors or regions. The then Czechoslovakian government, for example, argued that environmental upgrading would cost more than $30 billion, while in 1990 the Polish Ministry of the Environment stated that $260 billion would be required if the country was to be able to satisfy the EU standards by the year 2000 [*Marwaha, 1993: 117*]. In general, however, it was acknowledged that the sums concerned were enormous, and that it would therefore be best to concentrate initially on those activities with which substantial results could be achieved for a relatively low investment.

Although Western donors have not made any specific commitments on the final scale of their environmental aid, nor have they tied themselves down to assuming responsibility for any particular area, there were nevertheless certain expectations in many ECE countries. The collapse of the Berlin Wall was the signal for extensive speculations about how the need for economic reforms and a reinforcement of the process of democratisation, would result in large-scale Western aid. Environmental improvements were seen as part of these reforms, with the added belief that Western concern about transboundary pollution would ensure that funds for pollution clean-up and control would be provided.

It is not easy to obtain an accurate picture of the environmental aid which Western donors provide to ECE, as until recently very few statistics were available. Some information was released during the run-up to the Sofia conference, although there are still a number of points which need clarification. They mainly concern the difference between commitments and disbursements; these two categories may diverge widely as a result of, *inter alia*, bureaucratic delays and the absence of projects which meet the right requirements. In the case of Poland, for example, which received almost one-third of all of the environmental funds allocated to ECE, by the middle of 1994 only roughly one-quarter of the aid had produced specific results in the form of completed projects [EBRD, 1995: 22]. It is also important to know what kind of aid is involved – grants or loans – and if they are loans, the interest rates, maturity periods and other conditions. These are relevant aspects for both donors and recipients, but they are not dealt with properly in most surveys. The available figures are not usually mutually comparable, nor are they always equally reliable.

The most detailed statistics are those of the Task Force for the implementation of the EAP. For the purposes of the Sofia conference, a picture of the total size of Western environmental aid was obtained from data provided by the donors themselves. Table 1 provides a picture of the aid committed to the former Soviet bloc region during the 1990–95 period by the main donors; no distinction is made between loans and donations. The total for this period is ECU 3.5 billion, but most of this at any rate consists of loans. The share of the international financial institutions listed in Table 1 is almost 60 per cent of the total, and they mainly provide loans. It is not known what the ratio is of loans to donations in the case of bilateral environmental aid; the aid provided by the EU consists almost exclusively of donations (see opposite page).

A number of points emerge if total environmental aid during this period is broken down by recipient country (see Table 2; calculated from Environment for Europe [1995a: 7]. The ECE countries receive more than 70 per cent of the aid to the region as a whole. There are also significant differences between the various countries: Poland stands out in a very favourable light, followed by the Czech Republic, Bulgaria and Hungary. In relative terms, these four countries receive 58 per cent of the total environmental aid committed (31 per cent, 11 per cent, nine per cent and seven per cent respectively). In many cases aid follows the flow of foreign investments. The unstable economic situation, the limited creditworthiness, and the uncertainties with which investors are confronted make it difficult for most of the countries in the region to attract foreign capital. Most investments, in order of importance, are made in Hungary, the Czech Republic and Poland.

In order to obtain a better indication of the share of the donations in the total amount of environmental aid, it is possible to examine the statistics provided by the group of 24 (the industrialised countries). According to this information, the environmental aid committed during the 1990–93 period amounted to ECU 774 million [EBRD, 1995: 91]. This sum consists almost entirely of donations, and also applies to the states of the former Soviet Union.

Large 'pure' sums of aid, in the form of donations, come from the EU. Under PHARE, one-sixth of the total sum was earmarked in 1990 for the

TABLE 1

COMMITMENTS OF ENVIRONMENTAL ASSISTANCE IN THE
PERIOD 1990-95 (in million ECU)

Donor	Amount
Austria	59.93
Denmark	117.90
Finland	36.04
France	10.83
Germany	392.42
Japan	13.01
Netherlands	71.57
Norway	29.13
Sweden	51.68
Switzerland	41.49
United Kingdom	10.16
United States	231.40
EU	351.17
EBRD	667.08
EIB	256.90
GEF	49.43
NEFCO	29.49
NIB	35.30
World Bank	1033.10

Source: Environment for Europe [*1995a: 6, Table 3*].

Notes: (1) EIB: European Investment Bank; GEF: Global Environment Facility; NEFCO: Nordic Environment Finance Corporation; NIB: Nordic Investment Bank.

(2) In the case of the World Bank, only environmental projects are included (which excludes the ECU 2182.63 million lent to projects with environmental components).

TABLE 2

LARGEST ECE RECIPIENTS OF ENVIRONMENTAL ASSISTANCE (COMMITMENTS)
IN THE PERIOD 1991-94, TOTAL (in million ECU) AND PER CAPITA (in ECU)

Country	Total	Per capita
Poland	1017.9	26.4
Czech Republic	361.4	34.4
Bulgaria	291.2	32.7
Hungary	239.9	22.8
Romania	190.9	8.2
Slovakia	170.4	31.6

Source: Environment for Europe [*1995a: 7, Table 4*].

environment (ECU 49 million out of a total of ECU 300 million) [*Jachtenfuchs, 1992: 32*]. In practice, however, environmental funds did not rise above ten per cent during the first five years of the programme (calculated from EBRD [*1995: 12, 108*]). This is a clear reflection of the reduced priority accorded the environment by the CEE countries: allocation under PHARE is only made at the request of the countries themselves.

Most of the money goes to Poland and Hungary. A total of ECU 337 million was committed during the 1990–94 period, of which 26 per cent was earmarked for Poland, 18 per cent for Hungary, 12 per cent for Bulgaria and 11 per cent for the Czech Republic (calculated from PHARE [*1995: 21*]). As already stated, these are committed funds, which can differ considerably from the amounts actually provided. For instance, in the 1992–93 period, only 30.6 per cent of the PHARE environmental budget was actually spent; similar discrepancies occurred in other sectors as well, and the difference in the case of the environment was more or less average [*Wiersma and ter Welle, 1995: 31*].[1]

These delays in spending are due to both national and international factors connected with the drawing-up of priorities in tackling the environmental problems, the relatively long preparatory period, the terms on which the aid is granted, the scale of the projects, the co-ordination and the institutional capacity. In many cases these are run-up and transitional problems which have been alleviated by now. These aspects and the recent changes will be dealt with more extensively below.

Changing Insights

The level of Western aid remains lower than the high expectations originally entertained on that score in ECE. In the past transition period, the high expectations regarding the role of international environmental aid have been tempered. International environmental aid is thus only a very small part of total environmental expenditure.[2] Even in Poland this accounted for less than five per cent of total environmental expenditure in the 1990–1994 period [*EBRD, 1995: 22*]; the donors' contribution in Bulgaria in 1994 was estimated at four per cent [*Environment for Europe, 1995a: 4*]. Western donors have in the meantime made it clear that the largest contribution will have to be provided by the countries themselves. International institutions are not prepared to cover more than approximately seven per cent of the total of Ecu 300 billion mentioned above [*PHARE, 1995: 29*]. At any rate, this percentage has never been achieved by Poland, which has received relatively large sums of aid. It is unlikely that the Western contribution to environmental expenditure in other ECE countries has corresponded to this seven per cent to date.

Besides their less ambitious expectations about the size of the aid, the ECE countries have also discovered that the spending of environmental aid does not always run smoothly. Finding the most suitable and efficient form of environmental aid is a learning process for all parties. This can also be seen from the changes in the form of environmental aid. The use of the instrument of debt reduction for environmental improvement, in which the environmental fund is administered nationally, is a clear example of this trend. The Ecofund in Poland is a success story which may well be followed elsewhere.

In 1991 Poland reached an agreement with its creditors which entailed a 50 per cent reduction of the outstanding debt. Part of the agreement was the opportunity to make 'debt for nature swaps' on the basis of negotiations with the individual creditors. This facility could result in a maximal 10 per cent extra reduction in the debt to fund those environmental projects which were of particular importance. If the maximal ten per cent could be agreed on with all creditors, the Ecofund would contain ECU 2.3 billion until 2010. During the 1992–94 period, the amount made available to the independent foundation on the basis of an agreement with three countries was ECU 16.9 million; in 1995 it was ECU 21.3 million [*EBRD, 1995: 118*].[3]

Within the Ecofund, contracts for the execution of projects are only granted after tenders have been submitted. Although this takes place in a situation of open competition, there is a certain preference for companies in Poland or in the countries involved in the debt arrangement; care is taken to ensure that the share of the donor countries in the contracts is reasonable in relation to their financial contribution [*EBRD, 1995: 118*]. The percentage of the project costs covered by the fund depends on the type of project; it can be as high as 100 per cent for nature conservation and environmental education.

The positive example of Poland is now being followed in Bulgaria. Partly thanks to mediation by the World Bank, a debt reduction agreement was made between Switzerland and Bulgaria in 1996. It concerns a sum of approximately 20 million Swiss francs, more or less 20 per cent of the total Bulgarian debt to the Swiss government [*Nederlandse Delegatie, 1995: 4*]. There seem to be even wider possibilities for debt reductions of this kind, but some Western governments are rather wary of them. This is probably due to the belief that the donor has less say in how the money is spent and that the direct advantage to the donor's own economy is limited. The latter is not always the case; as the case of the Polish Ecofund shows, companies in the donor country may enjoy a privileged position when it comes to contracts. At any rate, this way of funding environmental projects is a good illustration of the trend to shift responsibility primarily to the recipient countries themselves. That is where the environmental protection has to be carried out, and it is also where most of the funds have to be found.

National Environmental Funding

The environmental budget is fairly small in almost all of the ECE countries. The size of environmental expenditure is important in that it is now generally recognised that the majority of environmental investment must come from national sources. In most cases environmental expenditure, financed by state budgets, amounts to less than one per cent of the gross national product (GNP), except in Poland, where it was 1.3 per cent in 1992. The Polish environmental budget corresponds to what is regarded as realistic in Western countries: one per cent to two per cent of GNP [*EBRD, 1995: 17*]. Expenditure lies within this range in a number of other countries too if foreign aid and private sources are included: in 1993 this was 1.3 per cent in Bulgaria, 2.2 per cent in Slovakia. It should be noted, however, that reliable figures for all ECE countries are not available [*Environment for Europe, 1995a: 4*].

With the adoption of the polluter-pays priciple, a proportion of national environmental investments can now be funded by levies or ecotaxes. A special environmental fund has been set up in a number of countries which is fed from these revenues: in Poland (in 1989), the Czech Republic and Slovakia (1991), Bulgaria and Hungary (1993). However, the share of the levies and taxes has been limited so far, although a rising trend can be discerned. These funds cover around 20 per cent of environmental expenditure in Poland and Slovakia, and around ten per cent in the other three countries [*EBRD, 1995: 17*]. Studies have shown that, if levies are exacted, they are generally too low and are not in proportion to the environmental damage caused [*HIID, 1995: 5; Klarer, 1994*] – a phenomenon which is certainly not confined to ECE. Sometimes the levies have not kept up with inflation, and increases are resisted from the fear that they will push up the prices of goods and services or that companies will simply not be able to pay them because of their poor financial situation. In the case of state enterprises, the higher costs are simply passed on to central government. The result of all this is that it is far too often cheaper for companies to pay the levies than to adopt measures to reduce environmental pollution.

The fact that the levies sometimes yield disappointing results is also connected with the difficulty of imposing them in practical terms. Cuts in government spending have hit environmental agencies particularly hard. In combination with the general exodus of skilled workers to the private sector, this has meant that very few people, often not properly equipped for their task and working for low wages, have to enforce compliance with the measures. This difficult situation is exacerbated in some countries where more attention is paid to a lot of small polluters than to a limited number of big ones [*HIID, 1995: 6*].

The small contribution of the polluters to the total environmental budget means that the vast majority has to come from government funds at a time when political support for the environment is declining. Social pressure is low because of the uncertain economic situation, low wages and unemployment. There is more concern about the survival of the welfare state system, which is seen as a much more urgent problem in the short term, especially for the elderly, than the environmental situation.

In addition, the persistence of strong centralisation in decision making impedes local environmental problems from finding their way to the national government. Environmental organisations are often active at the local level, but usually have little influence on national policy. Nevertheless, some decentralisation has taken place at the executive level as a reaction to the centralising tendency. In a number of countries the spending of environmental funds is above all a local and regional affair. In Poland, for example, 54 per cent of the revenue goes to the regions [*EBRD, 1995: 21*]. However, given the rather low revenue involved, the effect of this breakthrough is fairly limited at the moment. The problem has, however, been recognised: during the preparations for the Sofia conference specific recommendations for the decentralisation of the funding of environmental expenditure were discussed [*Environment for Europe, 1995a*]. In addition, strengthening of institutional capacity is one of the new spearheads of Western aid policy. Particularly at the local and regional level, there is a recognition of the need for more expertise, assistance in legislation and in the implementation and enforcement of environmental regulations.

The idea that the countries in the region themselves must do the most work to release funds has evidently taken root by now. Together with the trend towards delegating the allocation of international funds to national institutions, execution is now coming closer to the level at which the problems themselves are to be found. There are grounds for hope, since it often also implies a better spending of the aid funds. One condition for improved effectiveness is an improved prioritisation.

Prioritisation

In view of the extent of environmental damage, in the initial transition period ECE countries found it difficult to determine which problems were the most pressing. The absence of a list of priorities in the countries themselves meant that the donors could exert considerable influence in this respect. This in turn meant that projects primarily targeted those environmental problems which were regarded as very important in the West, either because these countries directly suffered the negative consequences of them or because Western public opinion focused on them. This resulted in emphasis on combating transboundary air pollution.

The international agreements on transboundary air pollution in Europe and the pollution of the Baltic Sea also played a part in the selection of projects for foreign aid. Agreements had already been cautiously made on these two areas during the cold war. Some contacts and some experience had thus already been built up, which made implementation and selection simpler. This was particularly important during the first few years after the transition in the light of the lack of familiarity with Western aid in the ECE countries.

Spending on air pollution increased dramatically in the immediate transition period in Poland, Hungary and Slovakia. In Slovakia it almost quadrupled as a percentage of the total environmental investments between 1988 and 1991; in Poland it doubled, and in Hungary it tripled between 1988 and 1992 [EBRD, 1995: 19, 93]. Foreign influence was conspicuously present in the growth of interest in Poland in gaseous emissions. A considerable proportion of the population is exposed to these particulates, which carry highly toxic compounds, while the technology required to counter it is relatively inexpensive and simple. As a result of the campaign against acid rain, which particularly menaced the forests in the Scandinavian countries, and the international concern about the hole in the ozone layer, projects in ECE often target reductions in the emission of the materials responsible. These are not, however, the emissions which cause the most direct damage in the countries themselves, but it is appreciably easier to obtain funds for these projects because of their direct concern to the West.

The setting up of the EAP was a first step towards prioritisation. Within the EAP countries were advised to concentrate primarily on health-related problems and on projects which benefit both the economy and the environment. The need for prioritisation was driven both by the realisation that Western aid would not continue to rise and by the limited availability of national resources. On the basis of the EAP, a process was launched in 1994 to formulate National Environmental Action Programmes (NEAPs), for which national environmental ministries receive international support.

Although these NEAPs were originally written mainly by the World Bank for the poorer countries in the region, the countries themselves are gradually assuming a more active role. Western donors are increasingly demanding a prioritisation of this kind, and they provide funds and expertise for this purpose. The NEAPs also have the advantage of facilitating the participation of an increased range of actors in policy-making. In addition to the Ministry of the Environment, actors such as government bodies, business and industry, and non-governmental organisations can participate.

This in turn can lead to less involvement of Western donors, allowing domestic actors to assume a more direct role in the preparation of environmental projects.

Preparations

International organisations and donors follow specific procedures with which project applications must comply. There is a heavy emphasis on submitting a well-prepared proposal whose feasibility has been extensively researched. These feasibility and preparatory studies are often produced by foreign consultants because of the lack of familiarity and experience with all kinds of procedures and conditions within the ECE. This is no guarantee of quality, however, as can be concluded from the poor quality of the reports sometimes produced [*EBRD, 1995: 56*]. What is sometimes a one-sided involvement of Western consultants is a missed opportunity to transfer knowledge about feasibility and project management to ECE experts, who usually have a lot of mainly technical knowledge at their disposal. Involving local experts can also be very important during implementation. In the meantime these problems have also been noted by Western countries, as can be seen from the many recommendations for the Sofia conference which point to the need for more involvement by local consultants in the preparatory stage. Here it is argued that Western consultants can be more effectively deployed for counselling and training local consultants.

The absence of a follow-up to the preparatory studies is another point of concern to both parties. It can happen that a project is not approved and is therefore not implemented, despite all the time, effort and money that have gone into writing the proposal. In some cases the preparations account for no less than 20 per cent of the total costs of the project [*Amann et al., 1995: 31*]. In the worst scenario, the ECE country concerned has to bear a considerable part of the costs. Even in the case of projects which have received approval, it may still take a long time before the money can actually be spent because of the donors' procedures and obstacles in the recipient countries. Good co-ordination improves the chance that adequate funding can be found for projects (see below). On the receiving side, involvement could probably be intensified if the number of terms laid down by the donors were reduced.

In the case of bilateral projects, donors frequently require the projects to be implemented by organisations and companies from their own country. Besides reducing the pollution of the environment in ECE, this tied-aid serves domestic purposes too, which are often of a different kind. We have already discussed targeting the kind of pollution which is a national priority in the donor country or whose negative effects are directly felt there. The fact that the most favoured countries border on major donor countries is thus probably not fortuitous. Bulgaria and Romania are often treated unfavourably when it comes to allocating aid funds [*Berg, 1995: 1, 48*].

Export promotion, which is often a major aid objective as well, is expressed in the obligation to make use of manufacturers and consultants from the donor country. This is even a legal obligation in some countries. It does not always lead to the most suitable and least expensive solution. Supplements to specific technology have to be purchased from the donor concerned, and linking up with other projects is often hampered by the application of different technical standards. The fact that practically every donor brings in its own national industry without any mutual co-ordination taking place sometimes means that neighbours in ECE follow an entirely different approach and use divergent systems to deal with the same problems. This lack of co-ordination can be particularly problematic in border areas which often share common ecological features. In these cases, the self-interest of the bilateral donors clashes with the effectiveness of the aid. It should be noted that this issue was raised in the preparatory documents on financial aid for the Sofia conference, in which bilateral donors are called upon to untie their aid.

Project Scale

The aid procedures have a built-in prejudice in favour of large projects: the complicated, time-consuming and costly procedures are hardly worthwhile for small projects. This weighing up of costs and benefits is mainly carried out by the multilateral banks. It is known that the institutional pressure of the World Bank in favour of a large turnover with as few complications as possible is to the disadvantage of the usually small environmental projects [*UNDP/UNEP/World Bank, 1994: 134–5; Kolk, 1996: 171–243*]. This diverts attention away from small-scale projects which could have a significant, positive environmental effect, help increase local involvement, and the promotion of local, ecological techniques.

The importance of small-scale projects has started to be recognised by various donors. If put into practice, more opportunities will emerge for Western aid to be directed towards, for example, energy-saving projects, which are almost always small-scale. Energy-saving demands considerable local labour power and small investments, a blind spot in Western aid policy. Nuclear energy expansion and increasing the efficiency of energy production are still the predominant concerns in the energy field, while the opportunities for savings on the consumption side are very large. Supported by international NGOs, environmental groups in the region have protested against the emphasis on nuclear energy projects, often financed by Western donors.

NGOs have gradually become recipients of project aid. The best-known examples are the extensive network of the Regional Environment Center for Central and Eastern Europe (REC) in Budapest and that of the American Environmental Partnership for Central Europe. There has also been an international Small Grants Programme for Poland since 1995, funded from the Global Environment Facility. This programme is running very successfully: there are a lot of applications for small-scale, local investment projects, a *lacuna* among many of the funds already mentioned. Small NGOs can tackle all kinds of problems by themselves, which leads to more active involvement of the population. Thus it contributes to a strengthening of civil society and in this way, to the process of democratisation. The Sofia decision to prepare a European treaty on public participation and access to information may give a further impetus.

Co-ordination

A final point concerns the co-operation between the ECE countries themselves and the co-ordination between donors. The relations between the ECE countries are sometimes difficult and political conflicts can interfere with co-operation in the field of the environment. There is also mutual competition for foreign aid and investments, and for which country will be admitted first to the EU.

In ECE, there has not been much horizontal co-ordination on transboundary environmental problems and nature conservation, partly as a result of the fixation on the West. What has been seen to date is vertical co-operation, between the individual host country and the donor, and little horizontal co-operation, that is, between recipient and recipient. Nor is there much learning from positive and negative experiences in other countries. Patterns of co-operation, such as those on the Danube, which are largely realised with foreign aid, could well act as a catalyst. East–West co-operation is sometimes also carried out under a Western umbrella organisation. Under the guidance of the REC, NGOs have started to exchange information about successful cases of participation and are seeking to further increase such co-operation [*REC, 1996*].

For a long time the co-ordination of Western aid was equally limited, and the matching of various loans and donations to arrive at an affordable package created many problems. However, the Project Preparation Committee, founded after the Lucerne conference, has increased co-operation among donors. Good results have been achieved partly as a result of matching loans from multilateral development banks and donations from Western countries. This method has made it possible to fund a large number of extra projects which would otherwise probably not have been regarded as feasible because of the high level of costs for the recipients. Twenty-six projects, involving a sum of ECU 1.2 billion, were started in the period between Lucerne and Sofia [*Nederlandse Delegatie, 1995: 3*].

The opportunities have been greatly enhanced with relatively few resources thanks to the co-ordination of donations from bilateral donors and other aid programmes, loans and national sources of funding and executive bodies. The donations make the loans cheaper or the terms more flexible, so that poorer countries can make use of these facilities as well. This is a way of doing away with the unequal regional distribution.

The Sofia Ministers Declaration mentioned various ways of making loans softer and innovative financial instruments, such as green equity schemes and pilot projects for jointly implemented activities [*Environment for Europe, 1995b*]. Other recommendations discussed before Sofia, including loan guarantee schemes and a Long-term Environmental Assistance Facility for the poorest countries in the region, were not adopted.

The most innovative among the politically accepted instruments are the green equity schemes. Instead of providing loans or donations, donors can buy shares in income-generating environmental projects. These investments in equities can act as a catalyst on private equity, grants and loans to fund project companies carrying out environmental investments [*Environment for Europe, 1995a: 12*]. Companies in the environmental services sector, such as waste management and water supply, can profit particularly from this mechanism. The Scandinavian countries are already operating green equity schemes, and so are the EBRD and the International Finance Corporation. This fairly advanced instrument can, however, only be used in countries with a relatively advanced privatisation process.

Conclusions

Although it remains difficult to obtain exact figures on the scale and composition of environmental aid, it is clear that donors are only prepared to make a limited contribution. Foreign aid will act above all as a catalyst with the host countries expected to provide the bulk of the expense, and the majority of funds going to a limited number of countries. The initially high expectations in ECE have become more realistic, and it is recognised that most of the money will have to be found in the countries themselves. This requires strengthening of institutional capacity in order to improve environmental legislation, its implementation and enforcement, and thus the efficiency of project execution. In the past few years, the emphasis in aid has been shifting more towards the countries themselves as far as financial management and project implementation are concerned. More attention is being given to the transfer of knowledge and policy advice, and to the support of small-scale projects, sometimes carried out by NGOs. Changes are particularly noticeable at the local level, which may contribute to the process of democratisation, diminishing persistent centralisation in decision-making.

The 1995 Sofia conference has led to improvements in the funding of environmental policy. There was more international discussion amongst the donors and with the recipient countries during the preparations for Sofia, and coordination has increased as well. However, donor priorities and interests, especially with regard to the objective of export promotion, continue to play a considerable role.

While the prospect of future membership of the EU has a positive effect on environmental policy-making, EU priorities have had a large influence on the shape of ECE policies, an influence that is not necessarily positive for the host countries. Counterbalances will have to be found in better national prioritisation and higher public involvement, aspects supported by the EU countries themselves at the Sofia conference. The room for manoeuvre is, however, very limited in view of the EU's own emphasis on monetary and economic integration, and the exigencies of the transition to a market economy in ECE. The overall tendency towards deregulation comes at a time when most ECE countries are still trying to establish an appropriate regulatory framework.

It should also be noted that the almost exclusive focus on the EU carries the risk of an even stronger polarisation, with the likelihood that countries in the former Soviet Union and those ECE countries which are not deemed suitable for membership in the near future will lag even further behind. They may even drop out of the European framework altogether and fail to be involved any more in initiatives to tackle regional environmental problems. The activities in the framework of the United Nations' Economic Commission for Europe, covering all of Europe, therefore remain of utmost regional importance. In the many heavily polluted regions of the former Soviet Union, the lessons drawn from foreign assistance to ECE demand even greater attention.

NOTES

1. The percentages of money actually spent were considerably higher for humanitarian aid (74.2 per cent), education, training and research (72.4 per cent) and the financial sector (60.8 per cent), while the largest discrepancies were displayed by the sectors social policy and employment (15.5 per cent) and infrastructure (21.4 per cent).
2. Although falling outside the scope of this Special Issue, Estonia is an exception worth mentioning: it is a major recipient of international environmental aid (by far the largest per capita sum) and around 60 per cent of environmental investments is funded by external sources.

3. The three countries concerned are the USA (debt reduction of ten per cent), Switzerland (ten per cent) and France (one per cent).

REFERENCES

Amann, M., Klaassen, G., Smith, M. and P. Zapfel (1995), *The Effectiveness of Financial Instruments for Environmental Investment in CEE Countries: Recipients' Perspectives*, Laxenburg: International Institute for Applied Systems.

Berg, C. (1995), *The Environmental Support to the Baltic States, Poland, and Western Russia*, Stockholm: Swedish Environmental Protection Agency.

EBRD (European Bank for Reconstruction and Development) (1995), *A Strategy to Enhance Partnerships in Project Financing for Environmental Investments in Central and Eastern Europe*, final report by the Consultants, London, April.

Environment for Europe (1994), *Environmental Action Programme for Central and Eastern Europe*, edited and revised document, 31 March.

Environment for Europe (1995a), *Integrated Report on Environmental Financing*, Ministerial Conference, Sofia, 23–25 Oct.

Environment for Europe (1995b), *Declaration by the Ministers of Environment of the Region of the UNECE*, Sofia, 25 Oct.

HIID (Harvard Institute for International Development) (1995), *Impediments to Environmental Investments in CEE and the NIS*, final draft of paper prepared for US Agency for International Development, Washington, DC, 25 April.

Jachtenfuchs, M. (1992), 'EC Foreign Environmental Policy and Eastern Europe', in M. Jachtenfuchs and M. Strübel (eds.), *Environmental Policy in Europe*, Baden-Baden: Nomos Verlagsgesellschaft, pp.17–41.

Klarer, J. (ed.) (1994), *Use of Economic Instruments in Environmental Policy in Central and Eastern Europe*, Budapest: Regional Environment Center for Central and Eastern Europe.

Kolk, A. (1996), *Forests in International Environmental Politics. International Organisations, NGOs and the Brazilian Amazon*, Utrecht: International Books.

Marwaha, M. (1993), 'Environmental Degradation in Central-Eastern Europe: Response of the European Community', in C.K. Varshney and D.R. Sardesai (eds.), *Environmental Challenges*, New Delhi: Wiley Eastern, pp.107–21.

Nederlandse Delegatie (1995), *Verslag van de Paneuropese Milieuministersconferentie*, Sofia, 23–25 Oct.

PHARE (1995), *Environment to the Year 2000. Progress and Strategy Paper*, Brussels: European Commission.

REC (Regional Environment Center for Central and Eastern Europe) (1996), *Beyond Boundaries. The International Dimension of Public Participation for the Countries in Central and Eastern Europe*, Budapest: Regional Environment Center for Central and Eastern Europe.

UNDP/UNEP/World Bank (1994), *Global Environment Facility. Independent Evaluation of the Pilot Phase*, Washington, DC: World Bank.

Wiersma, J.M. and A. ter Welle (1995), 'Onbekend en Onderbelicht. Het PHARE-hulpverleningsprogramma voor Midden- en Oost-Europa', *Oost-Europa Verkenningen*, Vol.139, pp.26–33.

Environmental Movement and Social Change in the Transition Countries

BARBARA JANCAR-WEBSTER

The environmental movement in ECE has undergone profound transformation: the movement has shifted from being a mobilising agent for populist protest against the *totalita* of the Communist regime and in its place has emerged pragmatic, goal-oriented professional organisations. Western aid agencies and environmental peer groups have had a strong influence on this transformation. The transformation has brought advantages to environmental NGOs. However, it has also resulted in a loss of the local perspective, with its distinct *modus operandi* and bottom-up input, and this has impoverished political discourse in the transition states.

The environmental movement in East Central Europe (ECE) has undergone profound transformations since the heady pre-democratic days, when Hungary's Danube Circle could call out thousands to protest the construction of the Nágymaros Dam and pressure the Communist government to abrogate its obligations under the agreement with Czechoslovakia to share in building the complex hydropower system. For some, the transformed nature of the environmental organisations bespeaks the end of the symbolic populist protest against what the Czechs termed the *totalita* of the Communist regime. In its place is seen the emergence of a pragmatic, goal-oriented professional organisation that, under the tutelage of its Western peers, aims to influence policy decisions like its environmental counterparts in the West. For others, including the author, the inability of the pre-democratic movement, with its wealth of local experience, unique perspective on politics and distinct modus operandi, to conserve these characteristics in the transition period has impoverished political discourse in the transition states. In their search for security and identity, the ECE governments have opted either to imitate their Western counterparts, or have sunk into the quicksand of authoritarian neonationalism to consolidate political power. This article attempts to trace the impact of the transformation process on the environmental movement and concludes with some thoughts on the future direction of the ECE environmental movements.

The Pre-Democratic Environmental Movements

Although environmental movements emerged in each of the ECE countries at the end of the Communist period, they developed differently in each country. The contacts between the various groups both within and between countries was extremely limited. Eastern Europe's communication system was a product of the 1930s and 1940s. The abolition of censorship came slowly and at a different times, with Czechoslovakia, Bulgaria and Romania the last countries to abolish it in 1989.

Some groups like those in the Republic of Slovenia in the former Yugoslavia, and the Hungarian and Polish environmental organisations, had substantial contact with Western environmental NGOs, most notably with German and Austrian greens. The international contacts of the environmental groups in the other countries, particularly Czechoslovakia and Bulgaria, were much more limited. Some environmental groups embraced a strong nationalist agenda, and eventually merged into the broader nationalist movement. The Baltic, Ukrainian, Slovak and Moldovan environmental groups are cases in point. Some groups developed as a specific protest movement, with a specific ideology and approach, such as the Slovenian greens. In the freer climate of Poland, environmental groups openly recruited members. Some environmental groups declined the dissident protest path, preferring to act within the established order and effect change from within. The most notable example of this type of organisation was the Czech Ecological Section of the Czechoslovak Academy of Sciences. Finally, in all the countries, the government-sponsored conservation organisation, the Society for the Conservation of Nature, continued to operate more or less down to the end of the Communist period, and continues to function in a slightly modified guise to this day. These societies were apolitical from the start and have continued to remain apolitical.

The significance of the growth of environmental groups prior to 1989 resides in the fact that they were grass-roots social initiatives. To use Václav Havel's term, these groups represented the rebirth of *civil society* in states where free spontaneous interaction between individuals outside the government-sponsored institutions was rigorously and strongly discouraged. They were able to organise because the environment had never been put on the black list as a subject for public discussion. Environmental protest started in Poland in 1980, when environment activists succeeded in getting the big aluminum mill outside of Krakow closed down. From Poland, environmental protest spread throughout the region. Revelations of ecological crisis or of some gigantic government project harmful to the environment precipitated public response and calls for the end of the Soviet imposed order. The Chernobyl disaster revealed the extent to which the ruling regimes had compromised the health and welfare of their citizenry, in turn strengthening the development of environmental groups.

In Czechoslovakia, air and water pollution were the catalysts of protest. In February 1987 some 300 people from the Chomutov District of North Bohemian Region signed a letter sent first to the Chairman of the district National Council and then to the Czech Prime Minister and Presidium of the Communist Party complaining about an inadequate warning system to alert people to an increase in air pollution in the district. On 11 November 1989, just a week before the student demonstration in Prague which ended the Communist regime, there was a protest demonstration against living conditions in the North Bohemian town of Teplice, where coal mining had turned the land into a moonscape of craters and made the air unbreathable. In the preceding weeks, a determined group of women called the Group of Czech Mothers staged demonstrations in the streets of the capital against the quality of water. Water quality had so deteriorated that infant formula could no longer be made with tap water.

In East Germany, the Evangelical Church became the protector of small disparate environmental groups such as the green network *Ark*. The 1989 pursuit of emigration by East German youth through Hungary dominated the international mass media. However, as young East Germans were climbing over embassy walls in Budapest, others were gathering in huge numbers in the smutty industrial cities. At the mass-candlelit rally in Leipzig in 1989, environmental pollution was elevated to a major political issue.

In Hungary, the environmental issue that mobilised the country against the Communist regime was the controversy generated by the government's insistence on co-operating with its Slovak partners in a gigantic hydroelectric power project that called for the construction of a dam at Nagymáros (see Jancar-Webster [*1991; 1995*] for more details), situated on the beautiful Danube Bend where the river turns at 90 degrees from its eastward course and flows south. In October 1988, on the anniversary of the Hungarian Revolution of 1956, the square in front of the Hungarian Parliament building was filled with some 40,000 demonstrators. The wide popularity of the issue enabled the anti-dam movement to pioneer non-violent methods of protest. Through the distribution of handbills on the street, small local demonstrations, demonstrations of women and children at the dam itself, and other methods, the ecological movement developed and taught large numbers of people democratic methods of action.

1988 was also a key year for the ecological movement in Bulgaria. Air pollution in the town of Ruse on the Danube river had reached such proportions that it threatened the health and life of the resident population.

The source of the pollution were huge chemical plants on the Romanian side of the river. Public protest forced the Bulgarian government to take up the matter with the Romanian government. Out of this local protest movement came the first autonomous environment group: the Independent Committee for the Protection of the Environment. By 1989, groups had formed in virtually every large Bulgarian city. At their head was *Ekoglasnost*, established in early 1989. In October and November of that year, the organisation sponsored a series of protests in Sofia on the occasion of the Helsinki Conference on Environmental Cooperation. The subsequent imprisonment of the demonstrators contributed in no small part to the fall of the Zhivkov regime [*Baumgartl, 1995*].

The environmental movement played a more ambiguous role in Yugoslavia. One of the major successes of the late 1980s was a nationwide effort, primarily led by scientists, to rescind a federal government decision to build a hydroelectric plant at the Tara River Canyon, one of the wildest and most scenic canyons in Europe, preserved under the United Nation's 'Man and the Biosphere' programme. A second success was the stop-nuclear-power movement initiated by a Belgrade student in 1989, which spread across the republics, resulting in the federal legislature's vote for a moratorium on nuclear power until the year 2000 [*Jancar-Webster, 1985; 1992a; 1993b*].

Instances of transrepublican environmental co-operation were rare in the Yugoslav Federation. Although environmental groups did organise in each of the former republics, the environmental movement put down its deepest roots in Slovenia. The forerunner to the Slovenian greens was started in the late 1960s by a daredevil group of students. It moved to the forefront of the democratic agenda in the mid-1980s, and in 1989, without official approval, declared itself a party. In the 1990 elections, the Green Party allied with DEMO, the coalition of national democratic forces, and won. In joining DEMO, the Slovenian environmental activists were seen by groups in the other republics, as primarily proponents of Slovenian nationalism and their experience was not transmitted to the other republics. Suspicion between the environmental activists in the different republics was very high. Each group feared penetration by the secret police, and tended to see police collaborators in the faces of its counterparts in the other republics. As a result, the democratic tactics developed in the anti-nuclear movement and among the Slovenian greens did not produce a pan-Yugoslav environmental movement. When the Communist regime collapsed in Yugoslavia, the environmentalists remained in their national groups. Their deep-seated distrust of one another made them incapable of mobilising a cross-national following that might have saved the tottering federation and prevented the destruction that followed.

The 1990 Elections

During the 1980s and especially after 1986, the Eastern European environmental groups played a leadership role in the demands for political change and in developing constructive methods to bring about that change. In 1989, the Eastern European movements also played a key role in publicising environmental degradation and demanding environmental remediation. In 1990, the region held its first democratic elections. However, when the results were in, the saliency of environmental concerns did not translate into a green victory at the polls. The environmental issue did not prove to be significant enough for the greens to win on an independent issue. Greens fared best when they joined a coalition, preferably the leading coalition. In Poland, no green party organised, and there was no green ticket. All of the party platforms, however, had a green section, and candidates with a green agenda were elected to the *Sejm* from the different parties. In Hungary, the Czech Lands and Croatia, where green parties formed, the greens were accused of harbouring too many ex-Communists and concealing their true agenda. None of the party candidates obtained the required five per cent of the votes to qualify for a seat in parliament. Czech ecological groups did run several candidates registered under the winning Civic Forum and these individuals were elected. The three per cent electoral rule in Slovakia enabled the greens to obtain six of the 150 seats in the Slovak National Council. In Bulgaria, *Ekoglasnost* registered with the winning Bulgarian Union of Democratic Forces and obtained fifteen seats in the Bulgarian assembly of 400 deputies. In East Germany, the Greens won eight seats. In Romania, the Romanian Ecological Movement (REM) founded in December 1989, supported the winning coalition, called the National Salvation Front, and won twelve seats in the Assembly and one in the Senate. The rival Romanian Ecological Party, founded six days after the REM, joined the opposition coalition and won eight seats, bringing the total green representation in the Romanian legislature to 20 seats in the 396-member Assembly, and one in the 119-member Senate. Shortly before the elections, the self-constituted Green Party of Slovenia joined the DEMOS coalition. The alliance resulted in the greens winning 8.8 per cent of the popular vote, or 13 per cent of the DEMOS vote. This was the highest percentage of votes cast for green candidates over the whole of Eastern Europe [*Kusin, 1990*]. The victory of the greens gained them eight seats in the Political Chamber, eight seats in the Communal Chamber and one seat in the Chamber of Working Deputies of the then Slovenian legislature. In the executive branch, a green shared in the Presidency, a second became Vice-President of Parliament, and a third became Vice-President of the Executive Council of the Government. There were three green-sponsored ministers.

Although the 1990 elections failed to demonstrate strong popular support for green candidates and parties, each national legislature had its small number of pro-environmental deputies. Their presence would have placed the greens in a relatively strong position to influence the new transition governments. However, when the author interviewed in Hungary, the Czech Lands and Slovakia in the summer of 1990, she found environmental activists and officials very pessimistic about the ability or interest of the new governments to adopt, not to mention implement, the necessary environmental remediation measures. Pessimism regarding the public's commitment to environmental protection was also widespread. In a word, on the morrow of the elections, ECE's environmental movements were in disarray.

Subsequent elections did not reverse the greens' downward political path. As public concern turned to basic survival issues of food, clothing and jobs, many people who had previously been active participants in environmental organisations became instead preoccupied with the tasks of daily living. Many environmental groups that were dependent on a single charismatic personality fell apart when that one person moved on to other interests. In groups dominated by scientists, recruitment of scientists into the government made it impossible for the group to continue. This was the case with the Ecological Section of the Czechoslovak Academy of Science. Public money for even the well-established conservation organisations dried up and there was no money at all for the newer activist groups.

Perhaps the major cause of dysfunction among the environmental groups was their distrust of one another. This distrust operated within and between groups. With the collapse of the Communist Party, bureaucrats who had once held prestigious positions in the youth organisations found themselves out of a job. Many saw the environmental movement as an opportunity to save their livelihood and quickly joined what looked to be the most successful groups. Many groups had already been penetrated by informers. Those activists who had risked their lives and possibly careers in the Communist period were not eager to share the fruits of victory either with the informers or what they perceived to be the Communist turncoats. In Slovenia, the old generation of green activists told me that they only trusted those with whom they worked and no one else, least of all, environmental groups in the other republics.

Thus, not only was the rapid drop in interest in environmental issues a cause of the greens' loss at the polls. Lack of trust enabling routinised communication between the groups precluded the possibility of the groups uniting in a single political movement. However, hindsight suggests that even if the groups had been able to unite, the environment still would not have risen to the top of the public-policy agenda in the transition states.

The Legacy of the Collapse of Communism

Several factors prevented and continue to prevent the re-emergence of mass-environmental concern in ECE. These factors derive directly from the legacy of Communism and the Communist world-view. The first of these is what might be termed 'the victory of the one alternative'. As long as the Soviet Union was alive, it was possible for reasonable people to argue over the merits of socialism versus capitalism, and, as in the case of the Slovenian greens [*Jancar-Webster, 1993a: 202–4*], develop a third alternative. The collapse of the Soviet Union with hardly a whimper left the ideological field empty of any alternative save a 'free-market democracy'. Driving the transition to the Western model of development was the desire on the part of all the ECE countries to join the European Union and NATO. Membership in the former seemed to offer economic and political security, while membership in the latter offered military security from Russia. Furthermore, membership in the EU held out the promise to these countries that they could take their place as rightful members of Europe, contributors to European culture, with a right to the lifestyle and benefits accruing to the European status.

The arbiters of membership in these two institutions lay outside the ECE region. As a result, the leaders of the transition countries found they had relatively few options in the transition process. If they desired to 'go West', their main task was to bring their country's political, legal and economic infrastructure into line with EU demands.[1] Membership of NATO was much less assured. But if membership was ever to be achieved, it required the formation of democratic institutions and the creation of a Western-style professional military subordinated to a civilian government and the rule of law. While the Baltic countries, Poland, the Czech Republic and Hungary have responded relatively easily to this external stimulus, Slovakia, Bulgaria, Romania, not to mention the countries formed from the former Yugoslavia, have had more problems.

Another aspect of the choice of no-alternative is the relative poverty and, in some cases, economic instability of the transition countries. The arbiters of aid and assistance are once again the European Union, individual Western countries, including the United States, and international lending institutions, the International Monetary Fund and the World Bank. All of these give aid with very specific requirements. Aid to the ECE was the first in the world to be required to have an environmental component. Given the severity of environmental degradation in the area, the environmental requirement is objectively to be welcomed. It ensures that environmental management cannot be totally forgotten in the interests of economic development and at the same time provides a solid, international set of criteria by which environmental remediation can be evaluated and implemented. But the environmental mandate imposes costs and performance criteria that are not regularly imposed elsewhere in the world and tends to make economic decisions that impact on the environment even more politically sensitive than they might otherwise have been. A case in point is the viability of nuclear power. For now the discussion is not merely between the rulers and the ruled. Foreign nuclear-power plant manufacturers and fuel providers are also stakeholders in the decision. The cold war may be over, but in the battle to expand the use of nuclear power in ECE, Czechs and Russians line up on one side, and French, the European Bank for Reconstruction and Development (EBRD), the Canadians and Americans on the other.

The second factor in the low visibility of environmental issues in ECE today is the desire of the large majority of its populations to live the consumer lifestyle of Western Europe. That lifestyle includes not only the increased purchase of automobiles, preferably of Western European origin, but the demand for Western products complete with plastic wrap and packaging. As the author has written elsewhere [*Jancar-Webster, 1992b*], to argue that a person does not need a car, convenience appliances, a high level of consumption and easier access to energy is counter-productive in ECE today. ECE societies have been too long subjected to scarcity and deprivation. Integration into Europe ineluctably means an improved living standard along Western European lines.

For the peoples of the region, transition has brought increased insecurity into their lives, and an increase in negative attitudes towards elected government and its institutions. As events quickly proved, the adoption of the outward forms of democracy could not conceal the property grab by the former Communist *nomenklatura*. The names of the institutions or enterprises might be different, but with few exceptions, the *nomenklatura* remain in power in every country in ECE. Popular participation in the emerging democratic structures remains low. Scepticism is the preferred response.

These two aspects, the externally imposed conditions of European membership and popular expectations of reaching Western standards of living, create a dilemma for the transition governments. To stay in power, they need to assure economic development and integration into the global market, while at at same time, guaranteeing a social safety net during the transition. Environmental problems are nowhere seen as a high priority and only remain on national policy agendas because of external pressure.

Seen in this perspective, the legacy of Communism is more than a collection of environmentally dangerous 'hot spots', undrinkable water, polluted and unbreathable air, deforestation, and high rates of environmentally-induced diseases. For the transition governments, a principal legacy is the fixation on economic development above everything else. This pursuit of growth cannot merely be seen as the persistence of Marxism. One has only to look at the newly industrialised countries of South-East Asia to realise that the fixation on growth is a more widespread phenomenon. However, the promise of Marxism-Leninism was precisely that it provided not only a more efficient but, more important in the current situation, a *more just* path to growth than did capitalism, based on the selfish interests of private property ownership. Everywhere in the former Communist countries, income inequalities are becoming daily more visible. The message of the reconstituted Communist parties in electoral campaigns has not changed since the transition. Capitalism is selfish, profit-oriented, and cares little for the worker or the person in the street. Under socialism everyone works and no one goes hungry. The resurgent Communists pluck a responsive popular cord when they blame the 'capitalist' tools that attempt to correct the disastrous economic policies of the old regime in the interests of economic restructuring (price liberalisation, privatisation, and monetary discipline), for the collapse of production, the rise in crime, and inflation [*Aslund, 1995*].

The other side of the fixation on economic growth is that the majority of the new leaders are becoming increasingly committed to market reforms, not least because they are among the chief beneficiaries. Privatisation has resulted in many former Communist enterprise directors and managers becoming owners and managers of the newly privatised industries. These new owners are acquiring the profit incentive and reaping the benefits of the emerging market economy. However, they were raised with the old attitude, 'growth first, protection later'. Environmental pollution is seen as the price one must pay for economic development (see Szacki et al. [*1993: 11–12*]). Lacking a clear understanding of how the pursuit of economic growth without adequate environmental protection can in turn lead to a reduction in growth, the managers of the newly privatised enterprises are more disposed to repeat the earlier mistakes of the Western industrialised countries, particularly those associated with an end-of-pipe approach to environmental management. To be convinced that there can be no trade-offs between the environment and the economy, the new elite has not only to learn that win–win strategies are possible, but to see successful examples in practice.

It has to be emphasised that there is virtually no precedent in the region for the successful integration of environmental protection and economic development. Given their education and training, many administrators do not understand the importance of the environment to economic development, and without a push from the public, environmental protection gets little consideration. As before, environmental practitioners tell the author that their opinions are consistently not taken into consideration in policy decisions.

When an international panel evaluated progress on the environment in ECE in 1995 at Visegrad, the conclusion was that environmental reform was low on the area's political agenda. In the words of the Regional Environmental Center for Central and Eastern Europe (REC) Executive Director, Stanislaw Sitnicki, 'Some people feel that the environment must entirely be dropped from the reform agenda until the economy recovers' [*REC Press Release, Oct. 1995*].

Despite this rather negative assessment the reader should not infer that no progress has been made in environmental remediation or that governments in the region have consistently behaved negatively towards the development and implementation of programs designed to promote sound environmental management. One of the outcomes of the UNCED Conference at Rio de Janeiro in 1992, for example, was the co-operation and development by 18 of the former Communist countries of two important types of documents: the first was entitled *Guidelines on Integrated Environmental Management in Countries in Transition*; the second was the elaboration of national environmental action plans (NEAP) for every country in the region, describing the country's main environmental problems, and identifying policies, institutional measures and investments to address them, based on the guidelines [*REC, 1994b*]. The region now has in place a coordinated strategy for addressing environmental remediation.

A few countries have also been successful in reducing pollution within their borders. While some may say that pollution reduction is primarily the result of lower production, Cole, however, has argued that this is not the case with Poland. He attributes Poland's success to three factors: national investment in pollution control through the collection of pollution fines; improved legislation and enforcement; and competition leading to technological innovation in what he terms the 'new buyers' markets [*Cole, 1995*].

The Transformation of the Environmental Movement

The absence of strong government leadership places much of the onus for environmental protection with the public. This, in turn, requires public concern. The classic remedy for public indifference is education at all levels and ages: in schools, among the NGOs, environmental practitioners, managers and national leaders. Financing of educational, as well as environmental remediation programs, was originally expected to come of the Environmental Funds which all the former Communist countries agreed to set up in accordance with guidelines adopted at a conference in Jablonna, Poland in 1995 [*OECD, 1995*]. The Fund's financial resources come from the collection of fines and penalties from polluting industries, and the amount collected depends on the effectiveness of environmental monitoring and the management of the environmental project cycle [*Pezko, 1995*]. Bulgaria, the Czech Republic, Estonia, Hungary, Poland, and the Slovak Republic, had, by the end of 1994, successfully raised almost US$500 million. While a significant sum, it is not sufficient to cover programme demands. Poland leads the way in its use of environmental funds, paying for almost half of its environmental expenditure through the Fund. However, the effective implementation of the Environmental Action Programmes (EAPs) depends on foreign financing, from such lending institutions as the World Bank, the EBRD, PHARE, USAID and other national donors, particularly the Scandinavian countries and Germany.

In addition to monies for 'capacity building' and educational purposes received from the large international and national lenders, the NGOs have benefited from the attention paid them by the international environmental movement and by democratic institutions. These include the World Wide Fund for Nature (WWFN), IUCN, UNEP, Environmental Partnership, and the Open Society, Danish and Baltic environmental NGOs (the Clean Coalition Baltic, the Danish Center for Alternative Social Analysis, and the Norwegian Bellona Foundation, and the European Union, such as through the PHARE and TACIS Democracy programs). Coordination of the many projects and programmes sponsored by these institutions is provided by the most inclusive of the regional organisations, the Regional Environmental Center for Central and Eastern Europe (REC), located in Budapest, Hungary. Founded in 1991, with a US$1 million grant given by the then President, George Bush, by 1994 the REC had received financial pledges of ECU 15.25 million. On the list of donors, the largest are the European Union, the United States, Japan and the Netherlands.[2] Major private donors, such as the David Suzuki Foundation in Vancouver, BC, the Amaliegruppen in Copenhagen, the German Marshall Fund, as well as the European Union have representatives on REC's Board of Directors.

Out of these funds, the REC operates a carefully structured grants programme designed

> to concentrate on the development of an effective environmental NGO network. To achieve this goal, REC identified five main areas of concentration: training, capacity building, encouraging contacts between isolated NGOs, supporting independent initiatives and raising public awareness of environmental issues [*REC, 1994a: Introduction*].

The REC programme includes, for example, a grants programme, information exchange and 'personal capacity building' projects. The grants programme is most germane to our discussion because aside from information exchange, it is the major vehicle for NGO network development. The grants programme to NGOs administers two types of grants: the 'earmarked grants' and the local grants. The first year the REC initiated what it called the 'unearmarked' system. This was a system of 'learning by doing', of direct contact with the NGO by an REC representative working with the NGO to develop management skills. By 1993, 82 projects were completed. The system was subsequently changed to an 'earmarked' system, whereby the NGOs were asked to identify the most important problem areas from their perspective. These were collapsed into five areas and grant monies were 'earmarked' for each section. The five priority topics in 1995 were nature conservation, pollution prevention, sustainable agriculture, NGO institutional development, and environmental education. The local grants are grants up to US$5,000 to NGOs to help NGO institutional development. The money has been spent on operating expenses, training and educational activities, local projects and local events.

There is a large difference in the application for the 'earmarked grants' and the local grants. The local grant programme is administered by the local offices and applications are made in the local language to the local centres. Advisory boards of five to seven members are established to evaluate applications in countries where there are local offices. The boards are rotated frequently, and one of their tasks is to keep the REC main office appraised of local needs. Behind the local grants programme lie four REC assumptions: most NGOs lack basic skills to prepare projects and manage their organisations; the quality of projects needs to be improved; there are insufficient funding sources to support NGO projects; and ECE governments will support NGO development and activity.

The 'earmarked' grants award money up to ECU 20,000 and are highly competitive. Application procedure is formal. The NGO must apply within one of the five priority topics, there is a deadline, and applications must be made in English. The application itself involves the writing of a Project Concept paper in which the NGO identifies its needs in relation to the five priority topics, describes its planned actions, its known or potential co-operative partners and the estimated need of financial support. The project proposals are then given to an independent expert panel which together with REC grant professionals, evaluates them and determines the grantees. The winning NGOs are invited to a Winners Meeting to meet each other and the members of the REC grants team responsible for monitoring their projects. At the termination of the project, the NGO is required to write a formal final report. Among REC's assumptions in the development of this very formal procedure are that 'NGOs need to overcome a strong anti-organization bias. NGOs are reluctant to co-operate with each other and give up their newly acquired identity. Lack of cooperation partly stems from limited funds for travel and competition for funds.'³

The REC grants programme has been described in some detail because the procedures the Center has developed are ones that are familiar to any Western scholar or profit or non-profit institution seeking funding. From this author's experience, grant applications from ECE countries are frequently turned down or not given adequate attention in the USA because the English may not be fluent, or the grant writer has had insufficient experience in grant writing to write the proposal in such a way as to catch the review committee's attention. One may well ask: how many people in ECE know sufficient English or knowledge of adminsitration or science to write a grant of this complexity, even with REC help?

A similar type of grants project application procedure is utilised by the other large international environmental NGOs. There are some small differences. The Rockefeller Foundation's LEADS Program aims to provide experience and training for government, business and NGO leaders. The WWFN, the IUCN, Greenpeace, Friends of the Earth, and the Bellona Foundation have their special areas of interest. The first two have a conservation agenda. Greenpeace and the Bellona Foundation are particularly interested in nuclear issues, the latter in nuclear waste in the Arctic. These organisations thus tend to seek out experts or NGOs interested in working with them on their project, rather than asking the NGOs to identify their needs. The conservation projects of WWFN and IUCN necessarily involve the recruitment of local scientists and specialists to co-operate with WWFN or IUCN experts. NGOs are primarily drawn in where contact with the public and educational projects are involved. WWFN, for example, has been a leader in the protection of the Danube River through its 'living waters' programme. It provided support, for example, for the Danube Blues protest against the Nágymaros Dam at the end of the 1980s and is currently supporting local NGOs who are against any further dam construction. With foreign funding driving the NGOs as it is driving the entire transition process,⁴ it is not surprising that the organisation, activities and responses of the NGOs reflect the concerns and practices of their sponsors. As a result, the environmental NGOs of the late 1990s are far different creatures than their predecessors of the 1980s, not least in terms of their priorities and interests.

There are clearly positive and negative aspects to the current ECE NGO dependency on foreign donors. On the positive side, there is no doubt that environmental NGOs have staged a remarkable renaissance in the past three years. While the vast majority of pre-transition groups fell apart and new NGOs have taken their place. In its Directory of Regional NGOs published in 1994, REC lists some 1,700, operating in 13 countries. There is now a large network of environmental NGOs in ECE that are replicating the behaviours and practices of their international peers, as they are being integrated into the international environmental movement. The more internationally known organisations, such as *Ekoglasnost* in Bulgaria, the Green Circle and the Rainbow Movement in the Czech Republic, and the Polish Ecological Club, survived the transition, becoming coordinators or umbrella organisations for the emerging local environmental NGOs. On the negative side, the vast majority of pre-transition groups fell apart and new NGOs have taken their place. Of those that disappeared, perhaps the saddest case is the Slovenian Greens. The NGOs' inability to sustain their momentum helps explain why REC and other international organisations were able so quickly to assume the lead in defining the scope, activities and practice of the transition NGO network. With its primary definition outside the region, the transition process has required of the NGOs three fundamental shifts in attitude and behaviour. These are (1) the shift to democratic institutions; (2) the shift from protest to constructive lobbying; (3) the necessity for professionalism.

The Shift to Democratic Institutions

The shift to democratic institutional structures and practice is far from completed in ECE. Poland, the Czech Republic and Hungary seem to have advanced the farthest, while Slovakia, Bulgaria, Romania and Croatia appear to be in the early stages of the process. If institutions are to function democratically, they have to be accessible and responsible to their constituents. The concept of constituency is not intuitive, but develops in relation to the perceived relevance of voters to securing an individual's election. The public too has to believe that its participation in decision making will have an effect on the decisions that are actually made. For both government official and the public participant, the situation involves learning a whole new set of rules of the political game. The importance of legislative procedure and rules had yet to be fully grasped. And most of the new rules have not yet been written.

To learn democratic procedure, the ECE environmental groups have had to seek help from the democratic West. As the REC white papers emphasise, education is seen as a key factor in making the ECE environmental NGOs more effective, in mobilising the public and in changing the attitudes of government officials to be more responsive to public input. Organisations like REC, the Bellona Foundation and Greenpeace willingly organise educational workshops that focus on the specifics of proper and effective lobbying and organisation. To become an effective lobbyist has meant that the former unstructured freewheeling NGO environmental movement has had to reshape itself into more permanent organisations. Restructuring has meant overcoming one's distrust of rival NGOs and learning to develop successful strategies and tactics in co-operation with them. It has meant launching educational campaigns to influence public attitudes and develop public sensitivity to environmental issues. The largest and most successful already have a small permanent staff that is available for lobbying efforts. REC's local grants programme and programmes funded by the Open Society have developed in response to the need for training in democratic procedure. A citation from REC's own analysis of ECE NGO behaviour is relevant here:

> The NGOs exhibit a particularly strong anti-organizational tendency and anti-hierarchical tendency. While this has prevented bureaucratization and permitted a high degree of flexibility and dynamism, the resistance to building more structured organizations limits the degree to which environmentalists can expand their constituencies and become effective in fundraising and advocating on matters of public policy. Another factor influencing NGOs' behavior is a deep distrust of centralized agencies and the feeling that 'professional' and larger granting organizations monopolize information and aid [*REC, 1994a: 2*].

Nothing more needs to be added to this description to see the total attitudinal shift required of the NGOs, if they are to remake themselves in the image of their foreign donors. Transformation and change may indeed be necessary. But until all the democratic institutions are in place, such as full public access to information, legal rules for interaction with the legislative and executive branch of the government, and NGO standing in the legal system has been clarified, the NGOs perhaps are right in distrusting hierarchies, centralised agencies and large organisations. The foreign donors argue that professionalisation, organisation restructuring and democratisation leads to a larger, more effective role for NGOs in decision making. But many NGOs are still struggling with the question: 'What's in it for us? Why should we participate?'

The Shift from Protest to Policy-Making

The demands of democracy have forced the movements to become more focused, more politically sophisticated in the Western sense and policy-oriented in their actions. Underlying the environmental protests of the Communist era was a profound public distrust of the Communist system. Environmental decay came to symbolise the ghastly consequences of the regimes' megalomania and lack of concern for the public welfare. Under the conditions of democracy, elected officials become (at least in part) instruments to carry out the will of the electorate. The public is no longer a helpless bystander in the games of the powerful. Rather, each person is obliged to unite with like-minded individuals and make demands upon the government that are in his/her interests. If cynicism is the proper attitude for the person living under Communism, positive activism is more appropriate for the person living under democratic institutions. The shift from protest to positive participation cannot be made overnight, because it demands a fundamental shift in attitude towards the nature of government. The new NGO must now see itself as an integral part of the decision-making process. It must study existing legislation with a view to utilising it to the NGOs' benefit and work to propose new legislation where existing legislation fails to meeting NGO requirements.

Most of the ECE public has not made this shift; most continue to distrust elected officials as they continue to distrust like-minded groups. Trust in the government takes time to build and comes only if its efforts are perceived as beneficial to the individual voter. Given the economic disarray, political corruption and social anxiety created by the collapse of Communism, it is not surprising that few people from ECE express great confidence in their elected officials.

On their part, the elected officials have not given their constituents much cause for confidence. The 1995 amendment to the Bulgarian Environmental Protection Act is a case in point. In November 1989, as the old regime was falling apart, activists from *Ekoglasnost* staged a large demonstration in Sofia protesting the water-diversion project from the Rila Mountains. The police used nightsticks and clubs to break up the demonstration, resulting in many injuries. The protests appeared to have made their point. When the Communist government fell, the new government stopped the project and passed the Environmental Protection Act requiring Environmental Impact Assessment (EIA) on all projects having an impact on the environment.

On 8 February 1995, an almost identical demonstration against the diversion project took place in the town of Sapareva Banja where construction was to resume at the foot of the Rila mountains. Once again, the police beat up the protesters among whom were local leaders and a Member of Parliament. The activists demanded an international investigation, but none occurred. In March 1995, to avoid further disruption, the Bulgarian parliament voted an amendment to the Environmental Protection Act.

The *Ekoglasnost* memo asking for international investigation of the incident stated that 'the same violence [that occurred in 1989] happened in an effort to restore a part of the same project'. The Bulgarian activist might well wonder whether the transition had changed anything, given that protest was greeted by the authorities with the same violence as before.

The Bulgarian government is not alone in its attitude towards public demonstrations or attempts by interest groups to modify policy. The Polish parliament has also passed a measure excluding projects vital to the national interest, such as the construction of highways, from the necessity of doing an EIA. Even a government that has appeared to be proceeding more rapidly through the transition process, like the Czech government, aroused concern among environmental NGOs as to the impact its 1995 'NGO' law would have on the activities of environmental NGOs. In effect, the law states that non-governmental organisations are to become more financially independent and less dependent on the Czech government for funding. The environmental NGOs correctly wondered whether that meant that the public funding they had received to date would be cut off.

Another problem in the transformation of environmental NGOs from protesters to participants in decision making is the fact, in virtually all the countries, that enabling legislation is far from complete. Some environmental legislation dates back to the Communist period and has not yet been rewritten. Other newer legislation makes some provision for public participation, particularly in the EIA process, but omits any formal NGO role in legislation. Where there is enabling legislation, participation varies both between and within countries. Influence at the local level appears to be more consistent and more effective than at the national level, as local officials experience a more direct relationship with their constituents than do those at the national level. An intuitive reading of successful environmental NGO actions suggests that action is more effective at the local level as well. The huge demonstrations supported by the international organisations against construction of nuclear power plants have done little to change official attitudes. In every case, whether it be the Czech Republic, Slovakia, Bulgaria, Hungary, Romania, or Lithuania, the national government has pursued nuclear construction in the face of strong NGO opposition. Appeals for international NGO solidarity have had no effect. What is more, the governments are pursuing construction not necessarily with safety as their highest concern. The decision of Slovakia to accept Czech and Russian offers at Mochovce, and the Bulgarian interest in a similar Russian offer are cases in point. Once again, the lack of response from elected officials does not augur well for confidence building between the voters and their representatives.

A Western lobbying group or NGO might look at NGO activities in ECE and argue that the local NGOs are going at politics the wrong way. But Western help puts the local NGOs in a dilemma. In extreme cases, Western sponsorship and training risks the sponsor and the agent being labelled a 'Western agent', as the Russians labelled the Bellona Foundation and Vladimir Nikitin. Given past experience and practice under Communism, there is little doubt that learning Western modes of political behaviour is learning foreign behaviour. The adaptation or integrating of foreign experience into local practices raises the whole question of how far adaptation can go without becoming what might be unkindly labelled 'international green imperialism'.

On the other hand Western support and training makes it possible for NGOs to gain access to new technology, including computers and the relevant software to go on-line and access a network, such as Hungary's Green Spider that started up in March 1993. Communication facilities such as these are essential for the coordination of environmental NGO efforts, at both the domestic and international levels.

But this Western support and training risks alienating members of grass-roots organisations, especially those that have little or no opportunity to become computer literate and who may feel intimidated by the directives and programmes emanating from the international organisations. Once again, the past intrudes on the present. During the Communist era, the only participants at organised meetings were the bureaucratic appointees of an officially recognised group. While citizens of all countries now have the theoretical right of free assembly, the fact remains that representatives of those environmental NGOs with access to foreign financing and training in appropriate organisational and political behaviour are most likely to be engaged in networking, including attending national and international meetings. There exists the worrying prospect of a gap developing between grass-roots organisations, on the one hand, and, on the other, national NGOs working with the international organisations.

A final aspect of the requirement for more public participation in national decision-making is the issue of maintaining NGO independence from national politics as well as international politics. The Western international environmental organisations have their agenda, the national governments have theirs, and when they do not coincide, the NGO is forced to choose. If its leadership is a paid bureaucracy, more likely than not it will side with the national government to retain its credentials. Such participation in policy-making forces the NGOs to become deeply involved in politics, an activity that was considered dirty and inappropriate for a committed environmentalist during the Communist era. For those born under Communism, the threshold between contamination and participation has yet to be fully delineated.

The Shift to Professionalism and Expert Knowledge

With the need to be involved in policy making comes the need for accurate information and the need for the NGO representatives to act in a professional manner. It can be argued that information was so limited in Communist times that education by experts is today essential to the expansion of public awareness of environmental problems and public participation in NGOs. How else can an NGO be informed enough to take on local government let alone the national legislature? The REC discussion of its grants programme stresses the progress many NGOs have made in becoming more *professional* (REC's word) both in grant writing and in day-to-day administration. Environmental policy-making under the Communist regime relied heavily on experts who exerted the most sustained pressure in their quiet lobbying behind the scenes. Today the increasing reliance on expertise, coupled with the promotion of professionalism among NGO leaders, stands in sharp contrast with the popular spontaneity of the pre-democratic NGOs. If primary responsibility for problem solving remains with the experts, there needs to be a very good reason why the ordinary citizen in the street should get involved in NGO activity just to push a solution advocated by experts. There may be even less reason to get involved when the process of involvement is externally prescribed and directed.

Future Development of the Environmental Movement

For the foreseeable future, foreign direction and financial control of the ECE environmental NGOs will continue. The principal coordinating organisation will continue to be the Regional Environmental Center in Budapest. The succcess of international financing and foreign direction of NGO renewal is undebatable. Over the past four years, from unstructured, perhaps overly-idealistic groups of enthusiasts have been created typical Western-style professional NGOs with well-defined environmental niches. The increasing professionalism of these groups puts them in a good position to participate in environmental decision-making, if and when the legal infrastructure permits. Without international assistance, environmental NGO co-operation and activism would have been non-existent or at a much lower level. The success of REC's programme is such that similar centres are being opened to serve the former Soviet republics.

The reconstruction of the environmental NGOs is a very important development for ECE. However, the author questions whether these professional organisations can ever mobilise the ECE populations like the old dissident movements did. The ECE publics are becoming increasingly disillusioned with the Western concept of democracy. According to the highly respected 1994 Eurobarometer Survey, public satisfaction with the development of democracy in the region was negative for all countries except the Czech Republic. Public agreement with the direction of development had dropped in all countries, with a shift from 13 per cent agreeing in Poland in 1991 to 29 per cent disagreeing in 1994. The only three countries where there was positive agreement on the country's direction were Albania, Estonia and Hungary. In no case did agreement represent 50 per cent of the respondents (European Commission in Gati [*1996: 8, 11*]). The election victory of former Communists in 1994 and 1995 in virtually all countries save the Czech Republic indicates the depth of the disillusion.

To suggest that 40 years of misrule cannot be turned around in five is inappropriate. The ECE public demanded the fall of the Communist regimes because of their perceived misrule. The public had little information about the seriousness of the economic and political collapse, nor the difficulties to be encountered in efforts to remedy the situation. But the public certainly did not ask for more misrule. People were also largely ignorant of problems afflicting the Western democracies. Once the novelty of contact with the West wore off and the problems became visible, the promises of democracy no longer seemed as bright. The perceived attractions of employment and social stability of the Communist era returned in all their nostalgia.

The great strength of the pre-democratic environmental movements was that they were all indigenous. Western contacts and Western help came *after* the movements were up and running. The great weakness of the development of NGOs today is that they are organised, nurtured and sustained by the West in the name of democracy building. Should public opinion radically turn, the environmental NGOs would find themselves isolated and out of touch. Empowerment is not a push from above. If the public is to become empowered, the move needs to come from the grassroots level, to arise from among ordinary people.

In a telling article, the former Polish dissident, Adam Michnik, describes the 1995 electoral victory of the former Communist Party in Poland as the 'velvet restoration'. Comparing the elections to the French restoration of the monarchy after the fall of Napoleon in 1815, he writes: The revolution had grandeur, hope and danger. The restoration is the calm of a dead pond, a marketplace of petty intrigues and the ugliness of the bribe, [just as the] fall from Bonaparte to what happened afterwards was a fall from being into nothingness [*Michnik, 1996: 14–15*].

If the environmental NGOs merely imitate their foreign benefactors, they will surely develop the appropriate institutions for lobbying and pressuring their national governments and perhaps learn to co-operate and integrate their programmes at the regional level. However, in so doing, the professionals who head the more successful NGOs risk alienating themselves from a public that no longer sees them as representatives of its interests, but rather as hierarchy and part of the power structure. The public alone can give the environmental NGOs the excitement and dynamism necessary to effect real environmental and democratic change. It may be that the time is not yet ripe for new initiatives. Getting from day to day is enough for most in the unsettled times they now face. It may be that NGO professionalism is not seen as an alienating factor. As yet, this is an unexplored research area rich with potential findings. As this author has written many times throughout her work, it may be that there is no danger that international assistance may one day exert controlling and inappropriate influence on NGO activity and environmental policy decisions in some East European country.

Nevertheless, who is to say that where environmental activism is concerned, there is no choice but one alternative? Thinking globally and acting locally are both equally relevant to environmental practice. Global environmental management from a central authority is being advocated today as both a development in process of becoming and a positive value in global governance. The Slovenian Greens and the pre-transition Danube Blues lived through the experience of centralised management and protested the destructive aspects of modern society: bureaucracy, technocracy, political hierarchical power. ECE environmentalists risked their lives to advocate a different vision of society, where progress was seen in psychological, spiritual and cultural relationships. It has been said many times: ECE can go the way of the West with all its environmental mistakes and costly clean-up; or it can choose a more environmentally sustainable path rooted in community rather than consumerism. For the ECE NGOs, the search for an independent identity capable of mobilising their peoples entails a renewed commitment to 'grandeur, hope and danger'. In today's world that may be too much to ask. However, politics is the art of the possible. The author retains her optimism.

NOTES

1. The ECE governments understand the EU position very well: 'It would be an illusion to expect that the welcome approach of the West towards the post-communist countries is motivated by anything else than by their concrete particular interests and by the space for manoevring between the internal and external dimensions of these interests' [*Hybner, 1995: 15*].
2. From 1990 to 1994, the EU has pledged ECU 4.42 million and has given ECU 4.08 million. The US has pledged ECU 4.2 million and has given ECU 2.5 million. Japan has pledged ECU 3.5 million and has given that amount. Japan's donation is part of a special Japanese Fund designed 'to strengthen cooperation between the government of Japan and REC to help develop market-based solutions to environmental problems'. (Japanese Special Fund, Rec.hu on-line, Fall 1995.) The Netherlands has pledged ECU 901,000 and given ECU 853,000.
3. The descriptions of the REC programmes and the grants programmes in particular, as well as the citations, are taken from REC [*1994a: 'Earmarked Grants', 'Local Grants'*].
4. All the country reports in the REC white paper [*REC, 1995*] unhesitatingly admit that the major source of funding for NGO activities is foreign.

REFERENCES

Aslund, Anders (1995), *How Russia Became a Market Economy*, Washington, DC: Brookings Institution.

Baumgartl, Bernd (1995), 'Green Mobilization against Red Politics: Environmentalists' Contribution to Bulgaria's Transition', in Wolfgang Rüdig (ed.), *Green Politics Three*, Edinburgh: Edinburgh University Press, pp.154–91.

Cole, Daniel H. (1995) 'Poland's Progress: Environmental Protection in a Period of Transition', *The Parker School Journal of East European Law*, Vol.2, No.3, pp.279–319.

Gati, Charles (1996), 'The Mirage of Democracy', *Transition*, Vol.2, No.2, pp.8, 10–11.

Hybner, Jiri (1995), 'European Union as the Focal Point of the Czech Republic's External Political and Economic Relations on the Road to Prosperity', paper presented at the 36th Annual Convention of the International Studies Association, Chicago, IL, 21–25 Feb.

Jancar-Webster, Barbara (1985), 'Environmental Protection: The Tragedy of the Commons', in Pedro Ramet (ed.), *Yugoslavia in the 1980's*, Boulder, CO: Westview Press, pp.224–46.

Jancar-Webster, Barbara (1991), 'Environmental Politics in Eastern Europe in the 1980s', in Joan DeBardeleben (ed.), *To Breathe Free*, Washington: The Woodrow Wilson Center Press and Baltimore, MD: Johns Hopkins University Press, pp.25–55.

Jancar-Webster, Barbara (1992a), 'Environmental Protection in Yugoslavia', in Edward Allworth *et al.* (eds.), *Yugoslavia in Transition*, London and New York: Routledge, pp.164–87.

Jancar-Webster, Barbara (1992b), 'Technology and Environment in Eastern Europe', in James R. Scanlon (ed.), *Technology, Culture, and Development: The Experience of the Soviet Model*, Armonk, NY: M.E. Sharpe, pp.1271–98.

Jancar-Webster, Barbara (1993a), 'The East European Environmental Movement and the Transformation of East European Society', in Barbara Jancar-Webster (ed.), *Environmental Action in Eastern Europe: Responses to Crisis*, Armonk, NY: M.E. Sharpe, pp.192–219.

Jancar-Webster, Barbara (1993b), 'Former Yugoslavia', in F.W. Carter and D. Turnock (eds.), *Environmental Problems in Eastern Europe*, London and New York, Routledge, pp.164–87.

Jancar-Webster, Barbara (1995), 'Environmental Degradation and Regional Instability in Central Europe', in Joan DeBardeleben and John Hannigan (eds.), *Environmental Security and Quality after Communism: Eastern Europe and the Soviet Successor States*, Boulder, CO: Westview Press, pp.43–68.

Kusin, Vladimir V. (1990), 'The Elections Compared and Assessed', *Report on Eastern Europe*, Vol.1, No.28, pp.38–47.

Michnik, Adam (1996), 'The Velvet Restoration', *Transition*, Vol.2, No.2, pp.13–15.

OECD (Organisation for Economic Co-operation and Development) (1995), *St. Petersburg Guidelines on Environmental Funds in the Transition to a Market Economy*, Paris: OECD.

Pezko, Grzegorz (1995), 'Overview of Environmental Funds and Other Mechanisms of Financing Environmental Investments in some CEE and CIS Countries', paper presented at the Third Annual World Bank Conference on Environmentally Sustainable Development, 'Effective Financing of Environmentally Sustainable Development', Washington, DC, 4–6 Oct.

REC (Regional Environmental Center for Central and Eastern Europe) (1994a), *Grant Projects Summaries. Vol.1: Grants 1990–1993*, Budapest: Regional Environmental Center for Central and Eastern Europe and AQUA.

REC (1994b), *Strategic Environmental Issues in Central and Eastern Europe Vol.1*, 2nd edition, Budapest: Regional Environmental Center for Central and Eastern Europe and AQUA.

REC (1995), *Status of Public Participation Practices in Environmental Decisionmaking in Central and Eastern Europe*, Budapest: Regional Environmental Center.

Szacki, Jakub, Imrina Glowacka, Anna Liro, and Barbara Szulczewska (1993), 'Political and Social Changes in Poland: An Environmental Perspective', in Barbara Jancar-Webster (ed.), *Environmental Action in Eastern Europe: Responses to Crisis*, Armonk, NY: M.E. Sharpe, pp.11–27.

PART II:

COUNTRY STUDIES

Hungary: Political Transformation and Environmental Challenge

LAURENCE J. O'TOOLE, Jr. and
KENNETH HANF

Hungary is undergoing both radical economic transformation and political change. Presently a number of challenges converge and compete simultaneously for attention and resources. Hungarian environmental policy and administration are part and parcel of these changes and the competing demands they make on the limited capacities of the institutions of governance. Improving institutional capacity is likely to be difficult since the issues involved are deeper than merely technical and administrative improvements. While democratisation, in many ways, makes improving the institutional capacity for managing environmental quality in Hungary more difficult, it may also be a prerequisite for it. In Hungary institutional capacity is generally in short supply. Consequently, the broader challenges and institutional needs of the nation are also a piece of the explanation of the problems of implementing environmental policy. A significant expansion of institutional capacity is required as part of any concerted effort to address environmental issues.

Like other countries in ECE, Hungary is presently undergoing both radical economic transformation and political change. While in the longer run these transformations may be mutually reinforcing and, indeed, the one may be the prerequisite for the other, in the short run, there are often palpable tensions, even outright conflicts between them. Presently a number of challenges converge and compete simultaneously for attention and resources. On the one hand, the development of an effectively functioning market economy is seen as the prerequisite for providing the material basis for long-term social welfare and well-being. In the short term, the process of privatisation has disrupted existing economic relationships and led to high levels of unemployment and lower levels of production. On the other hand, the democratisation of the political system has infused new meaning into traditional institutions and created a set of new political actors who must learn to work under the new rules of the political game. A new civic culture must be created along with the associational infrastructure that will be necessary to carry the redefined relationship between government and society. New forms of co-operation and collaboration must be developed which rest on the new functional division of labour and a respect for the autonomy of different institutions and actors.

At present, however, the reaction against the defunct political and economic system of socialism, with its centralism, state control and politicisation of society via both state and party organs, has encouraged centrifugal forces that fragment and undermine the effective institutional capacity of the country and separate different sets of actors from one another. Newly resurrected local authorities jealously guard their autonomy and powers from unwelcomed intrusions by national authorities as well as from each other. Likewise, advocates of privatisation and the market are suspicious of interventions by the state to regulate and guide economic activities in the name of other societal values and objectives.

Hungarian environmental policy and administration are part and parcel of these changes and the competing demands they make on the limited capacities of both political and administrative institutions. Improving this institutional capacity is likely to be difficult since the issues involved are deeper than merely technical and administrative improvements. While the changes since 1989 have opened up a window of opportunity for far-reaching changes, they have also made more difficult the design and putting into operation of new institutional forms and relationships. For the enhancement of institutional capacity in this field is related to efforts to democratise and facilitate the growth of civil society. To begin with, there remain tensions between environmental objectives and social welfare needs. But, here too, at a deeper level and in the longer run, both are needed for democratisation. In addition to the tension between the commitment to rapid economic development, as a precondition for creating the foundation for social welfare, some of the initial consequences of democratisation create problems for environmental policy managers. The everyday challenges of survival, along with the desire for quick improvement in the material situation, compete with, and usually win out over concern for environmental quality and support for more vigorous action aimed at promoting more sustainable patterns of development. Both the legacy of the socialist political system and the initial form giving to democratic institutions undermine, or have negative consequences for, the need to build a flexible system of intergovernmental, but also private–public co-operation, and partnership required in confronting environmental problems.

While democratisation may, in many ways, make improving the institutional capacity for managing environmental quality in Hungary more difficult, it may, on the other hand also be a prerequisite for it. Building effective institutional links with the emerging private and industrial sector;

encouraging real civic dialogue by developing the capacity to involve, for example, non-governmental organisations (NGOs), in environmental deliberations and decisions; developing bridges for collaboration and joint environmental management between central ministerial actors, regional inspectorates and local governments are equally crucial for effective environmental management. The most fundamental challenges are, therefore, the adaptation of existing institutions to the new demands; the creation of intergovernmental and private-public linkages needed to manage the interrelationships between economic development, societal change and environmental quality; and the development of the management skills necessary to both construct and operate such a system. It is difficult radically to transform a system of governance while, at the same time, struggling to provide for the daily needs of society, itself a prerequisite for building the legitimacy and support for the efforts to bring about the needed changes.

The Environmental Legacy of Socialism

Hungary, a landlocked country in ECE, has a population of approximately 10.6 million, 20 per cent of whom live in Budapest, the capital. The relatively small size of the country (93,030 square km) and the geographic/topographic setting mean that Hungary is heavily interdependent in ecological terms with its neighbours. The interdependence has consequences for several environmental media and has occasionally resulted in high-visibility international conflicts and negotiations. For water, to take an example, Hungary is particularly reliant on supplies from abroad, and the increasing levels of contamination of ground water make this fact even more important. Indeed, threats to water quality are currently seen as the leading environmental challenge – unlike the situation in some neighbouring countries, where combating air pollution constitutes the first priority [*Hanf and Roijen, 1995*]. The ecological interdependence extends beyond water issues, which have attracted the most domestic and international attention in the case of Hungary, to air pollution and acid rain. But not only factors beyond Hungary's borders affect the country's agenda of environmental problems. The full set of environmental issues are affected as well by the processes of political and economic transformation currently under way within the country itself.

While Hungary has not experienced some of the severely devastating environmental catastrophes that some of its neighbours have had to face after decades of state socialism, there are a number of regions in the country where serious environmental problems have been identified and have been matters for discussion, particularly within government and among some NGOs.

At the start of this decade, Hungary ranked second in the dubious competition among nations of ECE for the highest quantity of sulphur dioxide emissions per capita. The national standing for nitrogen oxides in the region, again based on a per capita measure, was third. If emissions are standardised for level of economic activity, '[e]mission of both pollutants per $1000 of [Gross National Product] in early 1990 was almost 9 times higher than the average in the countries which make up the European Community in the West' [Bochniarz et al., 1992: 180]. A comparison of indices of productivity '... demonstrates the serious gap between Hungary and the most developed countries of Western Europe in terms of technologies and resources available for investment in environmental protection and restructuring' [Bochniarz et al., 1992: 180].

This particularly unfavourable situation reflects in significant measure the choices, and miscalculations, made by the government prior to the 1989 transition to a liberal regime with a goal of a market-based economy. Hungary's centrally planned industrial base was built upon a set of assumptions that have come back to haunt decision-makers today. From the 1970s until nearly the time of regime transformation, the nation embarked on a set of industrial investments based on an expectation that the economic future lay in large mass production enterprises. This choice placed Hungary behind most of its Western neighbours, who were moving toward service-based and knowledge-based economies.

The investments also concentrated on energy-intensive industries, thus placing further burdens on both the economy and the environment. In fact, the political regime treated the oil price increases of the 1970s as aberrations. Instead of adjusting economic planning away from energy consumption in view of an expectation of higher energy prices over the longer term, the country chose instead to safeguard, even increase, energy supplies and production.

As a consequence, Hungary entered its transitional period toward a democratic political system and market economy with great reliance on heavy industry [Kerekes, 1993: 140–41] and little investment in energy saving and environmentally friendly technologies. Currently, Hungary uses energy at approximately twice the intensity of Western European measures, although Hungarian energy efficiency is one of the highest among the nations of ECE [Hungarian Commission on Sustainable Development, 1994a: 11–12].

The ill effects of these choices were further exacerbated by the centrally-planned suboptimal allocations of investments over time, particularly the under investment in essential infrastructure – including environmental infrastructure – and environmentally threatening concentrations of polluting facilities in the same vicinities [Ministry for Environment and Regional Policy, 1991: 16–18].

Political Transformation

Even though the former Hungarian state socialist system was known to be somewhat more open to the West than were regimes in some of the surrounding countries, the setting for political expression and policy-making on environmental issues differed in important respects from systems in the West. Particularly important in this regard were the following: limitations placed on political expression, gradually giving way to environmentally focused political protest in the 1980s; one-party central governance, with little overt political conflict and therefore little sensitivity to, or tactical positioning on, environmental policy issues; a consequent lack of 'green' political parties and strong, effective NGO efforts (until the time just prior to the political changes, in the case of the latter); state established investment plans and pricing schedules that paid little attention to environmental questions and, indeed, encouraged environmentally destructive choices; lack of independent local governments with capacity to exercise autonomous choices regarding environmental issues; and the inevitable placement of issues concerning the international dimensions of environmental problems in the context of political competition between larger national powers to the East and West.

The political changes since 1989 – resulting in a conservative coalition national government for the first four years of post-socialist governance, subsequently followed by a left–liberal coalition beginning in 1994 – have drastically altered the context within which environmental policy is developed and executed. Among these changes are more open political processes and agitation for more participation and involvement on the part of NGOs, citizens, and others, including on issues of environmental policy; political competition, which creates some possibilities for political leaders to advance their careers and party interests by pursuing environmental questions (though this incentive is limited by the perceived precedence afforded economic issues, as explained later); a significant reduction of the role of the state in controlling investment choices and the management of key industrial sectors, with privatisation and similar initiatives now well under way; establishment of the beginnings of independent local governments and, as a consequence, the initiation of both problems and opportunities for local involvement in policy-making and execution on environmental questions; and a complex and dynamic set of challenges now facing decision-makers in Hungary, many stemming from the multiple difficult adjustments necessary in the transition to a market economy.

An Economy in Distress

The political changes were accompanied by widely supported decisions to develop a market economy in part through the privatisation of a substantial portion of state assets. The several privatisation programs, and the inevitable liquidations that followed for numerous unprofitable enterprises, placed additional strains on the developing institutions of the mixed economy as well as on the government that was seeking to stimulate economic success.

The Hungarian economy has faced exceedingly difficult circumstances since the political changes of 1989. The Eastern markets, and Comecon, collapsed. The economy was poorly structured to take advantage of markets to the West. The country was further handicapped by a huge foreign debt (more than US$21 billion). Although the decision to privatise much of the economy was widely accepted and resulted in the largest foreign investments in the region, and although many new businesses were founded, the picture on balance has remained bleak.

Bankruptcies escalated, particularly among firms that were forced to deal with market conditions for the first time. The privatisation process experienced significant implementation difficulties [O'Toole, 1994], and in the early years was executed without substantial attention to the environmental problems inherited from firms' earlier period under state control. Industrial output dropped by 30 per cent by 1993 and then stabilised, and the Gross Domestic Product (GDP) fell by 20 per cent [REC, 1994a: A5–6]. Unemployment escalated, from virtually nothing to 12 per cent between 1990 and 1992 (see, for instance, United Kingdom [1995]).

The Environment as a Domestic Issue

Under the earlier socialist regime the government was at first relatively unresponsive to the emergence of interest in environmental matters. For instance, Hungary did not participate with representation at the United Nations Conference in Stockholm in 1972, although the country did accept the recommendations developed at that meeting. The mass development of citizen involvement in pressing for the addressing of environmental issues awaited the Danube movement in 1984, which sought to halt construction of the Gabčíkovo–Nagymáros dam.

Even now, public opinion is 'ambivalent' regarding environmental matters generally. There is an increasing amount of concern, but 'the general level of ecological consciousness is still rather low' [Ministry for Environment and Regional Policy, 1991: 24]. The economic stresses of the current period contribute to the restrained interest on the part of the broad public. In a recent public opinion survey the issues receiving the highest rankings in terms of salience were those associated with the economy (inflation, unemployment, social welfare, and pensions). The environment ranked in the middle of the list. While it may not be literally true, as one recent analysis reports, that the environment has 'fallen off the political agenda' [REC, 1994a: A4], it is clear that there is little popular support for environmental measures that pose a risk to the fragile economy. This circumstance is expected by most analysts to persist for the foreseeable future.

On the other hand, some recent evidence indicates that environmental perceptions on the part of private corporate executives and managers in Hungary are virtually identical to the perceptions held by managers and executives in other parts of the world [Vastag et al., 1994]. Hungarian executives and managers do differ somewhat from their counterparts elsewhere on the most appropriate means of addressing environmental issues that affect their companies. For instance, Hungarian business executives are more supportive of indirect regulatory measures and the use of incentives to encourage environmentally sound company decisions – this despite the general lack of such policies in the current Hungarian setting.

The Hungarian private business community itself, collectively speaking, has recently begun to consider environmental questions as a part of its agenda. The Chamber of Commerce has created a position for an environmental officer to deal with such issues on behalf of business interests. Nevertheless, Hungarians are currently burdened with many serious problems and do not see the environment as most urgent. While many people recognise the seriousness of the environmental situation, they are so pressed they feel they cannot become active themselves on the issue. Moreover, their experience with government over the decades provides a negative context for their assessment of the ability of such activism to have an impact. In the light of the overall situation in Hungary, this appears to be a sober but not unreasonable or unrealistic perspective [Flaherty et al., 1993: 93].

The highly visible environmental activism of the 1980s was based on real public concern but was also used opportunistically by both citizens and those with political ambitions as a vehicle for opposing the regime more generally. It has since given way to less overt and highly fragmented, but still significant, efforts by a huge variety of NGOs. NGOs have begun to participate in the public debates surrounding environmental issues in the post-state socialist setting. For instance, they provided input in the extensive discussions surrounding the general new environmental policy considered by Parliament during the last couple of years. But the general waning of salience of environmental issues in the public at large and among the political leadership affects their degree of influence. The lack of regular access on the part of these organisations to government decision makers also limits their involvement.

Several hundred NGOs currently operate in the environmental sector in Hungary. Some of these are well known, a few internationally, while the large majority are small and narrowly focused. Almost all are poorly funded, and competition for financial support from foreign or international sources is keen. The environmental movement, as expressed through the NGO community, is not organised into a broad coalition; nor is it experienced at acquiring and analysing information from government or other sources. The government, for its part, is in the early stages of learning how to interact productively and with openness with environmental NGOs and others. Some officials in certain ministries have developed working relationships and some level of mutual respect and trust with representatives of certain environmental NGOs. These links, however, are relatively few.

Developments in Environmental Policy

Leaving aside governmental policies enacted as early as the nineteenth century and designed primarily to provide some protection against industrial hazards, Hungarian policy on the environment began in the 1960s and 1970s, with a series of laws enacted by the state socialist regime to cover a range of issues. Besides the law on the protection of air purity (1973), however, these were largely aimed at preserving resources important to processes of production.

For environmental policy in general, the most important piece of legislation adopted under the state socialist system prevailing was the Act on Environmental Protection, enacted in 1976, and still in force in 1989, when the old regime fell. This law, which was the first explicit establishment of principles of environmental policy, established the (formal) right of citizens to live in a healthy environment and proclaimed protection of the human environment a responsibility of the broad society. Although the regulations stemming from the 1976 Act were quite stringent, at least on paper, they have proven unsatisfactory in dealing with the practicalities of environmental pollution.

Until late 1995, no broad, comprehensive environmental policy existed in Hungary. The 1976 law, with its several amendments, together with numerous narrower pieces of legislation and more specific regulations, continued to be the primary policy in the field. While the political regime had changed and the economic system had been dramatically altered, the formal policy on environment remained essentially constant.

An Hungarian Commission on Sustainable Development was created in

1993 to coordinate the national efforts in working out the principles and implementing concrete tasks of sustainable development. It was also intended to bring about the effective incorporation of environmental considerations in various long-term sectoral plans, and to increase public awareness of relations between economic development and environmental issues [*Hungarian Commission on Sustainable Development, 1994b: 3*]. Still, even now there are no national programs incorporating principles of sustainable development into the routines and regular decisions of the government or the implementers of environmental efforts. The most visible sign of acceptance of such principles has been the adoption of a governmental resolution on 2 April 1993 regarding a commitment to follow up on the UNCED initiatives on sustainable development by incorporating such priorities into actions within the country (Decree of the Hungarian Government No. 1024/1993). Another indication of this commitment is the acceptance of a new environmental policy in 1995.

The extent to which such formal commitments will influence the concrete actions and programs of Hungary remains to be seen. Available evidence suggests that there has been hard fighting, since the political changes, between a number of economic experts and environmental advocates, both within and outside government.

The former, along with some politicians, assert that there is currently not enough income for the government to initiate the technical changes needed to improve environmental conditions. The argument here is to opt for the strategy of focusing on economic growth now and using the income generated to convert technology, as necessary. Those advocating a more environmentally focused agenda argue that the time is ripe to eliminate archaic technologies and industrial operations, and to begin to alter consumer/household actions as well. In the three most environmentally central sectors – energy, transportation, and agriculture – the government's efforts should be directed toward change as a top priority. According to these advocates, the present time is ideal, since the economic transformations now create opportunities to undertake the conversion before major new investments are sunk into place.

The elections of 1994 resulted in a new coalition government consisting of parties in opposition during the first four years after the political changes. As far as the perspective and approach of the newer coalition toward environmental issues are concerned, most observers agree that the new government is not behaving much differently than the previous coalition. Indeed, the new government seems somewhat more interested in ensuring that the processes of privatisation and liquidation do not result in the ignoring of environmental damages or liabilities. To that end, programs have been initiated to deal with some of the environmental aspects of the privatisation process.

Moreover, national policy on environmental matters has recently begun to be modified. New legislation accepted in Parliament in September 1995 aims to begin a process of updating and systematically revising the Hungarian approach to environmental issues. Many aspects of the new legislation could eventually be significant. Newer approaches to environmental issues, particularly those founded on principles of sustainable development, are officially espoused. However, once again there is little evidence of sustainable development principles being converted into practical action through government. Instead, public policy, as interpreted via programs adopted and in place now, focuses almost exclusively on regulating 'end-of-the-pipe' emissions through punitive regulatory controls that are neither very punitive nor broadly and carefully implemented. The broad endorsement of the use of economic instruments where feasible, as well as the explicit adoption of some important, if vaguely formulated, environmental principles are among the features of potential interest, as the legislation and other recent governmental statements are given concrete meaning in the future.

Agencies and programs focusing on environmental issues continue to be plagued by a policy of budgetary stringency, as the new government struggles to deal with the nation's economic problems. While the serious economic distress reduced some immediate measures of environmental difficulty (for instance, emission levels derived from industrial sources), the changes can hardly be viewed as long-term solutions to the country's environmental problems. In fact, the problematic economy has made it more difficult for those espousing environmental causes – whether within or without government – to be influential. In many circles, advocacy of environmental issues is viewed as antagonistic to economic, indeed social, welfare.

The Impact of the Environmental Policy of the EU on Hungary

An important influence on environmental policy has been the susceptibility of the new national regime to influences and events beyond the borders of Hungary. With the collapse of the Soviet bloc, new governments throughout the ECE region not only adopted the formal constitutional principles prevailing in much of the rest of Europe; they also explicitly proclaimed a reorientation of national interests and perspectives with openness toward the West. Nowhere is this clearer than in the strong desire expressed by the national governments of the region for full membership in the EU as a matter of high priority.

Hungary currently has associate member status in the European Union and hopes to be accepted as a full member as soon as possible. Support for

EU membership crosses virtually all political parties with any popular following within Hungary. With the choice to 'go European' has come an array of opportunities and constraints: the requirement to adopt European Union policies into national legislation, the chance to receive financial assistance in making the transition fully effective (particularly through the EU's PHARE programme), and so forth.

Some institutional changes with regard to the location of responsibility for coordinating activities on European issues have been made within the government as part of Hungary's increasingly European outlook in national policy. Moreover, a number of efforts are being made to alter Hungarian policy, particularly formal law, so that national legislation comports with the requirements of the EU. A portion of the harmonisation effort is being devoted to environmental policy generally. The general commitment to harmonisation is now expressed in broad national policy concepts on the environment [*Ministry for Environment and Regional Policy, 1995: 39*], and more specific harmonisation efforts are under way.

Some participants and observers in the environmental policy field in Hungary are nonetheless sceptical of the importance of environmental issues in the generally well-accepted Hungarian commitment to harmonisation and EU membership. Some see governmental discussions of harmonisation as focused almost exclusively on economic, especially 'market', considerations. Opening the markets, rather than regulating or controlling economic activities within generally market settings, is what the government most consistently emphasises. This leaves some observers worried about the ultimate fate of environmental considerations in the policy and implementation efforts to be undertaken in the coming period.

Initiatives have been under way to influence harmonisation on environmental issues, especially air pollution and acidification. Of importance is an effort funded by PHARE. Half of this sizeable project is being used for harmonisation of environmental law, the other half for training of environmental personnel regarding EU requirements and the importance of national compliance. This initiative is likely to have a significant impact on environmental law and its implementation in Hungary, and certainly the assistance can be expected to have a measurable effect on the institutional capacity of Hungarian environmental policy management.

As noted above, a revised national law on the subject has already been drafted, in part with a view toward the harmonisation objective. Its requirements are already affecting the informal communications developing between governmental officials, particularly in the Ministry for Environment (sometimes aided by information and contacts provided through the Ministry of Industry and Trade), and large industrial sectors over the statutory constraints likely to be in force in the future. In this way, some industrial firms, including some of the largest ones, are even now adjusting to EU regulatory constraints through this somewhat indirect route.

Institutional Arrangements for Managing Environmental Policy

The general approach taken by the Hungarian government to issues of environmental pollution has remained relatively constant, even through the dramatic political and economic changes. At the same time, the actual execution of the policy and the institutional framework through which the policy is carried out have undergone substantial change.

The institutional structure for carrying out environmental policy has been altered several times but remains subject to criticism from observers. Administration of environmental policy in Hungary is organised around, in the first instance, the Ministry for the Environment and Regional Policy, which in turn is divided into a number of specialised units. The current formal structure of this ministry is the latest of several reorganisations since the late 1980s. Further restructuring has been considered during the tenure of the current minister as well.

The Ministry, for instance, was reorganised in 1987 to place environmental issues and water management in the same administrative 'home'. However, this arrangement lasted only until 1990, when water management duties were removed from the agency and placed with the Ministry for Transport and Telecommunications. In 1990 additional restructuring resulted nevertheless in the distribution of some environmental duties among numerous other units. More modest structural changes have taken place a couple of times since 1990. Yet the Ministry has not enjoyed a strong reputation, even in its revised form.

This unit performs many of the national government's regulatory (and other) environmental duties, particularly in terms of establishing rules and broad policy guidance. Yet it also houses additional functions, certain of which appear to some observers to be tangential to the environmental portfolio. Furthermore, throughout the successive incarnations of the environmental presence within the Hungarian administrative apparatus over the years, the structure has always been an 'Environment *and* ...' arrangement, with the environmental issues always included with (and, some would say, in competition with) such other goals as water supply or regional policy. In other words, the environment has been a persistently weak and somewhat grudging portfolio both before and after the political changes.

The heart of the field presence for enforcing environmental regulation is in the Regional Environmental Inspectorates, of which there are 12. These units have remained in place through the recent reorganisations. They operate in practice with considerable autonomy from the central ministry in

Budapest, although the chief inspectorate, to which the regions report, is appointed by the minister.

An examination of the current position of the regional inspectorates makes clear some of the critical limitations in institutional capacity currently plaguing environmental administration in Hungary. Due to severe budgetary restrictions, inspectors lack the resources to conduct their official duties. This has led to a situation in which inspectorates work partly as government authorities and partly as private consulting firms because they are only partially supported from the state budget [*REC, 1994b: 40*]. One way in which this dual role manifests itself is through the process of environmental impact assessment. The inspectorates are charged with reviewing assessments before, for instance, construction of a new plant is begun. However, sometimes the inspectorate itself has been hired to conduct the review, thus involving itself in a conflict of interest.

This institutional insulation of regional decision-making from the central national policy unit is only one source of discontinuity in environmental policy implementation. Another important pattern of differentiation separates execution of national policy into a number of different functional authorities, depending on the issue under consideration. In practice, other ministries and agencies of the central government are involved on a day-to-day basis in issues affecting environmental decisions.

The regional environmental authorities control the emission of pollutants, and they are charged with establishing emissions standards. However, ambient air quality standards inside settlements are set elsewhere in government: the public health authorities of the Institute of Public Health, located within the Ministry of Welfare. Because of the organisational locus for this task, the ambient standards are set with human health concerns uppermost in mind.

Meanwhile, mobile sources of emissions are the province of the Ministry of Transport, Telecommunication and Water Management. Supervision of the vehicle inspection programme is in the hands of the Public Transport Supervision Offices, and private firms can also undertake inspections if the firms have been licensed by the Offices. Violations are to be enforced by the Offices or the police.

Furthermore, the National Meteorological Service, a fourth administrative presence in this sector, is responsible for the measure of background air pollution away from settlements. The nation's energy inspectorates have also been involved in providing technical assistance in this sector. However, the shift to privatisation has made it more difficult for these experts to advise firms, while firms themselves have been reluctant to employ energy experts during the recent economic difficulties. Some have even eliminated positions formerly devoted to this specialty.

An important actor during much of the period since the political changes has been the State Property Agency (SPA), a governmental unit responsible for – among other duties – selling state assets into private hands through the privatisation initiatives. The privatisation process itself has been complicated by the question of legal responsibility for environmental damage done by the firms. Thus the environmental ministry and the SPA have had to interact during and sometimes after the property transfer process.

These several kinds of units inform each other of pending new regulations by circulating drafts, but little regular and predictable coordination occurs following the setting of these central policies. No standing committees (below the level of the Cabinet) mediate regularly among them. In some locales, informal coordination among field officers of the units allows for a more integrated approach. But this depends on the individuals involved within a given region and varies greatly in practice from one part of the country to another. Such informal ties were, reportedly, functioning better several years ago, before the political changes disturbed the stable patterns of patronage and personalistic coalitions that had marked the previous regime.

In sum, the system for dealing with issues of environmental quality in Hungary is complex and difficult to administer. The standards are formally restrictive, but in practice enforcement provides loopholes. Nor has this situation been eased in the transitional period following the political changes of 1989. Many new laws have been passed, though these are largely uncoordinated with each other. Changes have been made in the rules for controlling environmental pollution, but these changes do not get to the heart of the enforcement and coordination questions. Although a comprehensive new environmental policy has been accepted by the Parliament, an overall new set of programmes, with implementation arrangements and realistic budgets, has not been enacted.

Local Government and Environmental Management

Prior to the political changes, independent local governments did not exist as autonomous public decision-makers. With some exceptions, local councils were largely subservient to the central-party controlled system. Since 1989, more than 3,000 local self-governments have been created. The Fundamental Law on Local Self-Government charges the new local units with a range of significant responsibilities for environmental matters and also provides a set of powers formally available to use for dealing with pollution problems within their jurisdictions. They can also determine the amount of penalties assessed against violators.

These local governments might have taken some of the responsibility for environmental protection. However, in practice, local self governments have had to contend with contradictory regulations established by the national level, and are overburdened with a daunting number of duties.

In connection with the current process of property shifts, some industrial firms have been placed in the hands of local self-governments. Environmental problems in these cases may be serious but the locals are often in poor position to fund clean-ups or shifts in technology to ameliorate recurring problems like air emissions. Local governments themselves are also initiating new businesses, some of which have the potential to generate significant quantities of pollution. Some of these units of government may be caught between the conflicting desires to use such businesses as centres of revenue for local purposes and the policy goal of limiting traffic and emissions in their jurisdictions.

Except in rare cases, these local governments are not well equipped in terms of expertise or financial resources to assume a significant role in environmental matters. Some local governments, especially the larger ones, have contracted with consulting firms to assist them in assessing their environmental problems, and this activity appears to be on the upswing. However, the majority of local units have done relatively little thus far about environmental matters.

Matters have not been made easier by the tendency of some in the regional environmental inspectorates to seek to retain primary control over air quality rather than ceding some to the localities. Friction between localities and regional inspectorates is not inevitable, but it has developed often enough to limit the effectiveness of localities in addressing their air quality problems.

Enforcement Overview

Standards for protection of the environment are central elements of Hungarian national policy, but serious problems of enforcement have long plagued the system. Many of these have their roots in Hungary's legal and political system. According to Bándi [1993], in the past, the State focused on technical issues, rather than regulation and enforcement. Monitoring, largely conducted by industry with poor equipment and very little regulatory oversight, produced little useful information. What enforcement and implementation there was tended to focus on sanctioning those who polluted rather than on preventing the pollution. When a penalty was imposed, it was often insufficient to provide an incentive to curb pollution. Perhaps most importantly, there was no public participation in the decision-making process, and the role of civil law and the courts was very limited.

Even when citizen intervention was permitted, non-governmental organisations were too weak to support successful public involvement. Bándi points out further that organisational weaknesses also limited Hungary's ability to protect the environment. As we have seen, the ministry charged with implementing environmental policy is much weaker than the economic ministries, in terms of both power and resources. Spheres of authority are poorly defined and are constantly being changed. This unclear division of power creates uncertainty and hesitation, not only for the environmental agencies, but also for the regulated community [*Bándi, 1993: 2*].

Environmental policy in Hungary from the days of state socialism until the present has emphasised punishment for violation of regulatory standards rather than other types of policy instruments. As one Hungarian environmental economist has explained, 'A strange paradox of our development is that Hungarian environmental protection regulations are in many respects stricter than the average EC standards and much stricter than justified by our economic development level. The standards are so strict, in fact, that industries cannot comply with them' [*Kerekes, 1993: 146*]. In particular, designing policies to prevent pollution in the first place has been neglected. A permitting process is activated prior to construction projects, but thus far comprehensive environmental coverage is not provided. The heart of environmental protection remains with the system of standards and associated penalties.

Some non-punitive efforts have recently begun with the aim of focusing more on preventive aspects of policy. But in most spheres, non-punitive and especially extraregulatory instruments are only sporadically employed. For example, economic policy instruments have been discussed but have been mostly notable for their absence in functioning programs. A superficial exception is the system of penalties for violation of standards, which actually functions as a fund-raising mechanism and not as a deterrent to pollute.

Although many aspects of Hungarian environmental policy can be criticised, a major difficulty stems not from lack of reasonable standards and boldly stated objectives but, rather, from a lack of adequate governmental implementation capacity in the field of environmental policy. An important reason for this situation has to do with what Hanf and Underdal have called the 'vertical disintegration of policy' as it moves from general national commitments to the specific demands (costs) placed on social sectors relative to the benefits they can expect to reap directly [*Hanf and Underdal, 1996*]. This disintegration, or perhaps benign neglect, is most apparent when environmental questions face economic ones in the difficult transitional period. Here the generally accepted environmental goals lose out in the competition.

In addition to the vertical dimension, there is a more 'horizontal' one: the ability of central government to involve important sectors of the public in policy discussions and, potentially, in mobilising support for new initiatives. On this score different political systems develop these links in different fashions. For instance, pluralist and corporatist patterns of interest involvement can be markedly different, with real consequences for policy and practice. In Hungary and other formerly one-party systems, of course, the mobilisation of public 'support' for official actions has left an aftertaste in the current transitional period. Those in the wider society with, for instance, deep environmental concerns have been wary and somewhat distrustful of government action; even on those occasions when involvement in real policy discussions has been possible, motives have been suspect. Nor have government officials had much experience with or interest in sharing influence and dealing in good faith with such 'outsiders' as NGOs. When combined with the lack of experience on the part of some NGOs and others, these inclinations on the part of government representatives have translated into relatively weak and unproductive horizontal connections with potential allies or sources of support in the broader society.

Conclusions

The domestic political changes in the country have affected the context in which environmental issues are considered. As the Hungarian transition continues, it is likely that a more open political system, with more coherent political groupings and a stronger environmental voice from NGOs and political parties, will emerge and that the way in which environmental issues are approached will change. Thus far, however, the most notable feature of the Hungarian system is how little the altered political landscape has influenced the way that environmental issues are handled. It could be argued that the lack of change itself reflects the broader sense among the public that economic considerations and social welfare concerns should take precedence over environmental questions during this period.

The property shifts and emergence of market forces in Hungary show signs of the double-edged impacts on environmental protection efforts. The most obvious implementation challenges derive from the proliferation of regulatory targets and lack of 'bridges' in the increasingly differentiated setting, as well as from the slowly emerging involvement of local governments. The very deliberate pace so evident in the introduction of incentive-based policy instruments is due in part to the 'market as prison' [*Lindblom, 1982*] aspect of the emerging mixed economy – as policy makers in Hungary seek to avoid further economic pain by keeping marginal enterprises in business. But market forces can also aid efforts to meet the environmental challenge – by discouraging waste, for instance, even if the increased costs of goods like energy impose social distress; and by providing entrée to efficient multinational firms, even if some of these seek to apply in Hungary technologies deemed unacceptable in some other national settings.

More specifically, with regard to the overall institutional capacity to plan and manage a transition toward sustainable development, we can conclude the following. The political changes of 1989 have removed several obstacles to the effective implementation of environmental policy: depoliticisation of enforcement is taking place; privatisation in any case alters the relationship between regulator and regulated; judicial review is now a standard part of the legal system; and broader participation by those outside government is gradually emerging. Obviously, policies can still be improved. Furthermore, government could increase the priority it now places on environmental issues. But even high levels of commitment on the part of a government matter little if the commitment cannot be converted into effective streams of action. In particular, the complexities of policy implementation continue to frustrate these efforts.

Years of lack of attention during the era of state socialism, a fragile economic system during the transitional period, shortages of financial resources and staff in the relevant ministries, a lack of effective channels of coordination among the several official units acting to execute national policy, and limited horizontal connections with those interested in stronger and more effective environmental efforts have all meant that limitations on institutional capacity have constrained what has been possible during implementation. The lack of capacity is manifest not only in the relatively limited resources, influence, and vertical linkages within government, but also in the very limited ties with, and networking opportunities among, NGOs and others who remain seriously concerned with environmental questions and might be able to help catalyse support for environmental action.

But the vertical disintegration and 'horizontal' gaps as sketched here are not the only considerations. It is not merely that environmental institutions are less powerful and exhibit less capacity than other, competitive sectors and institutions, although that is indeed the case. The explanation lies also in a broader institutional incapacity. In its transitional period, Hungary has faced the handicap of having to develop institutional capacity generally, across policy sectors, levels of government, and in the broader society rather than merely the state. All these sectors and levels are short on expertise, lacking in needed budgetary resources, and often handicapped by a lack of pressure group support from the broader society.

Explaining the implementation gap on environmental issues does require comparing the relative support for environmental *vis-à-vis* other institutions and interests in contemporary Hungary. But it is important to bear in mind that in Hungary and the transitional nations of ECE, institutional capacity is in short supply more generally. Any analysis that treats environmental policy in Hungary as merely an instance of environmental institutions losing in political competition would be somewhat misleading or incomplete. The broader challenges and institutional needs of the nation are also a piece of the explanation. In this context, then, the Hungarian government has had need for significant expansion of its own institutional capacity as a part of any concerted effort to address environmental issues.

REFERENCES

Bándi, Gyula (ed.) (1993), *Environmental Law and Management System in Hungary: Overview, Perspectives and Problems*, Budapest: Environmental Management and Law Association.
Bochniarz, Zbigniew, Bolan, Richard, Kerekes, Sándor, Kindler, Jozsef, Vargha, Janos and Harald von Witzke (1992), *Environment and Development in Hungary: A Blueprint for Transition*, Budapest and Minneapolis, MN: University of Minnesota.
Flaherty, Margaret Fresher, Rappaport, Ann and Maureen Hart (eds.) (with contributions from Arpad von Lazar and Sándor Kerekes) (1993), *An Environmental Brief: Privatization and Environment in Hungary. A Case Study, Center for Environmental Management*, Boston, MA: Tufts University.
Hanf, Kenneth and Marcel Roijen (1995), 'Water Management Networks in Hungary: Network Development in a Period of Transition', *Environmental Politics*, Vol.3, No.4, pp.168–96.
Hanf, Kenneth and Arild Underdal (1996), 'Domesticating International Commitments: Linking National and International Decision Making', in Oran Young (ed.), *The International Political Economy and International Institutions, Volume II* (Cheltenham: Edward Elgar), pp.1–20.
Hungarian Commission on Sustainable Development (1994a), *Energy Use and Carbon Dioxide Emissions in Hungary and in the Netherlands: Estimates, Comparisons, Scenarios. Contribution to the National Energy and Environmental Planning in Relation to the Energy-Climate Issues*, Budapest: Hungarian Ministry for Environment and Regional Policy and The Hague: Ministry of Housing, Physical Planning and Environment.
Hungarian Commission on Sustainable Development (1994b), *Hungary: Towards Strategy Planning for Sustainable Development. National information to the United Nations Commission on Sustainable Development*, Budapest: Hungarian Commission on Sustainable Development.
Kerekes, Sándor (1993), 'Economics, Technology, and Environment in Hungary', *Technology in Society*, Vol.15, pp.137–47.
Lindblom, Charles E. (1982), 'The Market as Prison', *Journal of Politics*, Vol.44, No.2, pp.324–36.
Ministry for Environment and Regional Policy, Government of Hungary (1991), *National Report to United Nations Conference on Environment and Development, 1992*, Budapest: Ministry for Environment and Regional Policy.
Ministry for Environment and Regional Policy, Government of Hungary (1995), *National Environmental and Nature Conservation Policy Concept*, Budapest: Ministry for Environment and Regional Policy.
O'Toole, Laurence J., Jr. (1994), 'Privatization in Hungary: Implementation Issues and Local

Government Complications', in Hans Blommenstein and Bernard Steunenberg (eds.), *Governments and Markets: Economic, Political and Legal Aspects of Emerging Markets in Central and Eastern Europe* (Leiden: Kluwer Academic), pp.175–94.

REC (Regional Environmental Center for Central and Eastern Europe) (1994a), *Strategic Environmental Issues in Central and Eastern Europe, Volume 1*, Regional Report, Budapest: Regional Environmental Center for Central and Eastern Europe.

REC (1994b), *Strategic Environmental Issues in Central and Eastern Europe, Volume 2. Environmental Needs Assessment in Ten Countries*, Budapest: Regional Environmental Center for Central and Eastern Europe.

United Kingdom, House of Lords. Select Committee on The European Communities (1995), *Environmental Issues in Central and Eastern Europe: The Phare Programme*, session 1994–95, 16th Report, HL Paper 86, London: HMSO.

Vastag, Gyula, Rondinelli, Dennis A. and Sándor Kerekes (1994), *How Corporate Executives Perceive Environmental Issues: Comparing Hungarian and Global Companies, International Private Enterprise Development Research Center*, Chapel Hill, NC: University of North Carolina.

Sustainable Development in the Czech Republic: A Doomed Process?

ADAM FAGIN and PETR JEHLIČKA

Somewhat paradoxically, after the important role that the green issue played in bringing down the old regime, the environment has now slipped off the political agenda in the Czech Republic. Moderate improvement of some environmental indicators has occurred mainly due to the slow-down in economic activity after 1989. The goals of the government's environmental policy are defined strictly in technical and market terminology. Preference is given to costly solutions addressing legacies of the past whilst little is being done to prevent new problems arising since the 'velvet revolution'. The government's effort to harmonise environmental legislation and standards with the European Union is motivated predominantly by the need to demonstrate a readiness to join Western organisations. Meanwhile, citizens have severely limited opportunities to participate in environmental decision-making and environmental groups are weak and almost totally dependent on Western assistance.

Environmental issues in the Czech Republic have gone through a very turbulent development during the last decade [*Jehlička and Kára, 1994*]. In the 1980s the Czech Republic (as part of the federal Czechoslovakia) had one of the most damaged environments in Europe [*Moldan, 1990; Beneš, 1994; Vavroušek, 1994*]. People who criticised the Communist government for being responsible for the situation were also among the chief proponents of democracy. They were publicly denounced by the Communist authorities and their views were portrayed by the controlled media as a threat to the progress of society.

Today, after more than six years of democratic government, the situation is, worryingly, similar. Although there has been improvement in the quality of the environment over the past five to six years, the Czech Republic is still one of the major polluters in Europe. The favoured method of dealing with this problem – investment in end-of-pipe technologies – has not changed either. As at the end of the 1980s, Czech environmentalists have appeared in the mid-1990s on a list of subversive elements which was drawn up by the state intelligence services. In addition to the accusation of being a threat to the well-being of society, this time they are also deemed to pose a threat to democracy. Thus, without significantly changing their views and goals, environmentalists in the eyes of the government and a certain section of the media have gone through a paradoxical transformation from being one of the major proponents of democracy to one of its major threats.

Similarly, during both the 1980s and 1990s, government efforts to reduce certain kinds of pollution were to a great extent the results of foreign influence. While in the 1980s it was the pressure of neighbouring Western countries on the Czechoslovak Communist government to ameliorate the negative impact on their environment, current efforts are mostly motivated by the desire to join the European Union. This requires the Czech Republic to meet certain EU environmental standards.

By focusing on attempts to reduce air pollution, the role of environmental associations, the Environmental Impact Assessment (EIA) process, external assistance including convergence with EU standards, and the overall approach of the Czech government to environmental protection, it is possible to identify a number of serious constraints on the long-term amelioration of the Czech environment and the realisation of sustainable development. Moreover, the environmental issue provides a valuable lens through which to identify the limitations of the so-called 'transition to democracy'.

Tackling Air Pollution

As air pollution was always regarded as the most urgent environmental problem in the Czech Republic, the example of coping with this problem was chosen in order to expose the constraints and deficiencies of the general approach to environmental management.

The amount of environmental investment and its pattern of allocation is a good indicator of what a government sees as pressing environmental problems. According to Černá et al. [1995], the share of environmental investment in total investment in Czechoslovakia declined between 1970 and 1985 (never exceeding 1.35 per cent in each five-year period) compared to the period between 1986 and 1990, when it achieved 2.81 per cent.[1] In developed countries environmental investment as a proportion of total investment during the period of installation of pollution control technologies in the 1970s and the first half of the 1980s was between four and eight per cent.

During the first phase of the period of transition (1990–93), both the share of environmental investment in total investment and its structure changed markedly. Mainly as a consequence of public concern about the environment before and immediately after 1989, real investment in the environment increased sharply by 37 per cent in the years 1990–93, against the background of a considerable fall of total investment.

As far as the structure of environmental investment over the period 1970–90 is concerned, most (about 60 per cent), was directed at water protection projects. After 1989, partly in response to the adverse effects of air pollution, in particular its links to the poor state of health of the population living in the most polluted areas, and partly to fulfil international commitments, much greater emphasis was placed on reducing air pollution. During the years 1991–93 36 per cent of environmental investment was accounted for by air protection projects [*Černá et al., 1995*].

However, the first signs of a serious effort to reduce air pollution began to appear during the last years of the Communist regime, when *České energetické závody* (ČEZ, Czech Energy Company) introduced a programme designed to remove solid particle from emissions. Under the provisions of the Clean Air Act passed in 1991, ČEZ had to adopt another programme, this time aimed at the reduction of sulphur dioxide (SO_2) emissions from their power plants by about 95 per cent by 1998 [*Fagin, 1994*]. These emissions are the cause of acid rain and the deforestation of vast, mainly mountainous, areas. Following massive investment (loans from the World Bank and various commercial banks) into the installation of flue gas desulphurisation devices[2] and the target will be almost certainly met. Another step taken by ČEZ was the decommissioning of some obsolete coal-fired power plants. It is envisaged that their capacity would be compensated for by the Temelín nuclear power plant, which is expected to begin operations in 1998.

The measures taken to date to tackle air pollution might give the reader the impression that the government's environmental strategy is sound. Government officials often argue that the massive investment in air quality as well as the decrease in pollution[3] is evidence of their successful environmental policy. They often support such claims by making international comparisons. The 'State Environmental Policy', approved by the government at the fourth attempt in August 1995 (that is, more than three years after the present government took power), states that total environmental expenditures in 1993, 30 billion Czech crowns, represented three per cent of the GDP, whereas 35 billion crowns a year later amounted to 3.5 per cent of the GDP [*MŽP, 1995*]. The document goes further to compare these figures with the 1990 data from Western developed countries, where similar figures did not exceed two per cent, and concludes that environmental expenditure in the Czech Republic is much higher than elsewhere [*MŽP, 1995*].

As Klvačová [*1995*] aptly points out, it does not seem fair to compare the 1994 figures from one country with the 1990 data from other countries.

Secondly, it is not always clear whether these financial means can really be identified as environmental expenditure. Thirdly, it is necessary to relate such environmental expenditure, which is essentially meant to be clean-up oriented, to the level of environmental damage. Despite some modest improvements, the level of environmental pollution originating in the Czech Republic continues to be much higher than in most Western countries.[4]

However, there are further deficiencies in the government's claim that their environmental policy has been successful and efficient. While the fall of industrial output over the period 1990–93 is estimated to have been 36.6 per cent and the decrease in GDP 20 per cent, there was a disproportionally smaller decrease in air pollution, energy use and particularly energy production. Moreover, Černá et al. [1995] came to the conclusion that the improvement in air quality is only temporary and is expected to worsen with the resumption of economic growth.

Bedřich Moldan [1993], first post-Communist Minister for the Environment, warned that while the total amount of air and water pollution had indeed been reduced, the fact that industrial output had dropped much more dramatically meant that the energy and material intensity of the Czech economy had become even greater than in the past and therefore that the amount of 'pollution per unit of production' had actually increased.

What is worrying in the long-term, is that the undoubtedly massive investment in environmental improvement is not used in the most effective way. In a more recent article, Moldan [1996] criticises the current environmental policy for the lack of emphasis placed on sustainable development (measures aimed at reduction of energy and material intensity, technologies reducing the amount of waste, recycling and so forth) and the preference given to expensive end-of-pipe measures. Although government officials claim that this is only the first stage in eradicating the worst legacy of the past and that more sustainable strategies will soon follow, signs of a different trend are observable.

After several years of lower electricity production and consumption, these are again growing and are soon expected to achieve the same level as that prior to 1989.[5] ČEZ plans to increase the export of electricity which now stands at about two per cent. Most electricity is still being produced in power plants burning brown coal (lignite). Managers of northern Bohemian power plants reveal that the phasing-out of some blocks under the provision of the Clean Air Act is regarded as a temporary measure and that they expect to restart the operation of some of these blocks (admittedly after their upgrading) in the near future. After a short period of recession, the amount of mined coal is growing again, partly due to sharply increased exports. All this points to lack of any long-term environmental strategy within government policies.

Unfortunately, some of these short-sighted policies are pursued on the recommendation, or with the support of, various EU agencies. A case in point is the chosen method of desulphurisation of lignite-burning power plants. An article published in New Scientist [*MacKenzie, 1994*] quotes a report made by the Czech environmental NGO Děti Země (Children of the Earth) for the Science and Technology Options Assessment Office of the European Parliament in which the impact of PHARE in the Czech Republic was evaluated. According to their findings, PHARE 'is operating without a long-term strategy. A project may solve one environmental problem while creating another'. The study was carried out as part of Phare which recommended flue gas desulphurisation as the best method of reducing SO_2 emissions. The study proposals were verified in the Prunéřov power plant. This single power plant will need 273,000 tons of limestone annually to absorb SO_2 from flue gases. The limestone will be quarried in a nature protection area of Czech Karst. In a separate project, PHARE spent ECU 100,000 on a study of the protection of these karst formations and their specialised flora and fauna.

The environmental part of PHARE concerning the Czech Republic is now divided into two parts: national (which started in 1990) and regional (launched in 1991). The former is supposed to focus on the country's specific problems (for instance safety of nuclear power plants, environmental education). Its total budget was ECU 20 million [*MŽP, 1994*]. The latter, always comprising at least three countries, was conceived of as a means of promoting European integration and cooperation.

These intentions are not always fulfilled, as the history of the Black Triangle Programme shows. It started as one of the PHARE regional projects in 1991 and since then has spent about ECU six million on various environmental projects. Territorially, the programme covers the area most affected by coal mining and electricity generation in Polish Lower Silesia, German Saxony and Czech Northern Bohemia. Since 1991, the original plans have been revised in two main ways. First, the recipient countries protested against the way in which the assistance was conducted. Western European consulting agencies drew large-scale studies on the environmental situation in the region with little attention paid to the feasibility of their implementation.[6] By 1993 both the Czech and Polish ministries for the environment were pressing for a change in policy – away from studies towards small practical and locally-based projects aiming at ameliorating environmental problems such as energy savings [*MŽP, 1993*]. Second, the emphasis on transboundary co-operation had to be moderated too, although it was not entirely abandoned, as the three participating countries often found coordinated measures difficult to agree upon.

The programme of desulphurisation of the Northern Bohemian power plants is an example of the Czech government's uncoordinated approach to environmental management. As stated above, desulphurisation is seen by the management of ČEZ as an unavoidable and costly measure which, once completed, enables them to declare their production as 'clean'. This removes the barrier to increasing production and export. While this method removes most of the SO_2 emissions, it does not reduce the amount of carbon dioxide (CO_2) emissions, a major greenhouse gas. Any increased electricity generation based on burning brown coal leads to the increased emissions of CO_2.

A similar project is under way not too far from the Northern Bohemian brown coal basin. FACE stands for 'Forest Absorbing Carbon Dioxide Emission' and its important goal is to reduce the amount of CO_2 in the atmosphere. The Krkonoše National Park authority, whose forest suffers badly from acid rain (caused by SO_2 emissions originating partly in the Northern Bohemian power plants), is currently cooperating with the Association of Dutch Electricity Producers on reafforestation of the mountains. The goals of the two participants are complementary – for the Dutch side it is a cheaper way of fulfilling their obligation to reduce CO_2 emissions generated in the Netherlands. The Dutch side provides money[7] which is used for better care for seedlings and young trees. For the Czech state (the national park is almost 100 per cent state owned), it is a welcomed method of reafforestation, which in turn brings other benefits such as prevention of erosion. The apparent paradox between the Czech government participation in this project aimed at reducing emissions of CO_2 and its complacency about the increasing amounts of the same gas generated in the Northern Bohemian power plants seems to pass unnoticed.

The Czech Government's Approach to Environmental Management

The cases described above illustrate the narrow understanding of environmental problems in the Czech Republic and disregard for global environmental problems. This comes as no surprise, given the current government's (as opposed to the first post-Communist government) fierce hostility to the very notion of sustainable development which extends as far as rejecting any references to the term within the official 'State Environmental Policy' [*MŽP, 1995*]. The document characterises the state environmental policy as '[a] dynamic approach leading to finding ecologically, economically, socially and politically optimal variants, not as a static dogma undermining economic development and resulting in state *dirigisme*' [*MŽP, 1995: vi–vii*].

The principles of socially acceptable levels of environmental and health risks and the protection of private property are defined as the two main principles of current state environmental policy. Accordingly, the goals and tools of environmental policy have to be constructed in such a way that the optimal level of pollution corresponds as closely as possible to socially acceptable levels of environmental and health hazards. The document goes on to state that 'where possible, the basis for identification of the acceptable level of hazard is private negotiation and private agreements between potential victims and potential originators of hazards arising from pollution, as only they know risks and costs involved and have an interest in reaching optimal solution'.

Thus, the principal government document on environmental policy does not seem to give citizens and victims of environmentally damaging action in general much chance to protect themselves and to exert an influence on the originators of the environmental problems.

In general, there is a considerable democratic deficit in terms of the capacity of citizens to influence decision making in the sphere of the environment. One factor severely constraining people's opportunities in this respect is the highly centralised structure of the state itself – there are only two levels of democratically elected bodies: municipal (local councils) and state (parliament). While the former are weak within the environmental sphere and their capacity to act is both legally and territorially very limited, it proves difficult for a public group to influence the latter, particularly in the effective absence of a green party and strong environmental organisations. The following two sections of this article show that there is still a long way to go before the Czech citizens will be able significantly to influence environmental policies.

The EIA Process

Acts 17/1992, 244/1992 and 499/1992 on Environmental Impact Assessment (EIA) are, taken together, potentially the most radical and progressive pieces of legislation to have emerged from the immediate post-1989 period, and a crucial device for achieving sustainable development. However, if the effectiveness of any legislative act depends on its subsequent implementation, then the Czech EIA process is in need of substantial improvement if the radical potential of the legislation is to be realised [Braniš and Kružíková, 1994]. In general, the EIA process is a valuable lens through which to assess democratic practice in the Czech Republic. The implementation of the EIA legislation exposes the various constraints on an active civil society in the so-called democratic era, and the change of emphasis with regard to the environment since the immediate post-revolutionary period.

The Czech EIA legislation is not remarkably dissimilar from procedures elsewhere [*Sheate, 1994*]. However, the fact that the public are excluded from the early, and vital, stages of the process is a serious deficiency. In the absence of a scoping stage, the public are denied access to the often controversial decision as to whether a proposed construction requires an EIA or not [*Dusík, 1994*]. By stipulating in some detail the circumstances under which an EIA is required (Annexes 1 & 2 of the EIA Act), the Czech legislation denies the process the benefits of public knowledge of a particular area when deciding if an EIA is necessary. Defining environmental impact is sufficiently difficult without excluding members of the public who, as residents of a particular area, are often likely to have a greater insight into the negative aspects of a proposed construction than policy-makers and bureaucrats. As one of the greatest deficiencies of the centralised command system was its inability to incorporate and respond to growing public concerns about the state of the environment during the 1980s, the absence of a scoping process as part of the EIA legislation in the post-Communist period is a particularly controversial omission.

Public participation is further limited by the fact that once it has been decided that an EIA is required, the experts who prepare the EIA documentation are instructed to analyse the potential social and economic impact of a proposed construction, but are not required to communicate and liaise with the local community. The public review of the documentation stage of an EIA is the first instance when the public are legally ascribed a role, though even this stage is deficient. Whilst the legislation stipulates that the EIA documentation compiled must be made available to the public for a period of 30 days, there is no requirement to advertise availability in the local media. This has the direct effect of limiting participation to those with a specific interest, or those members of the public who happen, by chance, to see the information on the notice board of the local authority office. In a number of the EIAs that have taken place in the Czech Republic, participant members of the public have complained that they were unaware of the 30-day inspection period.[8]

Certain measures are required to encourage a passive citizenry, unused to active involvement in political decision-making, to participate in a potentially radical democratic venture such as EIA. It must be acknowledged that in a post-authoritarian period, legal instruments are not in themselves sufficient to bring forth the degree of participation that environmental abatement and democratic governance requires. The public requires assistance in using the formal democratic process now available to them, and need to be made aware of the various stages of the EIA process, including their rights as potentially affected citizens. Campaign groups that emerge as a result of a pending EIA require certain help in organisation and effective articulation of their position *vis-à-vis* the proposed development, and in using the media effectively to challenge officials in a constructive and organised way. Thus, beyond the creation of legislative acts, attempts to maximise and facilitate participation are vital and ought to be taken by officials in the interests of environmental amelioration and democratic participation in general.

Environmental Associations – From Radical Activism to Ephemeral Conservatism

Immediately after the 'velvet revolution' all registered environmental associations were encouraged to participate in the environmental policy-making process [*Ministry of the Environment, 1990*]. The then environmental minister, Bedřich Moldan, created the 'Green Parliament' as a forum for the articulation of environmental proposals in which a diversity of groups and associations were encouraged to participate. The lessons of the Communist era fresh in the memories of all concerned, the emphasis was on cooperation and partnership between the state and the newly emergent civil society.

Unfortunately the sentiment survived only slightly longer than the institutions it spawned. By mid-1991 the Green Parliament had all but ceased to exist and environmental associations were divided and their activities uncoordinated. Although the Green Parliament initiative had faltered during the so-called 'enthusiastic period' [*Jehlička and Kára, 1994*], in which dissidents were in positions of power, the electoral success of Klaus's *Občanská demokratická strana* (Civic Democratic Party) in June 1992 put paid to the ethos of radicalism and a progressive approach to environmental protection. The intention of the new government was to deliver the Czech Republic Western-style polyarchy, characterised by professional political parties rather than broad-based movements, a power elite sanctioned by periodic elections, and a narrowed political power base that essentially reduces the influence of interest groups. In the ensuing months the majority of officials at the Ministry of the Environment were replaced, and the relationship between the leading associations and the Ministry deteriorated rapidly.[9]

When evaluating the development of environmental associations in the Czech Republic since 1992, two main trends are observable: a reduction in political influence, and a concurrent increase in conservatism and professionalism of the larger associations. In contrast to the early post-revolutionary period, the influence of even the largest associations has declined significantly. The relationship between the Ministry of the Environment and the non-governmental sector is based on suspicion bordering on outbursts of hostility [*ČTK, 1995*]. The paucity of environmental legislation drawn up by the Ministry since 1992 has been constructed by officials with little or no consultation with environmental groups. Certain members of Český svaz ochránců přírody (Czech Union of Nature Conservation) or Děti Země are shown drafts of amendments, though such contact is entirely ad hoc. Since late 1994 formal monthly meetings between officials, the Minister and associations have been reintroduced at which issues and policy drafts are discussed. However, it is widely felt by members of environmental associations that such meetings are of little or no value in terms of gaining influence or exerting an impact on the policy agenda of the Ministry.

Whilst the relationship between associations and the Ministry has quite clearly deteriorated, the ability of the larger associations to forge links with deputies from opposition political parties appears to have improved.[10] However, such a development ought to be greeted with caution: despite gaining the overwhelming support of opposition party deputies for a series of amendments during the passage of ozone legislation in 1995, the alliance of environmental groups and deputies was ultimately defeated by the government who enacted the legislation without their recommendations.

With regard to relations with the public the situation is slightly more encouraging. Environmental associations such as Hnutí Duha (Rainbow Movement) and Greenpeace have worked closely with local community groups over the proposed construction of nuclear waste storage sites in 11 regions across the country. The larger environmental associations have performed a vital role in providing support and expertise as well as linking local campaigns in order to address the issue of nuclear waste in general. Backed by the established environmental associations, local protest groups have courted the support of local mayors and officials, many of whom have adopted the issue of nuclear waste as a key political platform. The future development of such a tripartite link between environmental associations, citizens and local politicians depends heavily on reform of local government.

However, the changed relationship between the government and environmental associations overshadows other developments and is of grave concern in terms of democratic representation and the future course of environmental policy. In February 1995 it was revealed that four of the larger associations (Animal SOS, Děti Země, Duha and Greenpeace) had been included on a security services' list of so-called extremist organisations threatening public order and were the intended target of surveillance. The ensuing media uproar over the inclusion of the four green organisations, all incidentally committed to non-violent protest, on a list alongside an array of extremists, resulted in their eventual removal [e.g., *ČTK, 1995*]. However, the incident left the relationship between the government and the environmental sector fraught and dysfunctional. To many, the incident proved that the era of mutual co-operation and a round table approach to environmental policy is well and truly over.

A concurrent development amongst environmental associations has been the gradual demise of radicalism in favour of a more conservative approach to campaigning, which had come to focus increasingly on lobbying parliament and the formal political machine. In the aftermath of the revolution of 1989, the environmental sector reflected the sheer diversity of environmentalism and the so-called 'new' politics of contemporary protest. Activists adopted a global perspective and a commitment to radical action. However, during the past two years much has changed. Groups no longer reject formal strategies, and have compromised on their ideals in order to form alliances with political parties. On a positive note, they now display a level of professionalism almost worthy of their British or German counterparts; for example, they now are able to use the media effectively without excessively disturbing societal codes. The vital difference is, however, that whilst some of their counterparts in Western Europe have once again embarked on a phase of radicalism – witness the protests over road extension in the UK – Czech environmental associations have donned conservative clothing at a vital juncture in their country's environmental history. With nuclear power firmly on the agenda and the prospect of extensive nuclear waste storage across the country a likely reality, the environmental associations talk of the need to proceed cautiously and consider compromise on nuclear storage sites. The once radical organisation Děti Země has compromised to such a degree that it negotiates in terms of where storage sites should be placed rather than whether they should exist at all.

The tragedy of such a shift in approach is that the non-governmental environmental sector has received no dividends for its professionalism and increased conservatism. They have not been welcomed in from the cold by the government, and greeted as new converts to democratic compromise. Whilst the main associations are desperately keen to emphasise their realism and willingness to negotiate, their ability to influence the environmental agenda of the government is not significantly greater than it was under Communism.

The attitude of the current administration aside, the difficulties faced by environmental associations can largely be attributed to the absence of a cohesive infrastructure able to sustain and nurture democratic participation. An immediate issue is the financial instability of even the largest associations. State financial support for the environmental sector, administered by the Ministry of Environment, is limited and is increasingly restricted to the funding of various projects with little money offered for the development of the overall infrastructure of the sector. Moreover, low levels of disposable income amongst Czech citizens in comparison to Western Europe force associations to depend heavily on foreign donations. Though the EU-funded PHARE programme has provided financial support for a number of the main environmental associations in recent years, future support cannot be guaranteed. Indeed, there is already evidence to suggest that such aid has been shifted away from the Czech Republic in light of the relative political and economic stability of the country. Against the background of such a trend, associations require indigenous financial support if they are to develop or even survive. The current legal situation governing donations to the non-profit sector provides insufficient incentives to Czech individuals and organisations to pledge financial support. Unlike the situation in the USA, the tax rebate on donations is insignificant in the Czech Republic. Moreover, the current legal position of non-profit organisations remains vague and uncertain, which serves to further discourage long-term indigenous support.

Financial uncertainty acts to undermine the non-governmental environmental sector. The larger associations, unable to offer employees secure and well-paid employment, continually lose staff to private consultancies. Against a background of a rapid increase in the cost of rented property, environmental associations have lost their offices and are forced to move out of the centre of Prague. Other related effects include denied access to accountants and legal services. The coordinating organisation, *Zelený kruh* (Green Circle), does provide registered associations with support, information and expertise. It provides premises for press conferences, and has orchestrated a number of meetings between officials, politicians, business and representatives from environmental associations. However, *Zelený kruh* itself stumbles from one financial crisis to the next and is thus unable to expand or provide the level of services the sector so desperately requires.

Harmonisation of Czech Environmental Legislation with Western Standards

In the absence of a domestic force advocating a more radical response to environmental problems, existing environmental measures, which are quite moderate and often have negative environmental side effects, are the product of two factors. First, the bulk of the legislation is a legacy of the 'enthusiastic period', between 1989 and 1991 [*Jehlička and Kára, 1994*] and consists of a solid framework of laws and regulations. Second, is the co-operation with Western institutions, stemming largely from the effort of the country to join the European Union and other Western organisations. As shown earlier, in the case of the recommended method of desulphurisation, the results are often ambiguous from an environmental point of view.

The Association Agreement of December 1991 between the EU and the then Czechoslovakia had to be renegotiated separately with each of the country's two successor states – Czech Republic and Slovakia – after the split on 31 December 1992. The new European Agreement between the EU and the Czech Republic was signed in October 1993 and contains an obligation to assist the Czech Republic in harmonising its law with European law. This is now being carried out within the framework of PHARE.

Despite problems, such as a lack of legal experts able to communicate in the European Union's official languages, by the end of 1994 more than half of Czech environmental regulation was compatible with the EU's. In no case is current Czech environmental regulation inconsistent with the European environmental regulations. At the same time, however, there are areas, namely chemical substances, industrial technologies and genetically modified organisms, which are not yet covered by the Czech legislation [*Romanovská, 1995*]. Even more importantly, formal adoption of environmental legislation does not automatically guarantee harmonisation in practice. Institutions and structures responsible for implementing common standards have yet to be built.

In autumn 1995 the Czech Republic became a member of the OECD and membership will have certain implications in the environmental policy arena. Member states are, for instance, obliged to prepare regular environmental performance reviews. This will enable Czech environmental indicators to be directly compared with those of the other member states. There are potentially two other and probably more important consequences of OECD membership: aid to the Czech Republic will undoubtedly be gradually reduced while the country will be expected to provide foreign assistance, which will most likely include environmental expertise, to other countries.

Conclusion

Environmental policy and the fate of the concept of sustainable development perfectly reflect the two distinct phases of post-Communist political development in the Czech Republic. The initial enthusiastic preparation of environmental laws and institutions framed within the context of inclusive citizen participation illustrate the democratic radicalism of the first dissident dominated post-Communist administration. The subsequent demise of a two-pronged strategy with regard to environmental regeneration – to clean up the most affected parts of the country and make preparatory steps towards sustainable development – coincided with the electoral success of Václav Klaus and the right-wing coalition in June 1992. In the ensuing four years, the emphasis has shifted from long-term preventive measures in favour of haphazard short-term amelioration. Ironically there is little difference in essence to the response of the Communist administration a decade earlier. The best example of this new approach is the programme of desulphurisation of Czech power plants. Several years since the 'velvet revolution' and the prominence of the environmental issue, domestic pressure for radical abatement has essentially evaporated and has been replaced by an external actor, the EU. Instead of far-reaching environmental reform, the country is now oriented towards compliance with the minimum environmental requirements of the EU. Whilst the ecological impact of such a shift is potentially devastating, the political implications are also grave. The government of the post-Communist Czech Republic excludes pressure groups and citizens' organisations from the policy process, refutes the suggestion of a long-term perspective based on sustainable development, and allows the direction of its environmental policy to be dictated by external authorities. To what extent has there really been a democratic transition?

NOTES

1. Czech government documents define environmental investment loosely as 'all costs contributing to the reduction of pollution, that is, to the improvement of the quality of the environment (cost of building and running facilities such as sewage treatment plants, introducing environmentally friendly technologies, costs of phasing out polluting productions)' [Héniková and Beneš, 1994: 215]. While prior to 1989 all investment was directed and made by the state, the post-1989 environmental investment has a more diverse structure. The other sources, apart from the direct government investment, are the State Fund for the Environment (whose income is based on collecting payments and fines) and private sector.
2. Flue gas desulphurisation of one power plant block costs 1.5–1.7 billion Czech crowns [Pissinger, 1994].
3. From 1990 to 1993, solid emission decreased by 30 per cent, SO_2 by 24 per cent and nitrogen oxides by 23 per cent [Černá et al., 1995].
4. Selected items comparing emissions in the Czech Republic and OECD (data from 1993).

Emissions	Czech Republic	OECD average
SO_2 (kg per capita)	149	52.6
NO_x (kg per capita)	68	43.3
CO_2 (kg per capita)	14.3	12.1

Source: MŽP [1994].

5. Consumption of electricity in the Czech Republic was in 1995 only by 0.6 per cent lower than in the record 1989. The structure of consumption is changing: consumption in households is growing, partly due to the government's policy of promotion of using electricity as a medium of domestic heating.
6. In its initial phase about 80 per cent of the financial means earmarked for the Black Triangle

programme by the EU were spent on Western consultancy (interview with Dr Blažková, Czech representative to the Black Triangle coordination unit, July 1995).

7. The Dutch contribution towards the costs of replanting was 150 million Czech crowns over the first three years of the project (1992–94) and the total contribution should amount to 1 billion Czech crowns.

8. The four EIAs used as case studies include a proposed private recreational park, a dam project, and the construction of two motorways. All four occurred during the period between August 1993 and June 1995.

9. A great deal of the information on the relationship between environmental associations and the state was obtained from a series of interviews with leading environmental associations in April 1994, November 1995 and June 1995.

10. Interview with Martin Bursík.

REFERENCES

Beneš, J. (ed.) (1994), *Environmental Year Book of Czech Republic 1993–94*, Prague: Ministry of the Environment.

Braniš, M. and E. Kružíková (1994), 'The Environmental Impact Assessment Act in the Czech Republic: Origins, Introduction and Implementation Issues', *Environmental Impact Review*, Vol. 14, pp. 195–201.

Černá, A., Tošovská, E. and P. Cetkovský (1995), 'Economic Transformation and the Environment', in J. Svejnar (ed.), *The Czech Republic and Economic Transition in Eastern Europe* (San Diego, CA: Academic Press), pp. 377–94.

ČTK (Česká Tiskova kancelář) (1995), 'Greenpeace Strongly Rejects Accusation of Extremism', *ČTK Daily News Bulletin*, No. 30, 4 Feb.

Dusík, J. (1994), 'Evaluation of the Public Participation Process in EIA – The Czech Republic', unpublished manuscript.

Fagin, A. (1994), 'Environment and Transition in the Czech Republic', *Environmental Politics*, Vol. 3, No. 3, pp. 479–94.

Héniková, S. and J. Beneš (eds.) (1994), *Životní prostředí České republiky. Ročenka 1993–1994*, Praha: Český ekologický ústav.

Jehlička, P. and J. Kára (1994), 'Ups and Downs of Czech Environmental Awareness and Policy: Identifying Trends and Influences', in S. Baker, K. Milton and S. Yearley (eds.), *Protecting the Periphery: Environmental Policy in Peripheral Regions of the European Union*, London: Frank Cass, pp.152–70.

Klvačová, E. (1995), 'Ekologická politika. Pocity přinejlepším smíšené', *Ekonom*, Vol.39, No.41, pp. 19–21.

MacKenzie, D. (1994), 'Experts Clean up as Eastern Europe Stays Dirty', *New Scientist*, Vol.142, No.1920, pp.8–9.

Ministry of the Environment (1990), *Rainbow Programme – Environmental Recovery for the Czech Republic*, Prague: Academia.

Moldan, B. (ed.) (1990), *Životní prostředí České republiky*, Praha: Academia.

Moldan, B. (1993), 'Míč v hřišti. Diskuse o vládní ekologické politice musí začít co nejdříve', *Respekt*, Vol.4, No.52, p.3.

Moldan, B. (1996), 'Ekologie 1995 – Česká republika', *Lidové noviny*, 11 Jan. 1996, p.8.

MŽP (Ministerstvo životního prostředí ČR) (1993), 'Černý trojúhelník: od velkých studií k lokálním konkrétním projektům', *Zpravodaj Ministerstva životního prostředí*, Vol.3, No.10, p.3.

MŽP (Ministerstvo životního prostředí ČR) (1994), 'Zpráva o stavu životního prostředí České republiky v roce 1993', *Zpravodaj Ministerstva životního prostředí*, Vol.4, No.9, pp.3–15.

MŽP (Ministerstvo životního prostředí ČR) (1995), 'Státní politika životního prostředí', *Zpravodaj Ministerstva životního prostředí*, Vol.5, No.10, i–xi.

Pissinger, R. (1994), 'Životní prostředí pánevní oblasti severních Čech', *Zpravodaj Ministerstva životního prostředí*, Vol.4, No.10, pp.3–6.

Romanovská, L. (1995), 'Co je Evropská Unie', *Zpravodaj Ministerstva životního prostředí*, Vol.5, No.7, pp.x–xii.

Sheate, W. (1994), *Making an Impact: A Guide to EIA Law and Policy*, London: Cameron May.

Vavroušek, J. (1994), 'Environmental Management in Czechoslovakia and Succession States', *Environmental Impact Assessment Review*, No.14, pp.1–31.

Rejecting Green Velvet: Transition, Environment and Nationalism in Slovakia

JURAJ PODOBA

Environmental issues played an important role in bringing down the old regimes in almost all Communist countries. Slovakia (as part of the former Czechoslovak Socialist Republic) was a special case in this respect. In this country, the green element played such a prominent role in the 1989 'velvet revolution' that it could have been called the 'green velvet revolution'. The current marginalisation of environmental issues and low profile of environmental policies in Slovakia are in sharp contrast with the high environmental concern and dynamic development of environmental institutions and laws in the late 1980s and early 1990s. This contribution describes the changing attitudes of Slovak society to environmental issues during the post-Communist transition and identifies its causes. It also explains the process by which environmentally harmful and previously unpopular symbols of the Communist achievements have been transformed into symbols of achievement of the Slovak nation and independent Slovakia. Two case studies – the aluminium smelter in Žiar nad Hronom and the waterworks Gabčíkovo on the Danube – illustrate this transformation.

Historical Background

Slovakia is a country of beautiful national parks, historic towns, castles and rural vernacular architecture. Pride of the beauty of the country is deeply rooted in the Slovak identity and has become part of a national ideology portraying Slovakia as the 'Switzerland of the East'. After the demise of Communism, this ideological stereotype from the 1930s and 1940s resurfaced in the rhetoric of Slovak political parties of national orientation.

Faith in industry and technology and the positive evaluation of the consequences of Communist industrialisation (despite its massive negative impact on the environment), features typical of the Communist period, were adopted by this post-1989 national political current. The coexistence of the two theoretically contradictory stereotypes of pride of the beauty of the

The author acknowledges the constructive comments of David Humphreys on an earlier version of this contribution. Any remaining errors are the responsibility of the author.

country on the one hand and pride of achievements of Communist industrialisation on the other, in the current national ideology promoted by the governing elite, is a very significant obstacle to an effective and progressive environmental policy in Slovakia.

The key to understanding current attitudes of Slovak society to the environment and its value orientation is the character of Communist modernisation in Slovakia in the twentieth century. A sweeping modernisation process has taken place during the last 50 years. The steep and environmentally destructive power of this process in Slovakia is unique in Central Europe. At the turn of the century Slovakia, with its backward agrarian economy and conservative, post-feudal society, was ill-prepared for the modernisation brought about by the industrialism of the twentieth century. The major phase of the industrialisation process, accompanied by fast and massive urbanisation, increased educational level and fundamental changes in the social and professional structure, is bound with the building of Communism which started in the late 1940s. Communist industrialisation in Slovakia is characterised by its extensive character, construction of large plants in relatively small settlements and the priority given to heavy industry (chemicals, mining, metallurgy and heavy machinery). The process of urbanisation lagged behind the process of job creation in industry. As a consequence, a wide gap opened between the technical and economic aspects of modernisation on the one hand and the social and cultural processes on the other [*Musil, 1993: 14, 20*].

The Environmental Movement Prior to 1989

The key role of the *Slovenský zväz ochrancov prírody a krajiny* (SZOPK, Slovak Union of Nature and Landscape Protectionists) in the anti-Communist opposition of late 1980s resulted in many of its members occupying high positions in the post-1989 governments and parliaments (both Slovak and federal), an indication of the prominent standing of the Slovak environmental movement amongst Central European anti-Communist groups. This was partially due to the very weak support for other opposition groups, such as dissidents focusing on civil rights, or Catholic activists co-operating with the 'underground church'. During *perestroika* the atmosphere in the society grew more dynamic and criticism of the regime increased. The empty civic political space was filled by small groups of intellectuals, artists and, most relevant to this study, environmentalists.

The fight against the liquidation of Bratislava's historic cemetery in 1982, which started the confrontation with the regime [*Budaj, 1986*], also marked the beginning of the phenomenon of the 'Bratislava protectionist movement'. Following the publication of Bratislava/Nahlas in 1987, a report drafted by the Bratislava branch of the SZOPK criticising the environmental, social and cultural conditions in the Slovak capital, environmental activists faced political persecution [*Budaj, 1988; Pravda*, 3 Feb. 1998 p.3]. The protectionist movement subsequently played an important role during the 'velvet revolution', particularly in the capital. Many of its leading activists assumed posts in the 'government of national reconciliation' or became members of both Slovak and federal parliaments. However this achievement, while promising for the future of environmental policy, was a turning point of the movement's history. Paradoxically, it marked the end of its unity and authority in the society.

The Environmental Movement and Greens after the 1989 Change

After November 1989 the 'nature protectionist movement' split into three groups. The largest group continued activities in the SZOPK along the 1980s model. Many members of the SZOPK were appointed to posts in the newly created regional environmental authorities. The second group took part in building the administrative and managing structures of the *Verejnosť proti násiliu* (VPN, Public against Violence) as a political movement. The third group – many well-known personalities – entered post-revolutionary politics often in high official positions. Despite the fact that during the 'velvet revolution' and before the 1990 elections representatives of the VPN with the 'protectionist' background employed environmental rhetoric, their real political orientation was often very different. Paradoxically, environmentalists and the leaders of the Green Party were often blamed for idealism and naivety by former nature protectionists in the leadership of the VPN who had been delegated to their posts by the movement [*Jehlička and Kostelecký, 1995: 213*].

The atmosphere in society dramatically changed during the winter and spring of 1990. The attention turned away from environmental reform and civil rights to issues such as the economic transformation, European integration, the emerging Slovak–Czech dispute, the role of the Slovak Republic in the federation and the question of the Hungarian minority in Slovakia. Euphoria disappeared and was replaced by the fear of freedom as well as the fear of new, until then unknown, social problems.

After autumn 1990 the internal division of the Slovak Green Party reflected the overall pattern of political orientation in Slovak society. The Greens were divided between the pro-federal (anti-nationalistic) and nationalistic (in effect anti-reform) lines. During the debate about the Language Act in the Slovak Parliament in October 1990, all Green Party deputies except one joined the nationalistic parliamentary bloc seeking to restrict the rights of the Hungarian minority. During 1991 leading figures in the Green Party lost contact with the environmental movement. Some green deputies preferred attending meetings of the radical nationalistic organisation *Matica slovenská* to joining protests of Slovak and Hungarian environmentalists on the site of the waterworks on the Danube in summer 1991. Eventually, the Green Party split into two: the Slovak Green Party and the pro-federal Green Party. After electoral failure in 1992 the pro-federal Greens disbanded. Despite having two MPs elected in the 1994 elections on the joint list of three left-wing parties, by 1992 the Slovak Green Party had also effectively ceased to exist as a relevant political force.

The first half of the 1990s brought two contradictory tendencies to the environmental movement. On the one hand, the traditional environmental organisations from the late 1980s, the SZOPK and the youth organisation *Strom života* (SŽ, Tree of Life), were affected by these changes. Many activists left these organisations and the interest of the public and the media in the environment also declined. The major environmental organisations lost the financial subsidy provided until the beginning of the 1990s by the state. They were unable to adjust to the new conditions and come to terms with falling support from the society and shrinking membership. The local branches which are still active represent the more conservative shade of today's environmental activism.

On the other hand, political freedom bringing new ideas and influences soon led to the emergence of dozens of new environmental NGOs and foundations supporting environmental aims and activities. Although some of these exist only formally, others have evolved into respected organisations. Unlike the 'traditional' movements, they are based on small clusters of activists rather than on mass membership. The new environmental NGOs are more narrowly specialised, campaigning on issues such as nuclear energy, protection of rivers, opposition to building new dams and so forth. However, their campaigning is usually entirely dependent on the financial subsidy from international environmental organisations and foundations. The Regional Environmental Center (REC) and Environmental Partnership are the most active sponsoring bodies in Slovakia.

Among the 'new' NGOs Greenpeace and *Za matku Zem* (For Mother Earth) are the most visible, both focusing on the state energy policy and nuclear energy in particular. During the last years these two organisations have succeeded in attracting the attention of the press and public. Activists of these new NGOs tend to be very young; most of them are under 25.

At the same time, there are other NGOs, whose members are mostly environmental specialists. The most active are *Ludia a voda* (People and Water) and *Slovenská riečna sieť* (Slovak River Network), both of which focus on hydroelectric power station issues. *Centrum pre podporu miestneho aktivizmu* (Centre for Environmental Public Advocacy) is, as its name suggests, promoting grass-roots activities, while *Spoločenstvo pre harmonický život* (Association for Harmonic Life) advocates alternative, sustainable ways of life. *Spoločnosť pre trvalo udržateľný život* (Society for Sustainable Living) is an umbrella organisation that provides a debating and publishing forum for activists from all NGOs, as well as intellectuals, artists and experts.

Domestic and Foreign Financial Resources and Investments

In the last three years the Ministry of the Environment received the least amount of money from the state budget out of all ministries. For instance in 1995, in comparison with 1993, it was allocated only 60 per cent of the financial means, while the state contribution to the State Environmental Fund (SEF) dropped steadily (1992: 950 million crowns; 1993: 440 million crowns; 1994: 300 million crowns; 1995: 250 million crowns – these figures are not adjusted for inflation). Environmental payments and fines are an additional, but negligible, source of income for the SEF. The number of projects financed by the SEF has dropped sharply. Meanwhile, state financial support to non-governmental environmental organisations has dropped to about one-tenth of that in the year 1992.

The major source of foreign environmental aid for Slovakia comes from the EU PHARE programme. Slovakia was involved in PHARE I, PHARE II and the Multi-Country Programme for the Environment. In PHARE I ten projects of ECU 11.2 million in total were selected. These projects were targeted at very different environmental issues, including the basic hydrogeological model of the Danube basin, creation of the ecotoxicological centre in Bratislava, monitoring of food quality, waste management, protection of karst regions, drinking water monitoring devices and security systems of nuclear reactors.

For PHARE II three projects of ECU 2.4 million were chosen. These projects focused on education and raising public environmental awareness and the relationship between contamination and human health as well as on upgrading groundwater monitoring. The Multi-country Programme for the Environment consists of two parts; a project aimed at concrete transboundary environmental problems and the strengthening of the institutional base by creating and supporting the Regional Environmental Center in Budapest (see Waller, this volume). Slovakia is taking part in the following projects: the Danube river basin; Programme Corine, Sustainable Forests and Biodiversity Protection; and the PHARE Institute for Environmental Technology (PIET).

Environmental Policy Since 1989

The most tangible positive outcomes of the 'green velvet revolution' are newly built state institutions and a new range of environmental laws. With respect to the former, the most important examples are the Ministry of the Environment and Nature Protection and newly created regional environmental authorities, separate from the general state administration, which were set up at district and local levels. In 1993, former state environmental organisations and some research institutes (for example, national park authorities and the Institute of Nature Protection) were integrated into the Slovak Environmental Agency.

Underlying features of current Slovak environmental policy are the concentration on the environmental consequences of economic development pursued from the beginning of 1950s, a narrow understanding of environmental issues in scientific and technological terms and a disregard for global environmental problems. Another feature of Slovak environmental policy-making during the transition is a lack of courage to solve enormous problems according to sustainable strategies. For instance, instead of concerted effort for restructuring the economy in order to reduce energy and material intensity, the state economic policy strengthens industrial production based on obsolete technologies consuming large amounts of raw materials and having severe pollution impact. In the energy sector, the result of this type of economic policy is a growing dependency on nuclear and fossil fuels and the need to build gigantic hydroelectric stations.

Apart from the vested interests of industrial lobbies another obstacle for effective environmental policy-making is insufficient capacity to implement and enforce new environmental legislation at all levels of the state administration and economic apparatus. Furthermore, codes of conduct for foreign companies and incentives for environmentally friendly technologies and products are not yet in place. Slovakia lacks environmental consultancy and advisory centres for business, local governments and the general public. This situation is deeply rooted in the still persisting social and political practices of the past including lack of environmental education, information barriers between environmental authorities, NGOs and the general public and the marginal standing of the environment and sustainable development in the eyes of both decision-makers and the public [*Huba, 1995a: 21–22*].

Nevertheless, several positive trends and successes during the past 5–6 years can be identified. Environmental degradation is less severe due to the overall decline in industrial output after 1990 and the closure of some of the unprofitable and most polluting plants such as a nickel smelter in Sered'. However, this environmentally positive trend results only from an economic slowdown that inevitably affects social interests. Another post-1989 positive feature is the significant fall in the use of artificial fertilisers. Their consumption in 1994 was almost six times, and in the case of phosphates and potash ten times, lower than in 1990. Decrease in the consumption of pesticides is also significant. At the same time, the decrease of per hectare harvest of cereals has fallen only by 15 per cent [Huba, 1995a: 20].

So far a moderate price increase of energy and sharp price increase of fertilisers are further factors behind the diminished environmental impact of industry and agriculture. In some areas however, it was the new environmental law which brought about positive effects. One case in point is an improvement in waste management. To conclude, certain positive changes in the physical environment have occurred partly due to decreases in industrial production, partly due to new environmental legislation and also, as Huba [1995a: 22] stressed, due to the personal involvement, enthusiasm and sense of responsibility of several hundred active people in influential positions.

The Contemporary State of the Environment in Slovakia

Despite certain positive trends mentioned in the previous section, the overall picture remains bleak. Forty-one per cent of the Slovak population still live in nine regions with a severely degraded environment. The following data document the extent of the industrial decline and the consequent reduction in the amount of emissions in the wake of the 1989 regime change. In 1985 the Slovak emission of sulphur dioxide was 120.4 kg per capita, in 1991 only 83.0 kg per capita. Emissions of carbon monoxide, which in 1985 reached 65.7 kg per capita are declining (to 59.4 kg per capita in 1991). On the other hand, emissions of nitrous oxides increased from 38.2 kg per capita in 1985 to 44.2 kg per capita in 1991. These data include only large domestic stationary sources, thus excluding emissions from transport, household heating and transboundary emissions. However, even after certain improvements in indicators of air pollution, Slovakia still occupies the ninth place among European states in sulphur dioxide emissions per capita and produces four times as much sulphur dioxide emissions as neighbouring Austria [Klinda, 1994; Huba, 1995b; Huba, 1996].

The aggregate production of radioactive waste by the year 2030 is estimated to be 38,000 cubic metres of liquid and 2,000 cubic metres of solid waste. In addition, there will probably be other waste from the damaged nuclear power plant A–1 in Jaslovské Bohunice, which was phased out in 1977 following a serious accident. The amount of nuclear waste which will have to be stored will further increase once another nuclear power plant of Soviet origin currently under construction at Mochovce is phased in.

The overall per capita consumption of primary energy is three to seven times higher than in Western developed countries. Despite very limited domestic sources of energy and raw materials the Slovak economy has specialised in metallurgy and related industries. For instance, in 1989 Slovakia produced 3.5 million tons of pig-iron and 4.7 million tons of steel. The result of this orientation of production was that industry consumed 63 per cent of electricity. Per capita consumption of electricity increased by 33.4 per cent between 1980 and 1990 [*Klinda, 1994; Huba, 1995b; Huba, 1996*].

Slovak rivers remain severely polluted. Between 75 and 80 per cent of their total length falls into the category of severe pollution. Almost one half of groundwater resources is endangered by pollution. The deterioration of the state of Slovakia's forests is perhaps the fastest in Europe. 2.4 per cent of forests were recorded as damaged by emissions in 1970, rising to 8.5 per cent in 1975, 15.6 per cent in 1985 and more than 50 per cent in 1990. By 1994 85 per cent of trees were affected.

Finally, it is estimated that due to geological and morphological conditions and irrational management of vast monocultural fields on the slopes 1.5 million hectares out of a total area of 2.4539 million hectares of agricultural land are endangered by water erosion [*Huba, 1995b*].

Rejecting the Outcomes of Green Velvet – Changing the Change

The economic power in the Communist state was in the hands of the top managers of state enterprises. Although the companies and businesses they managed were nominally the property of the people, in reality the managers behaved like owners and profited from the state and co-operative property. This social stratum originated in the post-Second World War decades in the atmosphere of 'progressive' Communist ideology of which 'taming nature' was an integral part. Lack of sensitivity to natural and cultural values and a propensity to see progress in terms of building large-scale projects were typical of this new generation of ambitious Communist technocrats.

The Communist regime created, due to the exclusion of society from participation in decision-making, favourable conditions for the realisation of extensive industrial development unimpeded by environmental considerations. The executor of this concept was the Communist top management, which was economically bound with this way of development.

Rapid changes after November 1989 – environmental legislation and institutions, high political positions occupied by leaders of the protectionist movement and discussions about former 'taboo' topics in the media – found the former Communist *nomenklatura* and the Communist management unprepared. The political change removed many of the *nomenklatura* from decision-making positions, but most of the top managers and technocrats, who had not reached the highest posts in the Communist Party hierarchy, kept their positions. After several months of disorientation and hesitation the management took steps to mitigate the impact of the November 1989 change. The representatives of various industrial lobbies started to contact suitable political parties as tools for achieving their goals and defending their interest. For example, the lobby connected with the building of the large water constructions on the Slovak rivers first sough the support of the *Kresťansko-demokratické hnutie* (KDH, Christian Democratic Movement) and only in 1992 turned to the perspective electoral winner *Hnutie za demokratické Slovensko* (HZDS, Movement for Democratic Slovakia).

Given that the process of modernisation and social progress took place under a Communist system that provided its citizens with certain social security guaranties, resistance to change and nostalgia for the past soon became an important feature of post-Communist Slovak society. The anti-reform political elite which after the 1992 elections replaced the 'velvet revolutionaries', in alliance with powerful economic lobbies, have used the prevailing resistance to change in society to prevent the adoption of new developing strategies. They have gained the support of large sections of the population by employing a combination of social populism resting on nostalgia for former social security and nationalist ideology. This curious blend facilitates co-operation between two seemingly contradictory political groups. The first group – the 'real right' – is an interest group composed principally of former Communist managers, the new rich (very often with a criminal or 'shadow economy' background) and political opportunists striving to privatise former state property. The 'far left' – neo-Communist extremists are the second group. As pure Communist ideology is now out of fashion it has been replaced by a special kind of Slovak nationalism which is enriched by many ideological stereotypes of the Communist period.

These two groups have one interest in common, namely to continue with the centralised model of the state-controlled economy, based on the patterns of Communist industrialisation and agriculture production. They have no interest in the democratisation of Slovak society, in decentralisation and in sustainable strategies of social and economic development. Former state-owned companies have been mostly privatised into the hands of supporters of the current regime.

Tangible results of the 'building of Communism', which in the pre-1989 era were celebrated as symbols of the progress and success of the Communist society, have changed into symbols of the capabilities and achievements of the Slovak nation. An important symbolic place in nationalistic propaganda is reserved for the major monuments of the Communist industrialisation and gigantomany, which almost invariably have had severe environmental impacts. In this respect nationalistic propaganda has adopted central features of Communist rhetoric, with the phrase anti-Communist now replaced by 'anti-Slovak' or 'anti-national'. One of the main goals of the current ruling political establishment is to suppress alternative and independent citizen groups and organisations in the country. In spring 1996 the ruling coalition of three anti-reform parties attempted to destroy, or at least to marginalise, all (not only environmental) NGOs by passing the special act on foundations and NGOs. Although the law was passed, the government had to make several concessions due to a well coordinated domestic campaign and foreign pressure.

The following two case studies document important aspects of the current struggle for democracy, future economic development and the adoption of sustainable strategies in Slovakia.

The Aluminium Smelter Závody SNP in Žiar nad Hronom

The aluminium smelter Závody SNP is the outcome of the first and most extensive phase of the Communist industrialisation of the 1950s. The negative impact on the environment and health of the population is enormous. Pollution is estimated to affect the health of 30,000 people living in the Žiar valley. The factory employs directly about 1,000 people. Closing it down would cause large social unemployment and possibly result in social unrest.

Modernisation of the factory commenced in 1986. In effect the whole new plant was built. The costs were estimated at four billion crowns. For these reasons the smelter became the target of severe criticism by environmentalists (SZOPK, Green Party) as well as the reform economists after November 1989. The aim was to put an end to the primary aluminium production. However, in May 1991 the Slovak government decided to support the extension of the factory's economically unsound and environmentally destructive production. Such an expansion has, besides a temporarily cheap labour force, no advantage as Slovakia lacks adequate sources of energy and raw materials (bauxite has to be imported from Hungary). Despite these obvious disadvantages, the need for restructuring the economy and the official emphasis on the need for enterprises to be economically viable, the government supported the extension of production of the single largest energy consumer in the country, thus effectively succumbing to the political pressure of the aluminium lobby. The courting of voters for the next election was also a factor.

The study which served as the basis for the final decision of the government did not pass the interministerial discussion and no other alternative to production of aluminium has been considered. The decision of the government preceded the results of an independent foreign expert study. The Norwegian company Hydro Aluminium (majority of shares owned by the Norwegian state) conditioned its participation in modernisation of the smelter by the long-term state-guaranteed supply of cheap electricity and a state donation for covering interests from the credit. The Slovak government's donation was 600 million crowns in 1992 [*Zamkovský and Žilinčík, 1992: 27*].

The smelter in Žiar nad Hronom is an example of how a complicated issue encompassing economic, social and environmental dimensions has been treated by the government of post-Communist Slovakia. The opposition of the Slovak Green politicians to the modernisation, as well as the attitude of the Czech and Slovak federal government, were interpreted as anti-Slovak activity. The fact that the federal government in Prague (and the Slovak government in Bratislava) supported the idea of restructuring the obsolete Slovak industry and the conversion of the military production and eventually carried it out, was considered in Slovakia as an imposition of the Czech interests.

In an extremely tense political situation a general strike was called in Žiar. The management of the factory capitalised on the anti-Czech nationalistic emotions to achieve their goals, namely to obtain the financial grant from the Slovak government and to continue the reconstruction of the factory. This case dynamised the Slovak–Czech dispute over the existence of the federation, boosted the rising wave of nationalism in the period of 1991–92 and firmly established its importance in political life of the post-Communist Slovakia.

Gabčíkovo–Nagymáros Waterworks on the Danube

The Gabčíkovo–Nagymáros waterworks on the Danube played a decisive part in shaping the attitude of society and consecutive Slovak governments to environmentalists and in the overall political development of Slovakia during the last decade. Political conflict over the future of the waterworks strongly influenced political developments in initially two (and after the break-up of the Czech–Slovak Federation of three) countries, the fate of democracy and environmental policy in Slovakia and the international relations and political stability of the whole Central European region.

The origin of the idea of the joint Czechoslovak–Hungarian project on the Danube dates back to 1952. On 16 September 1977 Czechoslovakia and Hungary signed the International Agreement on Building and Operating the

System of Water Constructions Gabčíkovo–Nagymáros. Czechoslovakia was expected to build the dam by Gabčíkovo and Hungary the dam by Nagymáros. While the Czechoslovak side started with the construction in 1978, work on the Hungarian side did not start before 1980 due to a lack of finance. For the same reason the Austrian building companies were invited in the late 1980s to participate in building the dam by Nagymáros. Hungary intended to pay its debt to Austria after the completion by selling cheap electricity.

The waterworks became the target of criticism from both Slovak and Hungarian environmentalists in the middle of the 1980s and later also of Czech dissidents from Charter '77. The first important activity of the Bratislava nature protectionists was an open letter to the Central Committee of the Communist Party in 1986. The campaign against the Danube dams gained momentum after publishing the Bratislava/Nahlas report. WWF has been actively engaged in the Gabčíkovo case since 1986. The political liberalisation of the Kádár regime in Hungary enabled the massive protests of the Hungarian public against the project. In 1989 the Hungarian government decided, without consultation with the Czechoslovak side, to stop the works on the Nagymáros dam.

The campaign against the waterworks on the Slovak side culminated during the 'velvet revolution' and the following months. The environmental initiative *Euroreťaz* (Eurochain) was created. But the technocratic conglomerate of supporters of completion of the water constructions in Gabčíkovo remained intact and continued their lobbying. Former Communist managers of companies involved in the project were replaced by technocrats with personal contacts to the new anti-Communist establishment, with a direct financial and political stake in the completion of construction. This powerful political force took over the professional and political responsibility for the future of the project.

Ivan Čarnogurský, vice-chairman of the Slovak Parliament and vice-president of the KDH between 1990 and 1992, was also the managing director of Hydrostav, the building company that was the main contractor of the Gabčíkovo project. He is also the brother of the then prime minister Ján Čarnogurský. During the summer of 1990 Slovak Radio and newspapers close to the government and to the Slovak nationalistic political parties (at that time in opposition) started a massive campaign in favour of the completion of the waterworks. Another, even more powerful, campaign took place during the summer of 1991. The attacks on the environmental movement were more aggressive than the campaigns in the Communist press after publishing the Bratislava/Nahlas report. In the summer of 1991, the Slovak government sent the special anti-terrorist police commando against environmentalists and citizens protesting peacefully on the construction site near the town of Šamorín.

In 1991 and 1992 objective coverage on the Danube issue disappeared from almost all media. Because the area is inhabited mostly by Slovak citizens of Hungarian nationality protesting against the 'dams monster', and because the Hungarian Republic discontinued the project on its territory, the Slovak media-led propaganda was accompanied by an aggressive anti-Hungarian hysteria. On 16 April 1991 the Hungarian Parliament charged the Hungarian government with negotiating with the Czechoslovak government about cancelling the Agreement from 1977. Since then the Hungarian side has not offered a proposal for an alternative solution of the basic functions of the water construction system. On the other hand the Czechoslovak/Slovak side has been willing to discuss only those alternatives that included fully operational Gabčíkovo waterworks. On 24 October 1992, the Danube was unilaterally diverted at the new diversion weir near Čuňovo, Slovakia, into the Gabčíkovo reservoir and canal.

The dispute on waterworks on the Danube became an international issue, steered by both sides towards the Slovak–Hungarian ethnic conflict. The Slovak technocratic lobby referred to the historical Slovak–Hungarian rancour to pursue their goals. Both Slovak and Hungarian nationalistic political parties have profited from the conflict and strengthened their political position. The case raised the danger of ethnic conflict in Central Europe and worsened the situation of ethnic minorities. The Slovak Greens were blamed during the political struggle for being anti-Slovak and as a consequence of biased reporting in the media lost much public support.

The above two case studies illustrate the most important environmental, political, economic, and social problems in post-Communist Slovakia. The way the issues were dealt with by the post-Communist governments and the attitude of the Slovak society towards them exposed a deep and widespread inertia in Slovakia and a reluctance to overcome the legacy of the Communist period and to change the Communist paradigm of development and economic management. Two symbols of the Communist regime's achievements have become the symbols of the bright future of the new, free and independent Slovakia.

Conclusion

The history of environmental issues and policies in post-1989 Slovakia can be conveniently divided into three distinct phases which aptly reflect the development of Slovak society in the post-Communist period. In the first phase, during winter and spring 1990, environmental reform was one of the priorities of public discussion in the free and optimistic atmosphere after November 1989. Proved environmental activists were accepted by the majority of the society and had access to the state-controlled electronic media and to newly established newspapers. The prominent role of green leaders in the 'velvet revolution' contributed to the creation of the new state environmental institutions, administration and legislation. During the first months of freedom it seemed very likely that the state environmental policy would change in a positive way and that the state of the environment would subsequently improve.

The second phase, after the first free elections in June 1990, was characterised by two contradictory tendencies. On the one hand, there was a radical improvement in terms of new environmental legislation and the presence of some representatives of the 'protectionist movement' in the Slovak Parliament. Many environmentalists gained key positions in the regional state environmental authorities. The Green Party had six deputies in the Slovak Parliament and dozens of new environmental organisations and foundations were formed. On the other hand, the general public's environmental concern soon evaporated. The autumn of 1990 and the following months were a period of growing nationalism and populism, directed against the open democratic society and sustainable strategies of development.

The conflict within the environmental movement and especially the Green Party's decision to partake in a nationalistic anti-reform bloc have, for the time being, discredited political environmentalism in Slovakia. The pro-reform government of 1990–92 concentrated on building democratic political institutions, privatisation and establishing a free market economy. Ruling political coalition did not have sufficient political will and power to solve the most negative aspects of the Communist legacy. The green goals of the 'velvet revolution' were replaced by a lack of interest in improving the worst environmental problems and in adopting sustainable strategies.

The third phase, after the elections in 1992, is characterised by the growing power of political groups and parties which in Slovak political life represent the anti-reform and anti-democratic political orientation. Following the 1994 elections won by HZDS, the new government implemented political purges in the regional environmental authorities and open attacks against environmental NGOs.

An overriding problem is a lack of interest in public matters and apathy to involvement in the civic life. This is partly due to the legacy of the Communist period and partly due to unfamiliarity with the new democratic ways of public participation. Despite the existence of legal provisions for public participation in environmental issues, the government has created an atmosphere which effectively discourages people from taking part in environmental activities [*Belčáková, 1995: 130*].

Due to the suppression of civil society during the Communist era, many

Slovak environmental NGOs remain poorly organised and managed. Sometimes there is a lack of co-operation among NGOs. Slovak NGOs also face problems with fund-raising, legal assistance and technical expertise. Activists are not always sufficiently experienced, adequately educated and prepared for campaigning and advocacy work.

The attempt to stabilise political environmentalism in the Slovak political context, based on the authority of the protectionist leaders from the late 1980s, has not been successful. The initial 'green velvet paradigm' was rejected by almost all elected representatives in Slovakia. No political party or movement has incorporated sustainable strategies into their manifestos or practical everyday politics.

It can be concluded that Slovakia is now witnessing the closing of the circle. After seven years of post-Communism, the renaissance of the state and party authoritarianism, state *dirigisme* and centralisation are dominant features of contemporary Slovakia. After a short initial spell of enthusiasm for environmental reform the population appears to have lost interest in environmental issues. Environmental interest is not deeply rooted in the value system of the people. The environmental movement of the late 1980s was a surrogate of political anti-Communist opposition in Slovakia, hence the reason for its short-lived popularity. In elections the majority of voters support political parties which overtly distance themselves from visions of an open civic society and sustainable development. The political change did not interrupt the economic and political power of the former Communist management. Instead, another process was started: the merging of this social stratum with the new political leaders to create a new political and economic elite, which abandoned the Communist doctrine concerning the unacceptability of private property while continuing the Communist model of industrial development. Hence the Communist economic policy based on energy-intensive and material-intensive heavy industry such as nuclear energy and gigantic water dams, continues. Slovakia is continuing with the directed economic growth from the period of the 'building of Communism', with growing authoritarian political power of the state and party bureaucracy, rather than embarking upon a transition of politics, society and the economy towards sustainable development.

REFERENCES

Belčáková, I. (1995), 'Slovak Republic', in Regional Environmental Center for Central and Eastern Europe, *Status of Public Participation Practices in Environmental Decisionmaking in Central and Eastern Europe*, Budapest: The Regional Environmental Center, pp.121–30.

Budaj, J. (1986), *Cintorínsky príbeh*, Bratislava: Príloha k zápisnici členskej schôdze ZO 6 SZOPK Bratislava.

Budaj, J. (ed.) (1988), *Ochranca prírody*, Bratislava: MV SZOPK.

Huba, M. (1995a), 'The Environmental Challenge for Central European Economies in Transition. Slovakia', unpublished manuscript, Bratislava.

Huba, M. (1995b), 'Životné prostredie na Slovensku v polovici roku 1995', in M. Bútora and P. Hunčík (eds.), *Slovensko v šiestom roku transformácie* (Bratislava: Nadácia Sándora Máraiho), pp.63–7.

Huba, M. (1996), 'Environment and Sustainable Development in Slovakia 1989–1995', *Südosteuropa. Zeitschrift für Gegenwartsforschung*, Vol.45, No.3, pp.282–94.

Jehlička, P. and T. Kostelecký (1995), 'Czechoslovakia. Greens in a Post-communist Society', in D. Richardson and C. Rootes (eds.), *The Green Challenge. The Development of Green Parties in Europe*, London and New York: Routledge, pp.208–31.

Klinda, J. (ed.) (1994), *Životné prostredie Slovenskej republiky v rokoch 1992–1993*, Bratislava: Ministerstvo životného prostredia SR.

Musil, J. (1993), 'Česká a slovenská společnost. Skica srovnávací studie', *Sociologický časopis*, Vol.29, No.1, pp.9–24.

Zamkovský, J. and P. Žilinčík (1992), *Environmental Policy in the Slovak Republic. (January 1992–May 1992)*, Bratislava: Center for Environmental Public Advocacy.

Environmental Policy in Poland

FRANCES MILLARD

Environmental policy in Poland after 1989 remains largely state centred and technocratic. The green movement is extensive but fragmented and divided and political parties have given little attention to environmental issues, while public concerns have shifted to the fundamental economic issues of daily life. Yet achievements have been substantial, albeit only partly as a result of government policy: industrial recession and restructuring have had a significant impact on the reduction of environmental degradation. Clean-up rather than 'eco-development' remains the key focus. The Ministry of the Environment remained weak, lacking a coherent strategy and proving unable to ensure the effective implementation of much new legislation.

The gravity of environmental degradation in Communist Poland had been appreciated for many years and by the late 1970s government rhetoric, if not its practice, had begun to take it seriously. From 1980 Solidarity provided a massive boost to environmental awareness [*Kabala, 1993: 114–33*]. Numerous independent national organisations such as the Polish Ecology Club, spontaneous local groups, and professional bodies publicised environmental concerns [*Hrynkiewicz, 1990*]. Environmental debate, though not uncensored, was permitted even after the suppression of Solidarity; it was a 'safe' issue, a safety valve for the expression of social discontent. A small Polish Green Party (*Polska Partia Zielonych*) held its founding congress in December 1988.

As elsewhere in Eastern Europe the primacy of heavy industry generated acute problems of air, water and soil pollution. In 1983 the Council of Ministers designated 27 areas as 'environmentally endangered', and subsequent years saw extensive prohibitions against developing existing industries and siting new ones harmful to the environment [*GUS, 1984*]. The densely populated agglomeration of Upper Silesia generated massive pollution from its vast concentration of mining and metallurgical plants, chemical factories and power stations, but the problems were nationwide in scope. Water resources were deteriorating, with 75.8 per cent of rivers classed by biological criteria (such as the presence of E. coli) as 'excessively polluted' in 1988 [*GUS, 1990a: 21*]. Heavy metal pollution of the soil was so severe that some areas were designated as zones of 'environmental catastrophe'.

The government responded with significant legislation [*Kramer, 1987*] and a clear strategy (*Rzeczpospolita*, No.25, 30 Jan. 1987). This was a consequence of a growing recognition of environmental barriers to further economic development, reflected in the dire warnings of academics and professionals (see, for example, Kassenberg and Rolewicz [*1985*]; Ginsberg-Gebert and Bochniarz [*1988*]) and also public concern, especially over the detrimental health consequences of pollution. However, the Environment Ministry was weak, and the industrial lobby was sufficiently powerful to prevent effective implementation of the growing body of legislation. Factory equipment was outdated; fines for polluting were low; inspectors demanding action against polluting enterprises were overruled on economic grounds.

In 1989 the Communist regime effectively acknowledged its own bankruptcy and established 'Round Table' discussions with Solidarity, which had maintained a tenuous underground existence since 1982. The negotiations of the Round Table's Ecology Subcommission achieved a substantial consensus on future policy direction. In the partially competitive elections of June 1989 several prominent environmental activists entered parliament under the Solidarity banner. Yet the salience of the environmental issue quickly waned, marked by the failure of Greens in the first free elections (October 1991) along with a pronounced reduction in environmental activism.

Successive governments pursued liberal economic strategies, inaugurated by the notorious shock therapy programme of January 1990. Removal of subsidies and price liberalisation generated a major industrial recession, with a severe fall in the standard of living; and the privatisation process proved long and tortuous. As expected, some existing environmental problems underwent amelioration and new ones emerged as a direct consequence of system transformation. For example, noxious emissions fell and energy use dropped sharply in consequence of the decline in industrial output, while price increases led to a drop in residential coal use [*Mayers* et al., *1994: 708*]. New problems arose from *inter alia* vast increases in the use of motor vehicles, the increased volume and changing content of household waste, the import of outdated, often dirty technologies by western industry, and the changing structure of energy supply.

By 1993 the economy was beginning to grow again, but the deep trauma experienced by the population did not disappear quickly. In 1993 the Communist successor parties, the Social Democrats and the Polish Peasant Party, won a decisive election victory. Welfare issues were paramount and the environment slipped well down the list of public priorities. Apathy was widespread, with public confidence in the political elites badly eroded. Early optimism regarding the development of pluralism and the vibrant pressure group universe of developed civil society gave way to a recognition that the pronounced weakness of such groups was likely to remain a feature of the post-Communist political process for some time. Nonetheless, the objective causes of environmental concern remained and policy initiatives were by no means absent. Substantial advances were made in the years 1989–96, despite the lack of favourable political conditions.

Public Consciousness of Environmental Issues

Indeed, public understanding of the implications of environmental degradation remained low, despite numerous opinion polls showing positive support for 'environmental values' [*Gliński, 1996: 127–32*]. After 1989 public concern focused largely on economic issues, especially unemployment, job insecurity, and rising levels of crime. The vision of consumer society proved attractive, with material aspirations to the fore. There was a distinct decline in media discussion of the environment; the 'fashion for ecology' [*Pawłowski and Dudzińska, 1994: 212*] waned quite rapidly. Yet, though generally debate remained limited in the mass media, by 1996 a burgeoning of the specialist environmental press had become evident.

Links between health and environmental pollution remain controversial and problematic. Eberstadt, for example, concluded that 'environmental catastrophe as such does not appear to be the driving force behind the post-communist health crisis' in ECE [*Eberstadt, 1994: 55*]. Yet it was difficult to dismiss the environmental factor in the presence of strong regional differences displayed by the data on morbidity and mortality. The World Bank found environmental concerns to be a 'significant determinant' of health status in ECE [*World Bank, 1994*]. The Polish Statistical Bureau also stressed the higher incidence of mortality from cancers and nutritional/immunological deficiency diseases as well as higher infant mortality in the most polluted areas [*GUS, 1993; 1994; 1995*]. These concerns received attention in the Polish press; but the quality of information was often poor: it was 'mostly catastrophic and usually not accurate' [*Pawłowski and Dudzińska, 1994: 212*]. This did not prevent widespread 'intuitive' consciousness of the threat to health, particularly in areas such as Silesia. Broadly speaking, those living in more polluted areas perceived greater environmental threats to health than those in less polluted areas [*Gliński, 1996: 132–40*].

Aside from its concern with health, there was public support for the development of national parks and reserves, significant for recreation but also for species management and protection of biodiversity. This aspect of environmental protection had a long tradition in Poland. Overall, there was a substantial pro-environmental element of the Polish population: about one-third of society, mostly highly educated, reasonably affluent urban dwellers fell into this category. In contrast environmental concerns were least developed among rural dwellers, the least educated and both the oldest and youngest (under 24) sections of the population [*Burger and Sadowski, 1994: 28–9*].

Actors in the Policy Process

The Ministry of the Environment

The Ministry of the Environment has always been justly regarded as politically weak in relation to the economic ministries. Frequent changes of government after 1989 meant a lack of continuity of leadership at the apex, though the Deputy Minister, the Chief Inspector and a number of other department heads remained in post for relatively lengthy periods. The first post-Communist ministers, Bronisław Kamiński, Maciej Nowicki and Stefan Kozłowski, were experienced professionals. Kozłowski's successor was Zygmunt Hortmanowicz, formerly deputy chair of Rural Solidarity, with less impressive credentials; indeed the *Sejm*'s Environmental Commission initially rejected his nomination. Hortmanowicz was unpopular with Parliament, with professional bodies, and with the environmental movement. In September 1992 a group of academics wrote to the Prime Minister accusing Hortmanowicz of ignorance, incompetence, breaking the law and self-aggrandisement. Among other things, Hortmanowicz demoted the Chief Nature Conservation Officer and, in violation of the environmental protection law, subordinated that post to the Deputy Minister of Forestry. The new Director General of Forests issued an order to 'reduce the elk population to zero' and a decision to bring forward the deer culling period to a time when mothers would still be suckling their young caused outrage. Hortmanowicz was ignorant of the regulations governing bodies such as the specialist advisory councils [*Nowakowska, 1992*]. The minister was also criticised for excessive use of patronage and using gifts from abroad to serve the aims of Rural Solidarity, rather than the environment [*Kaczyński, 1993*].

After the September 1993 election Stanisław Żelichowski of the Polish Peasant Party (PSL) became minister and survived successive reconstructions of the coalition. The association of the Ministry with the agricultural lobby again brought to the fore conflict between the Ministry's environmental brief and its responsibility for the forestry industry (Żelichowski's own background was in forestry). The PSL itself was notorious for rewarding loyal supporters with government posts. The Ministry enjoyed a reputation as a major source of patronage and financial opportunities arising from the large number of environmental funds and institutes which had been set up, often with Western assistance. The Ministry's functions embraced strategic and legislative initiatives. Here it made use of a number of advisory bodies with a reputation for skill and professionalism. The Institute of Environmental Protection had been reactivated in 1986 as an independent body with a research, monitoring, educational and policy advisory role. It developed links with the US Environmental Protection Agency, itself an influential model in ECE.

External influences proved central to environmental policy, notably because of Poland's determination to join the European Union. Successive governments accepted the task of ensuring that new laws (in all spheres) were compatible with EU legislation. On the EU side, after the Edinburgh summit and the White Paper (May 1995) the incorporation of *acquis communautaire* into the domestic legal systems of the associated countries was regarded as a key condition of EU membership. Further, the bulk of the funding of environmental projects after 1989 came from external sources, especially the European Union [*Löfstedt and Sjöstedt, 1996*], but also the USA and Sweden. External priorities effectively reinforced the Environment Ministry's primary focus on water resources and air pollution.

The main monitoring and implementing arm of the Ministry was the respected Environmental Inspectorate (*Państwowy Inspektorat Ochrony Środowiska*), known as the 'green police'. It focused on monitoring those industries regarded as the worst environmental offenders and on assessing compliance of new projects with environmental law. The Inspectorate issued more than 25,000 decisions between 1992 and 1996, with fines totalling over 800 million zloties. Among its most publicised decisions were delays imposed on the opening of Warsaw airport and a new Coca-Cola bottling plant.

Payments for environmental exploitation and the penalties exacted by the green police were central to environmental policy after 1989 and made up the bulk of resources for the National Fund for Environmental Protection (*Narodowy Fundusz Ochrony Środowiska*, NFOŚ) and its provincial counterparts (WFOŚ). The Fund also subsidised the Environmental Protection Bank (*Bank Ochrony Środowiska*, BOŚ), set up to provide cheap credits, especially for local government.

The EcoFund (*Ekofundusz*) provided another source of finance. Its original task was to allocate the zloty equivalent of a ten per cent reduction in Polish debts to the USA (and later Switzerland) to finance projects of significance not only to Poland but also to its neighbours. This included the reduction of transborder atmospheric pollution originating in Poland, protection of the Baltic, reduction of greenhouse gases, and protection of biodiversity. In 1995 the Fund was responsible for 47 significant investment projects, including a number using foreign production processes. It also contributed to the coffers of non-governmental organisations, for example, to 'Pro Natura' in Wrocław to rescue and reintroduce the mud turtle. However, hopes that the Paris Club's agreement regarding Polish debt conversion would entail eco-conversion with funds channelled through *Ekofundusz* remained largely unfulfilled. Managers' ignorance also proved a problem: the accounting systems of the market economy were unfamiliar territory for those brought up within the framework of central planning. Indeed, '... debt-for-nature transactions were, until recently, not understood even by some experts in the field of environmental protection' [*Budnikowski, 1992*].

Provincial and Local Authorities

After 1989 much environmental responsibility was decentralised, especially to the 49 provincial administrations (*województwa*) and also to elected local authorities (*gmina*). Provincial authorities administered the WFOŚ, the provincial funds for environmental protection and the arena for numerous conflicts. The environmental group representative on the Krakow Fund's Supervisory Council expressed disappointment at its lack of openness and failure to adopt formal procedures and criteria for allocating public funds: 'Subsidies are still allocated on the principal of first come first served or who makes the best impression' [*Peszko, 1994: 16*]. Yet he was also gratified by the enormous progress in creating such an 'innovative institution from scratch'. Indeed, Krakow placed environmental considerations high on its list of priorities (it was also the centre of the largest environmental movement in Poland).

The provinces have a varied record and in some areas they have palpably failed. In particular, they proved unwilling or incapable of dealing with the problem of waste. Little was burned, composted, recycled or used as landfill. In theory, waste was dumped at 614 legal communal tips and 1,245 industrial tips, but a vast expansion of so-called 'wild dumps' [*Pietrasik, 1996*] occurred after 1989, not least because of the increased cost of rubbish disposal services, both public and private. Even Krakow, an example of considerable achievements, found the problem of waste disposal intractable: the accumulated mountains of rubbish were estimated at more than 50 tons per citizen.

Three dimensions of the waste disposal problem proved particularly acute. There were the so-called graveyards for outdated pesticides and other chemicals, sealed in special cement containers and later stored in old bunkers, abandoned buildings or holes in the ground. Leakage of hazardous compounds (mercury, arsenic, phosphorus) was identified in numerous areas, but many were under 'no control whatsoever' [*Henzler and Kuziak, 1994*]. Self-igniting of rubbish dumps also became a significant problem, not least because of the range of harmful chemicals, including dioxins, released into the atmosphere [*K. Forowicz, 1994*]. The third aspect related to the unauthorised dumps: their contents were unknown, they were likely to damage wildlife, and they were aesthetically offensive. All these areas were finally subject to multifaceted legal regulation in the Draft Law on Waste Disposal, modelled on similar laws in Western European states such as Germany and Sweden, and presented to Parliament for its first reading in February 1996.

Below the provincial level lie the local communes. They are extremely diverse, with hugely varied funds, experience, expertise and initiative. Some took environmental concerns very seriously and displayed considerable creativity, particularly in recreational areas and areas of extreme degradation. Some communes actively promoted popular projects such as new sewage treatment plants. Many however did little. Communes neglected the monitoring and control function, especially where it 'interfered' with economic activity; and numerous communities were content to 'wait for the state to act' (Walewski, quoted in J. Forowicz [*1994*]).

Parties and Groups

Political parties have often donned clothes tinged with green in an effort to broaden their electoral appeal, but there was little evidence of this in Poland in the mid-1990s. In 1991 virtually all the parties proclaimed their environmental concerns in general terms. Three contenders described themselves as green or ecology parties, but none won seats, and their share of the vote was tiny. For the Polish Green Party, allied with the tiny Polish Ecology Party, the election was a disaster, and after the election it fragmented and effectively ceased to function.

In the September 1993 election green parties did not stand, nor did they support other parties, which they regarded (with some justification) as using the environment merely to win votes. The Krakow federation of independent environmental groups announced an 'antipolitical pact' and stated that 'there is now no Polish political grouping which could gain the support of the ecology movement' (*Życie Warszawy*, No.212, 10 Sept. 1993). Divisions among the greens themselves did not help their public image. Several former activists, including Janusz Bryczkowski of the Green Party, subsequently attracted attention when they joined a radical peasant movement, Self-Defence. After the election Bryczkowski fell out with Self-Defence's leader and later gained notoriety from links with the Russian radical politician Vladimir Zhirinovsky.

By and large party election manifestos contained indistinguishable general commitments to environmental issues. However, the Social Democrats, the Union of Labour and the Freedom Union retained green 'fractions' whose deputies played a major role in the parliamentary environmental commissions and in publicising proposed legislation to the environmental movement.

Environmental pressure groups flourished in the 1980s and expanded in the heady atmosphere after 1989, and the scope of activity soon rivalled that in Western Europe: it included deep ecologists, conservationists, leisure-oriented groups, tree planters, pacifists, vegetarians, animal rights' activists, cyclists and numerous others. However, many groups remained tiny and most limited their operations to the local level ('think globally, act locally'). Estimates of numbers vary considerably, from about 200 to about 500 groupings, organisations and movements. The largest was the Polish Ecological Club (PKE) and the most dynamic the Green Federation (*Federacja Zielonych*). Assessment of membership is also notoriously difficult, though one recent estimate suggests a figure of 25,000 members nationwide (*Rzeczpospolita*, No.25, 30 Jan. 1995; cf. *Gliński, 1994: 156–8*).

The groups' small clusters of active members made their professionalisation as participant non-governmental organisations very difficult (though some have seen professionalisation as a double-edged sword ['*Quo Vadis NGO?*', *1996*]). Many previous activists were syphoned off into government or lucrative posts as consultants in the business sector. Most groups remained poor and lacked fund-raising and financial management skills. Many local single-issue groups lacked effective mechanisms of coordination. Familiar divisions, for example, between conservation-oriented bodies and groups with deep ecology perspectives, were also an obstacle to concerted action. Nonetheless, the growing expertise and the sophistication of debate within green circles increased dramatically in the 1990s. Strong links developed quickly between the academic community and the NGOs, with the Polish Ecology Club playing a major coordinating role. A number of groups benefited in the 1990s from links with international bodies. Greenpeace International, Friends of the Earth International, the Marshall Foundation and many others demonstrated the importance of campaigning expertise and provided substantial funds for diverse projects, including educational initiatives, construction of sewage treatment plants, changes in fuel technology, local energy saving programmes, wildlife protection and scientific research.

Yet the absence of major national organisations proved a disadvantage in attempts to influence national environmental policy-making. Although most ministers of the environment have held periodic consultative meetings with group representatives, it is difficult to find examples where the green view has triumphed. In only two cases have massive protests really attracted public attention. The sustained campaign against the construction of a nuclear power station at Żarnowiec was successful in the short term; and although economic cost was the major factor in the decision to halt construction, public hostility to nuclear power (largely a product of the experience of Chernobyl) certainly facilitated the decision. In the second case, the construction of a large dam at Czorsztyn in the South, the protesters were singularly unsuccessful. Effectively, the political component of environmental policy making seems to have been largely absent. Policy is debated in narrow circles and couched in technical language by academics, professionals and consultants of varied ilk. The technocratic element was the predominant one in the early post-Communist years.

Despite their relative impotence, environmental pressure groups during the years 1989–96 were virtually the only vehicle for questioning the direction of government policy and raising publicly the possibility of alternative solutions. The environmental movement clearly has a major potential role for the future, despite its lack of influence in the early post-Communist political process. Meanwhile policy-making remained largely limited to the Ministry of the Environment and its attendant think-tanks (with considerable external support); and with crucial constraints, both in conception and in implementation.

Environmental Policy and Administration

Unlike other areas of post-Communist transformation where the need to reduce the role of the state is stressed, environmental policy making accepts the need for significant state intervention. The starting point for post-Communist policy was the 1981 Environment Act, generally highly regarded for its conception, if not the quality of its implementation [*Pawłowski and Dudzińska, 1994: 212; Budnikowski, 1992: 151*].

In accordance with the Round Table Agreements of 1989, the Environment Ministry gave early attention to identifying the most serious sources of pollution from heavy industry. The major starting point was the 1983 delineation by the Central Statistical Bureau of the environmental 'danger zones'. By January 1990 the Ministry had compiled and published an inventory of Poland's 80 'greatest poisoners'. 'If they do not take effective measures, they will cease to exist', said Minister Kamiński (quoted in *Rzeczpospolita*, No.11, 15 Jan. 1990). The polluter pays principle was placed centre-stage, and fines for violating emission standards were increased tenfold, with each 'poisoner' also required to present an environmental action plan. An assessment of progress in 1996 was reasonably optimistic, though only 17 of the 80 had wholly fulfilled their environmental obligations, either by ceasing production of certain products (for example, cellulose) or through investment in technology.

Another group had anti-pollution programmes in process and were given extra time to meet the required standards. Economic factors forced closure in some cases, such as the notorious carbide production unit (*karbidownia*) of the Bobrek mill in Bytom, which had exhausted all possibilities of appeal and delay. In January 1995 the final liquidation of Bobrek was begun. 'The basic reason for the mill's demise was its debts of over 850 milliard zloties', above all due to unpaid environmental fines and unpaid social security contributions [*Cieszewski, 1995*]. Two other enterprises were also in the process of liquidation. However, five new firms were added to the list, mainly for the river pollution they caused. The national inventory was later extended with a further list of the most harmful enterprises in particular provinces.

Investment in water resources took about 60 per cent of the ministerial budget (not, however, a large sum) to 1996, with emphasis on water management and water quality. Water management districts were established in 1991, with a computerised system introduced to control water consumption by industry and communities, water quality, and amount of waste, with charges for consumption and penalties for degradation. New criteria were introduced for the assessment of water quality, but not all criteria were used in practice [*Pawłowski and Dudzińska, 1994: 214*].The State Ecology Policy [*Polityka Ekologiczna Państwa, 1992*] was itself primarily a programme for air and water pollution reduction. The goals of phased reduction of emissions, especially of sulphur dioxide and nitrous oxides (an EU/World Bank priority), and of improved water management and treatment drew heavily on EU requirements; though the programme was less impressive in detailing the means to achieve these goals. An exception was the Baltic Marine Environment Protection Programme: an international programme for dealing with pollution of the Baltic, where Sweden and Denmark contributed substantially to Polish investments. Polish river pollution was acknowledged as a major contributor to Baltic pollution, especially of nitrates and phosphates [*GUS, 1990a; 1990b*]. By 1995 the Baltic inventory had identified 132 most blameworthy polluters, of which 38 were in Poland. Of the 47 identified as of the highest priority, 20 were Polish. Indeed, Poland was widely regarded as the worst offender. The Helsinki Commission's programme for Poland stressed investments for treating municipal and industrial waste and activities to improve the quality of management.

Special programmes also emerged, such as that to deal with the horrendous damage caused by Soviet military garrisons, especially from the dumping of petroleum-based products, leaching into soil and ground waters. A three-stage policy to the year 2000 would begin to deal with the damage through: (1) stopping further deterioration; (2) cleaning up the mess; and (3) recultivation. By 1994 the damage had been fully surveyed in the worst 21 bases, out of a total of 59. Petrol, detergents, phenol and numerous heavy metals were found in large quantities, but not radioactive elements or chemical weapons residues (*Rzeczpospolita*, No.257, 4 Nov. 1994).

Effectiveness and Constraints

In January 1995 the Minister of the Environment presented a report to the *Sejm*, including an analysis of the realisation of environmental policy 1991–93. The Minister claimed that the policies of successive governments had been highly effective due to progress in the efficiency of administrative structures, the restructuring and privatisation of industry, and the elimination of obsolete technology. For the first time in decades there had been an improvement in the state of the environment (*Rzeczpospolita*, No.16, 19 Jan. 1995). There had been a 15 per cent reduction in sulphur dioxide emissions, meeting the requirements of the Geneva convention (though Poland was not a signatory); while dust emissions had been reduced by 23 per cent and nitrogen oxides by 14 per cent. By 1994 all but six electricity generating plants had achieved 1998 standards for sulphur dioxide and dust emissions. 93 per cent of liquid waste was now treated, with 1,300 new treatment plants completed by 1994 and another 1,200 in the process of construction. As a result, only four areas were now to be regarded as areas of extreme environmental hazard: Upper Silesia, Krakow province, and the Legnicko-Głogowski and Tarnobrzeg regions. The Minister also reported that protected natural areas would soon cover almost one-third of Poland's territory: the twentieth national park was opened in January 1995, with three more scheduled.

The Environmental Inspectorate also claimed considerable success, especially in limiting the import of hazardous waste materials. After a period of rapid, virtually uncontrolled import of hazardous waste, new regulations came into effect in 1992. Better training and equipment also improved the situation, though efforts continued to import into Poland 'almost everything that the Germans and other Western countries throw away', from dirty Coca-Cola bottles to broken refrigerators, tons of dirty rags, wrecked cars and myriad toxic chemicals (Tadeusz Hadyś of the Frontier Guard, *Rzeczpospolita*, No.57, 9 March 1993). Between 1992 and autumn 1994 attempts were made to import over 9 million tons of allegedly usable materials, but only some 24,500 were admitted, while at the end of

1994 about 8,000 tonnes waited at the border to be returned to the sender [*J. Forowicz, 1994*].

The *Sejm*'s response to the Minister's report was mixed, welcoming the positive results but highly critical of the Ministry's lack of strategic thinking over the medium term. The programme was said to identify too many aims and to lack clear definitions of responsibility and lines of accountability. Radosław Gawlik of the Freedom Union's Green Fraction was particularly critical of 'eliminating the effects of pollution, rather than preventing them'. Generally there was too little integration of environmental policy making with that of other ministries (*Rzeczpospolita*, No.16, 19 Jan. 1995). Deputies strongly condemned the absence of a strategy for developing environmental education.

The *Sejm*'s criticisms were appropriate but by no means exhaustive. Huge problems of conception and implementation remained and the Ministry operated under serious constraints, not all of its own making. Firstly, there were barriers to the effective operation of the Ministry itself. Financial constraints were obvious, despite foreign assistance. According to the Ministry's own figures the Programme to the Year 2000 would require a doubling of annual expenditure to provide the 220 billion (old) zloties needed (*Rzeczpospolita*, No.16, 19 Jan. 1995). Questions also emerged in regard to the monitoring of funding. In 1994 investigations of the Environmental Bank by the National Audit Agency led to a number of judicial proceedings for fraud and misuse of funds and accusations of lack of effective mechanisms for issuing credits and auditing repayments. The quality of personnel was another problem characteristic of the public sector generally. For example, the equipment of the green police improved, but the low pay of highly trained personnel remained a major problem, leading to high turnover and risk of corruption [*J. Forowicz, 1994*].

The sheer volume of new legislation needed to transform the system also created problems for all ministries. Pressure to change the law in all spheres virtually simultaneously generated a huge backlog of legislation in Parliament. Many areas thus remained unregulated. For example, the market for washing powders quickly became dominated by foreign companies which, in the absence of legal prohibition of polyphosphates, sold only phosphate-based detergents [*Pawłowski and Dudzińska, 1994: 212*]. Further, laws once passed often needed amendment because of hasty drafting. The Law on the Protection of Nature was passed in 1991 but subsequently amended in 1992 and 1994. In 1996 extensive amendments gave greater precision to the Law on the Protection and Shaping of the Environment.

Also crucial to the environmental policy process were the problems of implementation. Despite numerous inventories, environmental impact assessments, and blueprints for eco-development, impressive sounding projects often remained largely paper exercises – as with the ambitious Green Lungs project, which won the Ford Foundation's European Environmental Award in 1993. Conceived in the 1980s, this covers the seven north-eastern provinces and Poland's neighbours, Belorussia, Latvia, Lithuania, Russia and the Ukraine. It aimed to develop transboundary protected areas for a region for which, according to the Central Bureau of Planning 'there is no alternative to eco-development' (*Rzeczpospolita*, No.33, 9 Feb. 1993). Indeed, the north-east lakes region of Poland is an area of great ecological value and deep economic crisis, with the highest unemployment rates in the country. Although the Institute of Environmental Protection was involved in developing proposals for coordinating environmental law and practice, the Green Lungs project appeared impressive only on paper. Former minister and presidential adviser Stefan Kozłowski attributed the 'poor record of implementation' to a basic lack of political will (*Rzeczpospolita*, No.192, 18 Aug.1994).

Monitoring implementation also proved problematic. We have already noted the lack of effective local control in regard to unauthorised dumping. The national inspectorate employs about 3,000 people for control purposes, but they concentrate on certain large enterprises, assessing only about one-quarter of enterprises estimated to have a substantial environmental impact. Small businesses had not yet been brought within the scope of environmental law in 1995, yet the private sector was the main engine of growth after 1992. Non-compliance was also rife. The polluter pays principle depends on the polluter actually paying. Yet the problem of enterprise debt to the state in 1996 remained enormous – including non-payment of taxes, social security contributions, and environmental payments and penalties. Firms also employed delaying tactics, utilising the many avenues of legal and administrative appeal.

At provincial level the situation was much the same. The environmental departments remained weak brethren. Both regionally and locally, funds were channelled to projects which were popular or had obvious direct economic benefit. For example, in 1992 provinces allocated funds for the protection of agricultural land primarily to 'building and modernising roads to meet the needs of agriculture'. Only two provinces spent any money on 'measures to prevent soil erosion'.

Parliamentary critics were certainly justified in their view that environmental concerns were rarely effectively integrated into the policy processes of other ministries. As the Chief Inspector laconically observed, 'Unfortunately ministerial specialists don't always remember their obligation to propagate pro-ecological solutions' [*J. Forowicz, 1994*]. The primacy of narrowly conceived, short-term economic concerns (without due appreciation of the economic and social implications of failure to deal with environmental aspects) remained a characteristic, if unsurprising, feature of policy making. Even with favourable economic indicators such as Poland enjoyed after 1993, governments remained preoccupied with immediate social and economic problems. 'Such a situation militates against the implementation of any policy which requires the complex synthesising of abstract and long-term interests, such as environment and development' [*Fisher, 1992: 9*].

In theory greater awareness of the environmental dimension existed throughout government from the mid-1990s. During the initial stages of the privatisation process environmental costs were not taken into account. What often occurred was the privatisation of part of a firm, leaving the rest along with its environmental obligations to the State Treasury (*Rzeczpospolita*, No.39, 16 Dec. 1993). Indeed, one-fifth of the original '80 poisoners' were on the list of 400 enterprises listed in the Mass Privatisation Programme. Later, the Ministry of Ownership Transformation accepted that the environmental obligations of firms for privatisation should be clearly defined.

Unemployment figured high on the list of economic arguments, especially against closure of firms. This was the main reason for opposition to the closure of the old, lignite burning Turów power station: closure would mean the loss of 100,000 jobs, according to the Ministry of Industry. When payments for environmental abuse were drastically reduced in 1993 – by 70 per cent for dust emissions and by 90 per cent for benzines, dioxin and mercury – two reasons were advanced by the Ministry. First, production would become unprofitable and unemployment would increase as factories went out of business; thus the Ministry 'had to compromise' with industry. Secondly, new elements were now covered by the payments system for the first time, while even with the reductions the charges remained 'high' (for example 100,000 zloties per kilo of untreated emissions of asbestos, zinc, and freons) (*Rzeczpospolita*, No.285, 4 Dec. 1993).

The Ministry of Transport has come in for particular criticism. Its decision to exempt cars with a capacity of less than 700 centimetres from the requirement that cars registered after 1 July 1995 be equipped with catalytic converters was certainly intended to protect the popular Fiat 126 (the *Sejm* criticised the decision as an example of 'anti-ecological protectionism', *Rzeczpospolita*, No.16, 19 Jan.1995). Pricing policy also affected transport: increased rail prices led to a shift of freight to private trucking firms, with the prospect of extensive line closures. (The Ministry of Finance blocked efforts to introduce economic incentives for unleaded petrol. It also preferred to leave the private sector as free as possible of government regulation.) Most important was the absence of an integrated transport policy, a glaring omission for a country desirous of improving its infrastructure to stimulate private (including foreign) investment. Price rises for public transport and the closure of many railway lines meant a shift to road transport and pressure for further development (even coal was often transported by road). The environmental movement opposed these developments and initiated campaigns against planned motorway development on a number of grounds [*'Autostrady', 1996*]. The first was the obvious point that public transport is more environmentally friendly than new roads, which are assumed to stimulate further the use of motor vehicles. It also objected to specific proposals. For example, in Warsaw new motorway routes were proposed without environmental impact analysis, while part of one planned route threatened natural and architectural resources such as the Otwock Landscape Park and Wilanów Palace.

Energy provided another area of obvious concern. Duncan Fisher's general observation regarding developments in Eastern Europe is entirely apposite in regard to Poland: 'The "energy production or energy conservation" debate is being turned into the traditional supply-side "what kind of energy production" debate' [*Fisher, 1992: 2*]. The demand-side solutions favoured by environmentalists have received little attention in Poland (as elsewhere in the region). Furthermore, despite the adoption in 1990 of a non-nuclear energy strategy, nuclear power was back on the Polish agenda by 1993. Parliament accepted 'in principle' the view of 'energy experts' that Poland should have a nuclear power station by the year 2010. The Polish Atomic Energy Agency (PAA) always supported the development of nuclear power, offered as a clean, environmentally sound solution to the problem of Poland's reliance on fossil fuels.

There was little counterweight to these views, though publicity concerning the continuing effects of Chernobyl fallout could arouse public anxiety. In 1994 several areas of high concentration of caesium 137 were the subject of public health warnings against the consumption of game and mushrooms (*Rzeczpospolita*, No.194, 22 Aug. 1994). Some environmentalists tried to reinforce public concerns about radiation by emphasising new studies linking radon to increased childhood leukaemia and adult laryngeal and lung cancers, especially among miners in Silesia. Here they had the support of the Solidarity trade union, but publicity was limited and confusing; and the respective ministries of industry, labour and health displayed little sign of concern [*Cieszewska, 1994*]. The environmentalists' press (notably *Gaja* and *Zielone Brygady*, Green Brigades) reached relatively few, but some respected mass circulation journals took up the issue. *Wprost* (Outright), for example, referred to the carcinogenic mines of 'the Silesian Chernobyl' (*Wprost*, No.36, 4 Sept. 1994). However, Polish greens were not themselves wholly united on the issue of nuclear power (e.g. *Zielone Brygady*, No.8, Aug. 1995).

Conclusion

By 1996 there had been substantial improvements in ameliorating some of the worst aspects of environmental degradation in Poland. The impetus to join the EU provided a benchmark for setting high standards. The removal of many subsidies and industrial recession and restructuring were initially more important in bringing this about than environmental policy as such; but after 1992 there were signs that investments in anti-pollution equipment, sewage treatment plants and the like, along with more efficient regulation, had led to some real improvements (say) in atmospheric emissions and water quality. Again, foreign assistance was of enormous importance. None the less, serious problems remained to be addressed and new ones emerged in the process of economic transformation. The constraints remained formidable.

After 1989 the major centre of environmental policy making in Poland was the pragmatic and technocratically oriented Ministry of the Environment. It proved politically weak in negotiations with other ministries, and it also lacked the resources to evaluate the environmental impact of their proposed legislation and administrative regulations. Despite generalised commitments to 'eco-development', clean-up rather than prevention of damage was the prime emphasis. In many spheres implementation of policy remained problematic, both at national and local level. Lack of financial resources remained a major constraint but far from the only one. Indeed, some evidence emerged as to the misuse of the special funds and easy credit arrangements provided. Technical expertise was often lacking, especially at local level, yet numerous environmental functions had been transferred to local government. Non-compliance remained widespread and regulatory and enforcement mechanisms were still inadequate.

REFERENCES

'Autostrady' (1996), *Zielone Brygady*, No.2, <http://www.uci.agh.edu.pl/pub/e-press/zb/9602/autostr.htm>.
Budnikowski, Adam (1992), 'Foreign Participation in Environmental Protection in Eastern Europe. The Case of Poland', *Technological Forecasting and Social Change*, Vol.41, No.2, pp.147–60.
Burger, T. and A. Sadowski (1994), *Świadomość społeczna: Niderlandy ekologiczna*, Warsaw: Instytut na Rzecz Ekorozwoju.
Cieszewska, B. (1994), 'Raport o izotopach radonu na Śląsku', *Rzeczpospolita*, No.174, 28 July.
Cieszewski, Jacek (1995), 'Trzystu z "Bobrka"', *Rzeczpospolita*, No.11, 13 Jan.
Eberstadt, Nicholas (1994), 'Demographic Disaster. The Soviet Legacy', *The National Interest*, No.36 (Summer), pp.53–7.
Fisher, Duncan (1992), *Paradise Deferred: Environmental Policy-Making in Central and Eastern Europe*, London: Ecological Studies Institute.

Forowicz, Jan (1994), 'Zarabiamy na chronieniu środowiska', *Rzeczpospolita*, No.257, 4 Nov.

Forowicz, K. (1994), 'Śmieć albo życie', *Rzeczpospolita*, No.39, 15 Feb.

Ginsberg-Gebert, Adam and Zbigniew Bochniarz (1988), *Ekonomiczne problemy ochrony środowiska*, Wrocław: Ossolineum.

Gliński, Piotr (1994), 'Environmentalism among Polish Youth. A Maturing Social Movement', *Communist and Post-Communist Studies*, Vol.27, No.2, pp.145–59.

Gliński, Piotr (1996), *Polscy Zieloni*, Warsaw: IFiS PAN.

GUS (Główny Urząd Statystyczny) (1984), *Obszary ekologicznego zagrożenia w Polsce*, Warsaw: Główny Urząd Statystyczny.

GUS (1990a), *Ochrona środowiska naturalnego 1989*, Warsaw: Główny Urząd Statystyczny.

GUS (1990b), *Raport o stanie, zagrożeniu i ochronie środowiska 1990*, Warsaw: Główny Urząd Statystyczny.

GUS (1993), *Ochrona środowiska 1992*, Warsaw: Główny Urząd Statystyczny.

GUS (1994), *Ochrona środowiska 1993*, Warsaw: Główny Urząd Statystyczny.

GUS (1995), *Ochrona środowiska 1995*, Warsaw: Główny Urząd Statystyczny.

Henzler, Marek and Dariusz Kuziak (1994), 'Śmieci górą', *Polityka*, No.10, 5 March.

Hrynkiewicz, Józefina (1990), *Zieloni. Studia nad ruchem ekologicznym w Polsce 1980–1989*, Warsaw: Uniwersytet Warszawski Instytut Socjologii.

Kabala, Stanley J. (1993), 'The History of Environmental Protection in Poland and the Growth of Awareness and Activism', in Barbara Jancar (ed.), *Environmental Action in Eastern Europe. Responses to Crisis*, London: M.E. Sharpe, pp.114–33.

Kaczyński, A. (1993), 'Kto daje i odbiera', *Rzeczpospolita*, No.259, 5 Nov.

Kassenberg, A. and C. Rolewicz (1985). *Przestrzenna diagnoza ochrony środowiska w Polsce*, Warsaw: Polska Akademia Nauk.

Kramer, John (1987), 'Environmental Crises in Poland', in Fred Singleton (ed.), *Environmental Problems in the Soviet Union and Eastern Europe*, London: Lynne Rienner, pp.149–67.

Löfstedt, R. and G. Sjöstedt (1996), *Environmental Aid Programmes to Eastern Europe*, Aldershot: Avebury.

Mayers, Stephen, Salayf, Jurgen and Lee Schipper (1994), 'Energy Use in a Transitional Economy. The Case of Poland', *Energy Policy*, Vol.22, No.8, pp.699–713.

Nowakowska, Ewa (1992), 'Radosna twórczość', *Polityka*, No. 39, 26 Sept.

Pawłowski, Lucjan and Marzenna Dudzińska (1994), 'Environmental Problems of Poland during Economic and Political Transformation', *Ecological Engineering*, Vol.3, pp.207–15.

Peszko, Grzegorz (1994), 'Raport z rocznej pracy w radzie nadzorczej wojewódzkiego funduszu ochrony środowiska w Krakowie', *Zielone Brygady*, No.8, Aug., pp.15–16.

Pietrasik, Sławek (1996), 'Jeszcze raz o zielonym stole i odpadach w krakowie', *Zielone Brygady*, No.3, <http://www.uci.agh.edu.pl/pub/e-press/zb/9603/smieci.html>.

Polityka Ekologiczna Państwa (1992), Warsaw: Ministry of Environmental Protection.

'Quo Vadis NGO?' (1996), *Zielone Brygady*, No.3, <http://www.uci.agh.edu.pl/pub/e-press/zb/9603/darek.html>.

World Bank (1994), *Health and the Environment in Central and Eastern Europe*, Environment Report No.12270, Washington, DC: World Bank.

Environmental Action during Romania's Early Transition Years

SIMINA DRAGOMIRESCU, CRISTINA MUICA and DAVID TURNOCK

As with other countries in ECE, Romania began its transition with some major environmental problems because legislation failed to deliver effective pollution controls. Although scarcely apparent during the last years of Communism, an ecological movement achieved early political success and some of the worst affected areas have now seen substantial improvements. In addition, the slow-down in the economy helped to reduce the scale of environmental damage, although rising unemployment helped to breed a survival mentality which had made the public wary of supporting radical environmental programmes. However, with the help of foreign capital and technology, progress continues to be made on a broad front and the legislative programme of 1995–96 should go a long way to bring Romania into line with EU practices.

The Romanian Environment

Although rich in natural resources, Romania is prone to a number of major environmental hazards including avalanches in the mountains, gully erosion, landslides and mudflows in the hills and plateau country, combined with floods and seismic risks in the lowlands [*Balteanu, 1992*]. However, the extent of the danger is increased in many cases by human mismanagement. There are, for example, 3.5 million hectares of potentially flooded lands along the Danube and its tributaries (Arges, Buzau, Ialomita, Jiu and Siret); the Banat-Crisana plain (Cris Rivers, Mures and Somes). Floods arise through heavy rain and snow melt in spring. Catastrophic floods follow heavy rainfall on a damp soil that cannot absorb more water. But floods are aggravated by the narrowing of rivers at bridging points and, much more significantly by deforestation.

The vegetation zones are under climatic control and large areas may be destroyed by gales, such as the 200 km per hour storms of November 1995 (the worst winter weather for half a century) which led to catastrophic damage over 9,000 hectares in Eastern Transylvania (Covasna, Harghita and Mures). But vulnerability is increased by planting inappropriate species for short-term economic gain. Moreover, the forest line may be artificially depressed by heavy grazing pressure [*Geanana, 1991–92*] and all woodlands will be progressively thinned if animals are allowed to destroy young trees [*Stoiculescu, 1990*]. In addition, extensive clear felling can result in accelerated run-off during heavy rainfall. Commercial cutting is gradually being brought under control but since 1989 there has been much illegal cutting, peaking at 281,000 cubic metres in 1992 and since falling to 195,000 cubic metres in 1993 and 145,000 cubic metres in 1994. Part of this damage arose because privatisation (which affected about seven per cent of all woodlands), led to immediate felling without the required authorisation of the forestry authorities and without replanting because the owners were not interested in taking a long-term view. Altogether some 6,000 hectares of forest was lost.

Most seriously, illegal cutting has affected the acacias planted to stabilise the Oltenian sand dunes. These have started to move again and nearby villages are threatened. Over the longer term, deforestation has contributed to erosion in the Subcarpathians, but in modern times it is inappropriate agricultural methods that have been most significant in aggravating the incidence of gullies, landslides and mudflows in areas with complex structures of sandstone, clays and shales like the Ramnicu Sarat and Ramna basins [*Surdeanu and Ichim, 1991*]. Muica and Zavoianu [*1996*] see dangers in overgrazing in areas with a particularly sensitive environment, like the Buzau Subcarpathians where landslides and mudflows could again become more prevalent. Also the quality of grazing will decline with greater prominence for low-productive herbaceous associations [*Muica and Muica, 1995*].

There is also a tendency to resume cropping (maize cultivation and potatoes) on hill land regained through restitution since 1989. For the results are generally poor and erosion may spread to other surfaces by regression, increasing the sediment carried off by streams to accumulate on river beds or in reservoirs [*Zavoianu, 1995*]. Cumulatively these problems are serious because there are some 2.0 million hectares of degraded land across the country where erosion may remove 300–5,000 tonnes per hectare per year. To total annual wastage of soil through erosion amounts 120 million tonnes (107 million tonnes of which comes from agricultural land). Only occasionally is the landscape positively enhanced by landslides which block valleys and cause lakes to be impounded: Lacul Rosu and Lacul Balatau have been in existence for some time but the lake in the Cuejdi Valley near Piatra Neamt has only recently been created.

Misuse of Resources: Water and Air Pollution

Further environmental problems arise almost exclusively as a result of the misuse of resources. Water pollution arises from the lack of adequate treatment of effluent, and so, for example, lakes in Bucharest are polluted with organic substances linked with sewage from the town of Buftea which should be directed into the main sewer system of the capital city. But in addition industry which discharges about 3.0 billion cubic metres of water into the drainage system each year. There is a big increase in the mineral content of water in the Somes River after the waste water from the industrial estates of Cluj-Napoca has been discharged [*Bagrinovschi, et al., 1991–92*] and ammonia levels in the Mures downstream of Targu Mures are 3.5 times the legal maximum due to the Azomures fertiliser plants. International concern has arisen over pollutants in both these rivers (and the Cris as well) which flow from Romania into Hungary. There is high chlorine concentration in the Trotus below Onesti (almost double the legal limit) where pollution is linked with wood processing and chemical plant [*Harjoaba and Conachi, 1993*].

Pollution has also affected the shallow water table which is critical for the fifth of the population that depends on wells. Underground waters are polluted in the vicinity of the major industrial complexes and although fertiliser use has declined, because the high costs cannot be afforded by today's private farmers, inappropriate use in the past has left a legacy of nitrate pollution of groundwater especially in the southern part of the country where eutrophication is widespread. There are drinking water problems where microbiological pollution of surface water exceeds treatment plant capacity. Large amounts of chlorine are used which itself creates risks of digestive infections [*Cucu, 1992*].

Air pollution became a serious problem by the 1970s due to the large scale of socialist industrialisation, allied with the increase in road traffic as well as the capacity of electricity generators and district heating stations. Emissions of dust, sulphur and carbon dioxide are a nuisance but a serious health hazard in areas of high concentration. There are problems for young children especially on account of respiratory infections, with heavy metals (especially lead) a special hazard. The health of schoolchildren has been affected by the cement works at Bicaz and Tasca [*Vasilov and Ichim, 1993*]. Once again, international relations may be affected because strong protests from Bulgaria about pollution crossing the Danube from the Giurgiu chlorine factory eventually brought about major changes in the town's industry. Monitoring has improved and pollution levels have fallen [*Mihu, 1990*], but in Bucharest maximum emissions levels are often exceeded and some industrial towns concerned with the manufacture of cement, chemicals and non-ferrous metals have become notorious. Wood processing units are relatively benign but, even so, they can emits high levels of dust and sawdust which should be intercepted in high-capacity filtering units.

Misuse of Resources: Unregulated Tipping

Unsightly accumulations of quarry waste are a problem especially when the material is toxic [*Armas, 1991–92; Talanga, 1991*]. The total amount of waste material in tips in mining areas is estimated at 3.43 billion tonnes [*MAPPR, 1994: 24*]. Much of the industrial waste (wood, paper, glass, metal, oil and rubber) is now being recycled; but relatively little of the mine waste or garbage generated in urban areas. The total amount of recycled waste is 22.7 million tonnes per year: 6.3 per cent of the total of 357.1 million tonnes per year, where the other principal components are the coal industry (243.1 million tonnes per year), extraction and processing of minerals (42.1 million tonnes per year) and garbage (17.6 million tonnes per year) [*MAPPR, 1994: 24*]. Dumps of noxious wastes are a particular hazard especially when there the danger of diffusion by streams draining the land. Since 1989 there have been problems arising from the storage of toxic material imported illegally from Western countries [*Ciulache and Ionac, 1995*]. Substantial amounts have been located and returned to the country of origin. Stricter controls are now in force at the frontiers to control this problem which covers not only chemical waste but rejected produce from farms and food processing units (tobacco and tomato puree). However, growing amounts of rubbish are still being generated within the domestic economy.

Misuse of Resources: Rural Areas

Rural areas are both victims and sources of pollution [*Rauta, 1992a*]. Air pollution damages crops and depresses yields [*Bran, 1996*], while heavy metals have been detected in the soil close to some industrial plants [*Rauta, 1992b*]. Pipeline fractures (such as occurred on the Ploiesti–Constanta oil pipeline at Pucheni) can causes considerable losses to agriculture. Acid rain damage to forests has become more noticeable in recent years [*Negulescu, 1990*]. Romania was doing better than other countries of South-Eastern Europe until 1993 but is now in a similar position. There are five categories of damaged forests ranging from Class 1 (slightly damaged) to Class 5 (dead) and Classes 2–4 have increased from 16.7 per cent in 1992 to 21.2 per cent in 1994. Fir and other resinous species are quite heavily damaged, along with acacia, while beech are most resistant (only 15 per cent defoliated). But generally it is the lower forests that are most seriously affected and the health of the forest increases with altitude. Regionally, pollution is relatively serious in the Western Carpathians and in the counties of Arges and Sibiu [*Enache, 1994*]. Damage is aggravated by drought and locally-generated pollution; also by inappropriate management which has neglected mixed woodland, use of unsuitable exotic species and approved irrational cutting.

Farmland is being lost through urban development and investment in infrastructure. In areas of strip mining there have been some environmental benefits through the canalisation of streams. But the landscape has been transformed by the pits and spoil heaps, while the underground water level has fallen and wells have run dry [*Popescu, 1993*]. After the mining has finished lakes in the hollows may be used for recreation and for fish farming, but apart from the first two or three years when cultivation is rewarded with the fertilising effect of the coal dust the land has little agricultural value [*Candea et al., 1993*]. On the other hand, agriculture causes considerable damage estimated at 50 million lei in 1992 (half the damage attributed to industrial pollution). Problems arise through soil compaction and degradation through excessive fertiliser dressings. Irrigation has helped to increase yields, especially in the south-east of the country and further schemes are advocated [*Benone, 1993*], but there can be a negative effect on soil fertility [*Varlan et al., 1993*] and problems of salinisation may also arise [*Rauta and Carstea, 1990*]. Polluted water draining off farmland has affected lakes of balneary importance like Techirghiol [*Serban and Simionas, 1990*]. Ecological restoration of the soil has been estimated to cost US$25 million [*MAPPR, 1994*]. Meanwhile, intensive agriculture has led to the almost total loss of wetlands in the Danube floodplain and the transformation of the silvosteppe and xerophilous pastures. Quite apart from the ecological significance of this change, the economic costs arising from the destruction of fisheries should be taken into account.

Environmental Action during the Early Transition Years

Recent environmental management has been based on the law of 1973 which placed responsibility in the hands of a National Council of Environmental Protection. However, under this organisation, which had responsibility between 1974 and 1990, law enforcement was generally weak on account of the priority given to industrial production. Now there is more effective action at the government level through the establishment of the Ministry of Environment in 1990 (renamed Ministry of Waters, Forests and Environmental Protection in 1992) which integrates the work of the old National Council with the Romanian Academy's Commission for Protection of Natural Monuments which has been active since 1932 on the identification of protected areas. Romania is seeking to adopt international standards and the policy is to include the recommendations of all international conventions signed by the Romanian government in the national legislative programme. Romania has been very active in adhering to international conventions in recent years: including Basel, Geneva and

Helsinki (all relating to aspects of transboundary pollution); as well as Ramsar (dealing with wetlands). From the end of 1997 all export of hazardous waste from OECD countries to non-OECD countries will be stopped (though import of such waste is already forbidden in Romania).

Priority Areas

Fourteen priority areas have been identified where there are serious pollution problems requiring immediate action. These are the industrial zones of Bacau, Baia Mare, Brasov, Brazi (Ploiesti), Borzesti-Onesti, Copsa Mica, Govora (Ramnicu Valcea), Isalnita (Craiova), Pitesti, Suceava, Targu Mures, Turnu Magurele, Tulcea and Zlatna. A particularly serious situation has arisen at Copsa Mica, a small town on the Mures near Medias badly polluted by the Sometra metallurgical plant, using old technology to produce lead/zinc concentrates as well as gold and silver, and the Carbosin petrochemical plant specialising in carbon black for the tyre industry.

The emissions of dust and gases included heavy metals and up to 67,000 tonnes of sulphur annually, while about 700 tonnes of metal (iron, lead and zinc) was contained in waste water discharged into the river each year. Acid rain affected the local woodlands while the accumulation of heavy metals (cadmium, lead and zinc) in the soil adversely affected agriculture and wild life. But despite the highest infant mortality in the country and damage to the normal physical and psychological development of all children [*Enache, 1994: 140–41*], plus the aggravation of bronchitis and asthma [*Thomson and Nachywey, 1991*], the option of factory closure was resisted by the workers anxious to hang on their jobs. The outcome was a reduction in emissions and a search for investment to modernise the plant.

Substantial improvements have now been made. In 1994, 3.0 billion lei were allocated to the small town of Zlatna in the Western Carpathians in order to clean up the Ampellum enterprise concerned with non-ferrous metallurgy and sulphuric acid [*Mihailescu and Ciobanu, 1990; Serban et al., 1993*]. The obsolete sulphuric acid plant was a particular problem at the so-called 'death works' but this section has now been refurbished and production was restarted in 1996. Pollution is also being eliminated at the non-ferrous metallurgical complex of Baia Mare where the Romplumb enterprise was assisted by the Swiss government to install filters to collect the fine lead powder that used to be pumped into the atmosphere. Furthermore, with help from Finland the Phoenix factory in the same city updated its filtering system and installed a new furnace to eliminate sulphur dioxide pollution currently dispersed through chimney 350 metres high (a European record), which was partly counterproductive because of the inversion phenomenon which forced the pollution back to ground level. Thus the Ministry of Waters, Forests and Environmental Protection was able to fulfil its promise of 1992 that flowers would grow on Romplumb's premises within four years. High levels of water pollution at Baia Mare (copper concentrations are 16.4 times higher than the legal maximum in the Sasar River because of the Pheonix Works and the Harja/Baia Sprie mining operations) are being reduced by further action at Pheonix and the river is also being transformed through landscaping and flood control measures. There should be a clean environment by the end of 1997. Elsewhere in the district pipes were installed for the hydrotransport of waste from flotation plants at the Baia Sprie and Baiut mines; and a decantation lake (Novat) was provided at Borsa.

Other Initiatives

The woodlands are being better protected, thanks to close co-operation between Ministry of Waters, Forests and Environmental Protection and the Ministry of Home Affairs. Stiffer penalties are now in force for illegal cutting and an improved supply of firewood for the rural areas in a benefit to people who do not have supplies of their own. Regeneration has increased from 18,854 hectares in 1993 to an estimated 25,500 hectares in 1996 [*Salagean, 1996a*] and, following the removal of fallen timber uprooted by the storms of the 1995–96 winter, plans have been drawn up for regeneration; with allowance for snow breaks and priority for trees which are relatively resistant to windblow and can therefore protect other species in vulnerable areas. The restocking of 500 hectares was planned for Covasna for Spring 1996 but there was a late start to forest work due to the long winter. Meanwhile, there is also greater activity in treating both degraded lands (1,506 hectares in 1993 and 1,530 hectares in 1994) and regulating torrential streams (50 km in 1993 and 81 km in 1994). And work has started on rebuilding of forests affected by pollution from factories in such towns as Copsa Mica and Zlatna.

Elsewhere a range of significant initiatives are being taken. In Iasi where organic substances in the Bahlui River at Holboca exceed the permitted norm by 2.5 times, a German company (Mannesmann of Dusseldorf) is to refurbish the sewage plant in the city in order to safeguard a river which flows into the Prut River and ultimately the Danube Delta. In Bucharest a start is being made on the problems of sanitation and garbage collection. An improved garbage collection system is operating in Sector 5 of the city, thanks to the Romanian–Italian joint venture Ecosal. Garbage is being collected in high capacity containers with separate compartments for wood, paper, plastic or glass waste. Residents are rewarded for their co-operation by tickets that can be exchanged for cash at the council office. Ecosal are also commissioning an installation to convert human waste into agricultural fertiliser. Meanwhile, the French company Sater-Parachini is providing for the ecological storage of waste in Bragadiru commune and another ecological dump for household waste has opened at Mioveni (Arges). The latter, with a lifespan of some 30 years, has a capacity 117,800 cubic metres and a stockpile for re-usable materials. Finally, on the Black Sea coast Navodari and Ovidiu have joined forces with Constanta in a joint venture with Sater-Parachini. The Consulab company is making a US$5.0 million investment, using the French partner's financial and technical resources in establishing an ecological waste dump comprising ten garbage pits over 32 hectares.

Energy Conservation

When the Agency for Energy Conservation was created in 1991 as a public body within the Ministry of Industry, Romania was the first of the former socialist countries to create a government organisation specifically for energy conservation. Emerging out of the former Energy Inspectorate, the Agency can help industrial enterprises both technically and financially in energy efficiency, with scope for expansion into the agriculture as well the commercial sector (including offices and public buildings) and residential areas. The aim is to achieve the efficient use of energy in all fields with the provision of financial and technical assistance [*Patterson, 1994*]. It is necessary to get round the public perception of energy savings as a 'sacrifice', because the country consumes three times as much power as the European Union (EU) per unit of GNP and also producers power inefficiently in large-capacity stations working way below full capacity. To help reduce consumption and so moderate the polluting emissions which cause the greenhouse effect, a 'competition' has been set up whereby the local authorities in Constanta, Craiova and Ploiesti submit organisational frameworks with the cost of US$7.0 million met by US and French Funds for Environmental Protection, the EU PHARE programme and the Romanian government. The project will include the development of local power generation strategies, improvement of fuel burning efficiency, recovery of heat in industry and better management in the power industry.

Other organisations are also playing a role in conservation, like the state electricity authority RENEL. While some staff believe that conservation is not in the company's interest (especially in the absence of strong environment protection legislation) others see the way forward to new electrical technologies which will enhance business in the long run [*Patterson, 1994: 113*]. By 1992 the Ministry of Industry had introduced energy efficiency standards (for example, thermal resistance for buildings and appliances) and provided resources for both research and financial incentives to enterprises. A comprehensive energy conservation programme is still in preparation. Until it is available there will be an attraction to buying cheap equipment (perhaps second-hand from abroad) with low energy performance [*Patterson, 1994: 114*]. What is needed is an ongoing programme of retooling guided by appropriate standards and incentives, financed from the state budget and from abroad. Romania's situation is not as bad as most other ECE countries because until the 1980s it was usual to buy factory equipment in the West or use Western technology under licence. However, operating below capacity creates considerable distortion. There is much potential for renewable energy, given the level of support within Romania for greater attention to biomass energy which could become far more important that firewood at present.

Western Technology and Regional Co-operation

Environmental protection laws are being harmonised with the EU and this process should be complete by the end of 1998. There is also a widespread appreciation that Western technology is essential for the solution of pollution problems. In the past foreign assistance was geared largely to industrial production. This meant that the organisation responsible for pollution monitoring and control equipment (set up in 1978 in Bucharest, with branches in Cluj-Napoca, Galati, Ploiesti, Suceava and Timisoara) was thrown back on domestic resources and forced to use outdated technology to produce various types of detection equipment. Since the revolution arrangements have been made for foreign collaboration and there have been discussions with the German firm Lurgi regarding the most serious problems at chemical factories. Black Sea Economic Co-operation aims at more effective pollution control to preserve natural beauty and encourage tourism. Since 1990 there has been the Bucharest Convention (1992) and the Odessa Declaration (1993) to deal with pollution and environmental protection. Water quality in the Danube is also subject to international agreement [*Equipe Cousteau, 1993*]. Romsilva (the Romanian silvicultural authority) has collaboration with Moldova and there is a Romanian–Ukrainian joint geo-ecological survey investigating the north-western part of the Black Sea. Monitoring is to be extended to the Danube Delta; for the main polluting agent of the marine environment in the Black Sea continental shelf is Danube water and sediment which provokes eutrophication [*Panin et al., 1992*]. There is also an intergovernmental commission for the Black Sea operating under UNESCO auspices on which Romania is represented by specialists from the Institute of Marine Research. The international 'Greenglobe' programme seeks to harmonise tourism with the natural environment and there are specific programmes for ecotourism in the delta and the wider Black Sea region.

Environmental Action and Public Opinion

Romania has made substantial progress since 1989 and this is in no small measure due to public opinion. Under Communism there was no significant environmental protest. The worst problems were not widely appreciated by the population at large and the intelligentsia was disinclined to go beyond professional publishing to underline the importance of the Communist Party's own pronouncements on the importance of environmental policy; sadly compromised by the drive for higher industrial output. Draconian plans for the restructuring of villages were much more widely and critically discussed, both within the country and abroad.

However, immediately after the revolution conservationists came out of the woodwork and many ecological groups arose at a time when the ruling Salvation Front was only too happy to see as many political parties as possible. The two Bucharest-based parties, the Romanian Ecological Movement (*Miscarea Ecologista din Romania*: MER) and the Romanian Ecological Party (*Partidul Ecologist Roman*: PER), did surprisingly well in the elections of May 1990, securing two senate places (one for each party) and a total of 20 seats in the Chamber of Deputies (12 for MER and eight for PER). The two parties attracted 591,000 votes (the average for the two sets of returns) or 4.05 per cent of the total. Exactly half the votes (295,800) came from Bucharest and eight other industrial areas where the share of support was more than 20 per cent above the national average. However it would appear that MER was much the more active of the two with membership estimated at 100,000. It had a well-developed programme and established close links with the green movement in Europe as a whole. Through its newspaper 'Eco' the party called for the close monitoring of pollution and for a new commitment to environmental protection, public health and respect for public opinion in the planning process.

However, this early process has not been maintained. As the scale of economic reconstruction became apparent people became concerned primarily with survival and showed little inclination to sacrifice jobs for a cleaner environment. Shortage of parliamentary time has delayed environmental legislation while some early pieces of legislation were not particularly well drafted: a decree on pesticides and fungicides 1993 did not make it clear whether or not local authorities had an obligation to enforce it. Action is also limited by an acute capital shortage.

Although some finance is obtained from PHARE and other EU sources, the major source has to be the state budget or the funds of the enterprises concerned. Thus government has probably done enough to convince most of the electorate that all reasonable measures are being taken. Government has been pragmatic over major public works (moving in favour of smaller-scale hydropower projects which are far less disruptive than the massive artificial reservoirs built under Communism). So when the chosen Candu technology has an excellent safety record and extra nuclear capacity will offer the prospect of an end to winter power shortages public opinion will see a far greater danger in Bulgaria's nuclear power station than in the domestic programme. Consequently support for ecological parties is now very limited, although the absorption of PER by the Democratic Convention means that its supporters are no longer counted separately. However, MER, which continues a separate existence, failed to gain any parliamentary representation in either the 1992 or 1996 elections. Even in local government elections of 1992 and 1996 its showing was generally poor although it topped the poll in Zlatna in 1992 taking 46.2 per cent of the vote.

Some of the more inspired leaders of the early days are no longer active, while MER has been compromised by involvement in the government coalition. One MER member (M. Bleahu) was Minister of Waters, Forests and Environment Protection at the time of the Sibiu waste scandal. Various deals in the first months of the transition involved importation of degraded tobacco and foodstuffs, along with waste paper and infected seed. But the Sibiu incident related to fungicides, herbicides and pesticides imported from Germany by the Montana and Pine Park companies, concealed as 'industrial goods' and 'German economic aid' [*Salagean, 1996b*].

The material was to be stored prior to incineration in facilities that were being installed under Romanian–German co-operation. However, the Greenpeace organisation alerted the Romanian government and public opinion in Sibiu was very effectively mobilised, but not before a critical situation arose at Apoldu de Sus where one of the stores was flooded by melting snow and 40 sacks of waste dissolved in such as way as to threaten local water supplies. After the installation of the Vacaroiu government in November 1992 all the material was returned to Germany the following Spring, but Bleahu lost his portfolio because, although he had no prior knowledge of the real nature of the consignment, he was widely believed to have mishandled the issue when the true facts came to light [*Ciulache and Ionac, 1995*]. In recent years many activists from the ecological parties have joined other parties, sensing that the lack of both resources and strong public commitment gives them little scope for action on the ecological front. However, Bleahu has just surfaced again as a winner in the 1996 parliamentary election since his party (now PER) has an allocation of places in the fielding of candidates by the Democratic Convention, now the largest single party. He is one of three prominent ecologists who have gained entry to parliament in this way.

Meanwhile there is a significant NGO movement which is able to take effective action (especially at the local level) and so act as a catalyst for further enhancement of public awareness. The number of environmental NGOs has been reckoned at over 150. They cover a wide spectrum ranging from large national groups with regional structures to small local organisation; and in political tone they range from the conventional to the radical [*Dinu et al., 1994*]. But NGOs might be encouraged by legislation, while further stimulus could emerge from receive ecological disasters such as the serious storm damage in the forests of the Eastern Carpathians in Autumn 1995 and the winter floods of 1995–96. The Cluj-based 'Transilvania' Ecological Club has produced a guidebook containing environmental information for the public now that public consultation on planning matters (including environmental impact) is a legal obligation. At the same time the public is being better informed about citizens' rights and more emphasis is being given to environmental education [*Jordan and Tomasi, 1994; Rascu, 1993*]. For although schools and universities were covering environmental issues before the revolution [*Turnock, 1982*], the emphasis has become stronger since. Moreover, there is a close connection with tourism which is another growth area in education. Energy is being included in the curriculum of some special industrial schools and energy centres are included in the higher education system. A Chair in energy and the environment has been created at the Polytechnic University of Bucharest with the support of UNESCO.

The New Environmental Legislation of 1995–96

Further environmental action requires new laws shelved during the first years of the transition when immediate survival was the most pressing priority. However, the long awaited legislation was published only at the end of 1995 and adopted in 1996. It seeks to conserve natural resources and maintain biodiversity by protecting air, soil and water and to safeguard designated protected areas (nature reserves and national parks) and natural monuments as well as settlements. Responsibility for environmental protection, including enforcement of pollution limits, will now rest with the central authority (the Ministry of Water, Forests and Environmental Protection) and the environmental agencies in each county which will record observations on air and water quality and monitor the situation in the nature reserves. There are other responsible institutions subordinated to the Ministry, like the Institute for Silviculture (ICAS), while the Romanian Academy and the National Committee of UNESCO help to decide the criteria for the designation of protected areas.

The new law lays down the responsibilities of central administration and local authorities for protecting the environment. It also provides codes for handing of dangerous substances including chemical fertilisers and pesticides. The new legislation will apply the polluter pays principle and compliance programmes will cover all polluters over a period of five years: thereafter failure to meet standards could result in closure. Provision has also been made for land management because new developments will require an impact study, which will have special significance in sensitive areas. In the case of a large project an 'accord de mediu' will have to drawn up by the Ministry or the local agency and scope for public debate and local authority resolution of conflicts are also built into the legislation. Finally it should be pointed out that the general law is an umbrella under which more specific legislation will shelter. These other laws will deal with such matter as water management, the forestry code and nuclear protection.

Water Management

The new Water Law establishes principles for water management. Rational water use must involve consideration of both environmental protection and economic development. But there is scope for public participation and the water authorities can only implement their management plans after consultation. The only exceptions are special situations such as drought or flood when emergency measures are necessary. There will be separate management for each basin through a committee set up under the public corporation 'Romanian Waters'. Each committee will include representatives from local government and local consumers as well as non-governmental organisations. The management plan will be implemented through a regime of bonuses and penalties in order to minimise pollution.

Despite the resources of the natural lakes (1.0 billion cubic metres in an average year) and the underground water supplies (9.6 billion cubic metres), the key resource comprises the national rivers (39.6 billion cubic metres) because the massive volume in the Danube (53.2 billion cubic metres) is peripheral and relatively impure. Hence, the mountains are Romania's natural 'water tower' and to safeguard supplies there should be further research and better management to bring about a reduction in pollution and controlled development of pastoralism, tourism and forestry operations [*Zavoianu, 1993*]. The water industry should be restructured 'so as to assure the circulation of first-degree quality water through the mountain space by means of purification stations and by self-purification' [*Gastescu, 1990: 92*].

Reservoirs are essential to cope with seasonal variations in run-off, but care will be needed to avoid the sedimentation which has been a problem in the Subcarpathian zone [*Tecuci, 1993*]. Also small storages should be encouraged to avoid the disruptive effects of very large projects. At present there are some 400 water storages with total capacity of 13.0 billion cubic metres. Further provision will be linked with an extra 930 megawatts of hydro capacity (currently 5,700 megawatts in total) [*Michael, 1993*]. In view of the central position of the mountains there should be gravitational supplies to the adjacent lowlands by underground pipes. At the same time care should be taken to minimise waste and distribution losses are to come down from 40–45 per cent to 15 per cent. Ultimately the aim is to increase Grade 1 water quality from 54.3 per cent to 90.0 per cent by improved purification and re-equipment of factories. The share of the urban population receiving piped water and sewage should increase from 87 per cent to 99 per cent; and in the case of the rural population from 19 per cent to 85 percent [*Ion–Tudor, 19966*]. This will require substantial pipelines such as the one proposed across the Transylvanian Plateau between the lakes of Rastolita and Somesu Cald [*Zoltan, 1996*]. Other aspects of the water programme include flood protection for 440,000 hectares in addition to the 2.13 million hectares covered at present; and rehabilitation of irrigation systems (total area 3.2 million hectares) with expansion of irrigation over a further 300,000 hectares. Irrigation systems should be managed so that waterlogging, soil degradation and salting is avoided.

Forest Policy

In 1996 a new legal framework ('Codul silvic')was also established for the long-term protection and rational exploitation of the forests through better management (backed by computing and remote sensing) to reduce losses and achieve a lower level of annual cutting level. Cutting is being restricted to 13.5–15.0 million cubic metres compared with 23.0–24.0 million cubic metres in the Communist era, but it is hoped that an improved age distribution will not only ensure continuity of wood production but allow an increase in annual cutting to 16.0–17.0 million cubic metres by 2000–2005. It is also considered necessary to return to the natural woodland structure where it has been artificially modified in order to increase the proportion of more valuable timber. The policy of species change has proved counterproductive in the face of severe storms; so 4,000 hectares will have to be reforested at a cost of 10 billion lei. This effort will require 18 million saplings and more than 1,000 kg of spruce tree seeds. In future therefore species will correspond more closely to natural vegetation with low altitude spruce and pine in plains where exotics have been relatively unstable. Such measures will contribute to a change in the balance of wood harvested so that three-quarters will be deciduous (and the rest resinous) compared with only 60 per cent at present.

Current forest growth of 4.1 cubic meters per hectare per year is below the potential because of 700,000 hectares of low productivity oak and beech forest; young beech forest in inaccessible areas; slow growth in polluted areas (150,000 hectares) and illegal grazing by animals. Grazing is now forbidden in publicly-owned forests (including afforested degraded land and protective forest strips) with stiff penalties for damage. However, exceptions will be made for flocks in transit; also to provide shelter and allow some routine grazing in well-established parts of the forest. Carts must keep to forest roads. Dwarf pine brushwoods ('jnepenisuri') are strictly protected. Private woodlands must be managed according to principles laid down by the local forestry office ('Ocol silvic'). Silvicultural diseases will be tacked more energetically, especially the drying phenomenon while fast-growing species crucial for the cellulose and paper industries will be encouraged. The hunting of wild animals will be managed on a sustainable basis and conserving biodiversity will call for protected areas amounting to eight to ten per cent of the forest stock, including many new protected zones in the hill and plain regions.

The forests are being made more accessible through better organisation by each 'Ocol silvic' and by a special fund for new roads ('fond special pentru acesibilizarea padurilor') financed by a levy on furniture and sawn timber exported. But at present Romania has only 39,200 km of forest roads: 6.1 metres per hectare, compared with the norm of 20-30 metres per hectare in the EU (45 metres per hectare in Germany, 44 metres per hectare in Switzerland, 26 metres per hectare in France). Only 65 per cent of the forest stock is accessible which means than 2.2 million hectares of forest cannot be effectively exploited. The annual rate of road-building has been only 50–150 km in recent years, with emphasis on Covasna and Harghita counties. But the cost is considerable with 100 km costing some 10 billion lei. In addition, a great deal of repair work is needed since 29,000 km of roads are in a poor state. Yet it will cost 77 billion lei just to repair the 2,300 km of road damaged in the 1994-95 floods.

National forest stock covers 26.7 per cent of the country but 30.0 per cent is considered the minimum that should be aimed at. In addition to large forest stands there will be provision for degraded land plantations, blocks of woodland on grazings, and belts of trees along streams, railways and roads (with action to ensure adequate management of those belts already in existence). For many years there have been programmes to protect eroded land [Baloi and Ionescu, 1986] and planning has extended across whole river basins prone to erosion [Traci and Ivana, 1990]. But now the foresters have been collaborating with the Agriculture Ministry to explore ways of taking over eroded lands that cannot be efficiently farmed.

In 1994 4,000 hectares of agricultural land were identified as being suitable for planting: 780 hectares were planted in 1994 and 900 hectares approved for 1995. Private owners requesting help will be given free seed. But in critical areas protective strips will be considered as public works. Meanwhile, a new programme has been launched to combat drought on the

Danube floodplain by regenerating 750 km of woodland belts on the Danube floodplain in Dolj, Mehedinti, Olt and Teleorman counties over a three year period with 6,000 hectares of additional land allocated. Protective forest curtains are to be established on 11,000 hectares of land in the east, south and south-east of the country to combat the drying phenomenon. Flood prevention will involve complex forest and hydrotechnical works on 2,500 km to protect areas periodically endangered by floods, mud and landslides.

Protected Areas: Nature Reserves and National Parks

Another important feature of the legislative programme of 1995–96 is the codification of the responsibilities of local government for environmental protection including nature reserves and national parks. The first Carpathian reserve was created in 1920 (Cocora in the Bucegi) and thanks to the Romanian Academy and the commitment of eminent scientists like Emil Racovita the National Network of Natural Protected Areas includes 534 protected areas covering 1.41 million hectares or 4.8 per cent of Romanian territory. But the network is still not entirely conducive to biodiversity and habitat conservation because it does not embrace the full range of conditions [*Dinu et al., 1994*]. Management also remains defective in many cases, with lack of finance a major problem. The National Conservation Strategy is considering various financial options including user charges and a nature tax on commercial operations from which protected areas would benefit through a Nature Protection Fund.

'Protection of rare species and representative vegetation types is essential at a time of increasing anthropic pressure; such action must be combined with measures to maintain landscape diversity and safeguard wildlife habitats' [*Muica and Popova-Cucu, 1993: 155*]. Reserves should be signposted and fenced so that access can be adequately controlled. Hitherto there has been no more than a general framework, though much good work has been done informally by the foresters and by NGOs in clearing up rubbish left by visitors. A good example is the volunteer camp organised by the International Civil Service Romania Group at Lacu Rosu, helping to protect the area through better management of solid waste which is now collected by the Gheorgheni local authority. A resort tax may now be levied in this area to finance environmental protection. However, in the Bucegi Mountains only a strict regime of protection can solve the excessive pressure from sheep grazing (with one grazing station for every 9.0 square km) and tourist pressure [*Velcea et al., 1993*]. The tourist authorities will need to become more involved in environmental protection so as to ensure that pollution is reduced.

National parks are needed to work on the concept of clusters of reserves surrounded by a buffer zone, with limited development of tourist facilities restricted to the outer zone beyond [*Abrudan et al., 1995*]. The only established national park was created in the Retezat Mountains in 1935. It now covers 54,400 hectares including a nature reserve of 18,400 hectares where no economic activity is permitted. The area has international recognition as a biosphere reserve with remarkable floristic diversity including circumpolar, Arctic-alpine and Carpathian-Balkan species. But another park has been designated for the Rodna Mountains (56,600 hectares), including the Pietrosu Mare biosphere reserve with it high mountain vegetation of Carpathian pine as well as floristic rarities such as the local endemic *Lychnis nivalis*.

The chamois was successfully reintroduced into this area. Other proposed national parks with alpine and sub-alpine vegetation have been scheduled in the Caliman (15,300 hectares), Ceahlau (17,200 hectares) and Piatra Craiului (14,800 hectares). Nine other areas have also been designated although the necessary legislation is still awaited. The list could well be longer because local specialists have further areas in mind; like the Parang where a cluster of reserves already exists [*Ploaie, 1995*]. Politicians in Hunedoara have succeeded in getting the Senate Commission for Culture to consider converting the Gradistea Muncelului and Sarmizegetusa historic zones to public property. This is because of acts of vandalism arising from land restitution. The activities of private land owners are endangering the historical monuments at Sarmizegetusa.

Most attention so far has been given to the Danube Delta, the largest natural wetland complex in Central Europe, where a biosphere reserve was set up in 1990 (including the existing nature reserves) and recognised under the UNESCO 'Man & Biosphere Programme' in the same year. It is also listed as a wetland of international importance under the Ramsar Convention. A special administrative regime was established in 1993: to assess the ecological status of natural resources and designate functional zones/restore damaged deltaic ecosystems; act as regional environmental agency and collaborate with local authorities to protect the interests of the local population; co-operate with relevant national/international bodies to promote research and exchange of information; allow concessions for renewable resources with a scale of fees; ecological education/public awareness; monitor waste disposal; regulate navigation in co-operation with the Ministry of Tourism. The World Conservation Union (IUCN) has made a major contribution [*Goriup, 1995*] and the World Bank US$4.5 million project will train the people responsible for ecological monitoring. Local authorities will monitor the species inhabiting the reserve and a database, using a geographic information system, will be set up for the drafting of management projects.

Implementation

Substantial improvements can be expected as a result of the new legislative programme. The importance of EU membership provides a stimulus to harmonise with European legislation and action over motor vehicles will soon be necessary in a country where lead-free is presently little used. However, the existence of legislation is no guarantee of enforcement and it may be some time before pollution limits are effective and planning procedures are followed everywhere in an objective fashion. It is too easy to blame inconsistency on corruption; rather, there is an ingrained culture of localism which legitimises accommodations which enable local authorities to coexist with their communities at the expense of the national interest. However, as pluralism advances even rural societies may become more fragmented and in this context authorities will need to be more neutral in their approach and the more traditional methods of problem solving may disappear in favour of greater standardisation. On the other hand, the intense competition for investment is likely to enhance the discretion shown by local authorities to existing industrial operations and the planning applications of others.

Education and research is an important contextual issue. Adequate research backing for the country's various ecological regions [*Vadineanu et al., 1992*] is delivered by the Ministry of Research and Technology which has drawn up a national programme ('Orizont 2000') for scientific research concerned with technology and environment which has now received government approval. A coordinated research programme is needed [*Jelev, 1992*] and World Bank funding is being coordinated by the Ministry of Waters, Forests and Environment Protection to formulate a Biodiversity Conservation Strategy and Action Plan. But mentalities will also have to be changed in the enterprises where managers lack practical experience in adapting strategies to meet realities. A new generation is required to confront problems inherited from the past as well as the new challenges which relate to international business as well as the domestic scene: both economic and environmental. Management training programmes concerned with human resources and innovation in restructuring will have implications for an improved R&D performance that will be particularly important for the environmental programme. The Urban Sociology Centre is also involved perfecting the R&D programme and improved laboratories are also being provided.

Conclusion

In comparison with the extreme pressures of public opinion over issues such as the Gabčíkovo-Nagymáros hydropower project in Hungary or the nuclear power debate in Poland it may seem that Romanians are relatively indifferent to environmental issues. It may be that further education is needed to stimulate a more critical approach to such matters. For it is interesting to see that the Danube Delta, which attracted a great deal of national and international attention, has been the subject of legislation and is now modestly funded. By contrast the national parks (although strongly supported by groups of professionals, including biologists, silviculturists, geographers and speleologists) have made little progress since the original intentions were noted. Yet progress has been made along a fairly broad front and the complexity of the Romanian transition means that careful consideration must always be given to job security. Moreover, pollution levels are rarely excessive outside the black spots where much work has been done over the last four years. And since the population is tired of shock therapy after the traumas of the Ceausescu era, the government has read the public mood correctly in maintaining a gradual reform process. Limited resourcing for environmental action has however enabled policy action to move in the right direction with international co-operation and environmental education to stimulate public awareness.

REFERENCES

Abrudan, I.V. et al. (1995), 'Woodland Management and Conservation in the Bihor Mountains', in D. Turnock (ed.), Rural Change in Romania (Leicester: Leicester University), pp.67–70.
Armas, I. (1991–92), 'Aspects of the Anthropic Landforms in Romania and its Mapping', Studia Universitatis Babes-Bolyai: Geographia, Vol.40–41, pp.91–97.
Bagrinovschi, V. et al. (1991–92), 'Le potential ecologique des eaux superficielles du basin hydrographique de Somes', Studia Universitatis Babes–Bolyai: Geographia, Vol.40–41, pp.29–38.
Baloi, V. and V. Ionescu (1986), Apararea terenurilor agricole impotriva eroziunii alunecarilor si inundatiilor, Bucharest: Editura Ceres.
Balteanu, D. (1992), 'Natural Hazards in Romania', Revue Roumaine de Geographie, Vol.36, pp.47–55.
Benone, Z. (1993), 'Contributii geografice la studiul zonelor irigabile din sud-estul Romaniei', Geographica Timisensis, Vol.2, pp.183–7.
Bran, F. (1996), 'Calitatea solului la nivel global si local in perimetrul judetului Braila', in C. Vert et al. (eds), Proceedings of the Second Regional Geography Conference: Geographic Researches in the Carpathian-Danube Space, Volume 2 (Timisoara: Universitatea de Vest din Timisoara), pp.187–92..
Candea, M. et al. (1993), 'The Coal Exploitation Influence upon the Geographic Environment in the Motru Coalfield', in C. Muica and D. Turnock (eds.), Geography and Conservation (Bucharest: Geography Institute), pp.99–102.
Ciulache, S. and N. Ionac (1995), 'Public Control of the Rural Environment: A Case Study', in D. Turnock (ed.), Rural Change in Romania, Leicester: Leicester University, pp.78–81.
Cucu, M. (1992), 'Poluarea mediului si sanatatea in Romania', Mediul Inconjurator, Vol.3, No.1, pp. 23–5.
Dinu, A. et al. (1994), 'Country Profile: Romania', IUCN/World Conservation Union East Europe Newsletter, No.13, pp.6–8.

Enache, L. (1994), 'The Quality of Environment in Romania', in P. Jordan and E. Tomasi (eds.), *Zustand und Perspecktiven der Unwelt im Ostlichen Europa*, Wien: Peter Lang Europaischer Verlag, pp.131–57.

Equipe Cousteau (1993), 'Environmental Programme for the Danube River Basin', *Mediul Inconjurator*, Vol.4, No.2, pp.21–32.

Gastescu, P. (1990), 'Water Resources in the Romanian Carpathians and their Management', *Revue Roumaine de Geographie*, Vol.34, pp.85–92.

Geanana, M. (1991–92), 'The Influence of the Geographical Position on the Upper Tree Line in the Romanian Carpathians', *Studia Universitatis Babes-Bolyai: Geographia*, Vol.40–41, pp.61–63.

Goriup, P. (ed.) (1995), *Management Objectives for Biodiversity: Conservation and Sustainable Development in the Danube Delta Biosphere Reserve, Romania*, Newbury: Nature Conservation Bureau.

Harjoaba, I. and M. Conachi (1993), 'Trotusul: un rau sacrifiat', *Terra*, Vol.25, No.1–4, pp.38–42.

Ion–Tudor, C. (1996), 'Development Strategies for Waters, Forests and Environment Protection', *Romanian Business Journal*, Vol.3, No.4, p.11.

Jelev, I. (1992), 'Programul unificat de cercetare in domeniul protectiei mediului in Romania pentru perioada 1991–1955', *Mediul Inconjurator*, Vol.3, No.2, pp.3–10.

Jordan, P. and E. Tomasi (1994), 'Environmental Management, Education and Policy in Romania', in P. Jordan and E. Tomasi (eds), *Zustand und Perspecktiven der Unwelt im Ostlichen Europa*, Wien: Peter Lang Europaischer Verlag, pp.159–69.

MAPPR [Ministerul Apelor Padurilor si Protectiei Mediului] (1994), *Starea factorilor de mediu in Romania*, Bucharest: Ministerul Apelor Padurilor si Protectiei Mediului.

Michael, I. (1993), 'Aspecte ale corelarii amenajarilor hidroenergetice cu mediul inconjurator', *Mediul Inconjurator*, Vol.4, No.1, pp.67–9.

Mihailescu, I. and C. Ciobanu (1990), 'Poluarea industriala a solurilor si a vegetatiei forestiere in Zona Zlatna', *Revista Padurilor*, Vol.105, pp.129–35.

Mihu, D. (1990), 'Proiectarea obiectiva a retelelor de supraveghere a calitatii aerului', *Mediul Inconjurator*, Vol.1, No.1, pp.21–5.

Muica, C. and N. Muica (1995), 'Landcover Change and its Ecological Consequences in Romania', in D. Turnock (ed.), *Rural Change in Romania*, Leicester: Leicester University, pp.64–6.

Muica, C. and A. Popova-Cucu (1993), 'The Composition and Conservation of Romania's Plant Cover', *GeoJournal*, Vol.29, pp.9–18.

Muica, C. and I. Zavoianu (1996), 'The Ecological Consequences of Privatisation in Romanian Agriculture', *GeoJournal*, Vol.38, pp.207–12.

Negulescu, M. (1990), 'Ploile acide', *Mediul Inconjurator*, Vol.1, No.1, pp.11–14.

Panin N. et al. (1992), 'Situatia ecologica in partea de nord vest a Marii Negre', *Mediul Inconjurator*, Vol.3, No.1, pp.27–34.

Patterson, W. (1994), *Rebuilding Romania: Energy Efficiency and the Economic Transition*, London: Earthscan Publications.

Ploaie, G. (1995), 'Tourism and Conservation in the Mountains of Valcea County', in D. Turnock (ed.), *Rural Change in Romania*, Leicester: Leicester University, pp.54–60.

Popescu, C. (1993), 'Mining versus Environment in the Newest Coal Basin of Romania', in C. Muica and D. Turnock (eds.), *Geography and Conservation* (Bucharest: Geography Institute), pp.103–8.

Rascu, P.E. (1993), 'Aspecte si propuneri in legatura cu degradarea patrimoniului natural si cultural-istoric in Romania', *Mediul Inconjurator*, Vol.4, No.1, pp.19–24.

Rauta, C. (1992a), 'Agricultura: victima si agent de poluare a mediului inconjurator', *Mediul Inconjurator*, Vol.3, No.1, pp.19–22.

Rauta, C. (1992b), 'Poluarea cu metale grele a solului din Romania', *Mediul Inconjurator*, Vol.3, No.4, pp.33–44.

Rauta, C. and S. Carstea (1990), 'Starea calitatii solurilor agricole din Romania la finele anului 1989', *Mediul Incorjurator*, Vol.1, No.1, pp.39–42.

Salagean, L. (1996a), 'Forest Code: Fundamental Forest Law in Romania', *Romanian Business Journal*, Vol.3, No.27, p.11.

Salagean, L. (1996b), 'Wastes Mafia' Connection Dismantled', *Romanian Business Journal*, Vol.3, No.44, p.11.

Serban, P. and S. Simionas (1990), 'Influenta antropica asupra Lacului Techirghiol', *Mediul Inconjurator*, Vol.1, No.1, pp.31–8.

Serban, R. *et al.* (1993), 'Impactul uzinei 'Ampellum' Zlatna asupra calitatii aerului: prezent si perspective', *Mediul Inconjurator*, Vol.4, No.1, pp.41–8.

Stoiculescu, C.D. (1990), 'Influenta exercitata de pasunat asupra radacinilor fine de gorun: factor de deterioare a echilibrului ecologic', *Revista Padurilor*, Vol.105, pp.127–8.

Surdeanu, V. and I. Ichim (1991), 'Alunecarile de teren din bazinele subcarpatice ale riurilor Rimnicu Sarat si Rimna ca surse de aluviuni', *Terra*, Vol.23, No.2–4, pp.33–36.

Talanga, C. (1991), 'Implicatii ale exploatarilor miniere de la Rosia Poieni asupra demografiei regionala', *Terra*, Vol.23, No.2–4, pp.37–9.

Tecuci, I. (1993), 'Solutii constructive si masuri pentru atenuarea fenomenului de colmatare a lacurilor de acumulare', *Mediul Inconjurator*, Vol.4, No.2, pp.51–3.

Thomson, J. and J. Nachywey (1991), 'Europe's Dark Dawn: the Iron Curtain Risis to Reveal a Land Tarnished by Pollution', *National Geographic Magazine*, Vol.179, No.6, pp.36–69.

Traci, C. and S. Ivana (1990), 'Efectele lucrarilor de amenajare in bazinul hidrografic al torentului Valea lui Bogdan (Prahova)', *Revista Padurilor*, Vol.105, pp.136–42.

Turnock, D. (1982), 'Romanian Geography Reunited: The Integrative Approach Demonstrated by the Conservation Movement', *GeoJournal*, Vol.6, pp.419–31.

Vadineanu, A. *et al.* (1992), 'Conceptul de regionare ecologica si diferentierea ecoregiunilor din Romania', *Mediul Inconjurator*, Vol.3, No.3, pp.3–6.

Varlan, M. *et al.* (1993), 'An Example of Modified Geosystem in the Moldavian Plain: The Irrigated Perimeter Tansa-Belcesti', in C. Muica and D. Turnock (eds), *Geography and Conservation*, Bucharest: Geography Institute, pp.33–8.

Vasilov, M. and R.I. Ichim (1993), 'Efecte ale poluarii aerului cu pulberi de ciment asupra sanitatii scolarilor expusi', *Mediul Inconjurator*, Vol.4, No.1, pp.15–17.

Velcea, V. *et al.* (1993), 'Geographical Elements Regarding the Environmental Recovery in the Bucegi Mountains', in C. Muica and D. Turnock (eds.), *Geography and Conservation*, Bucharest: Geography Institute, pp.119–21.

Zavoianu, I. (1993), 'Romania's Water Resources and their Use', *GeoJournal*, Vol.29, pp.19–30.

Zavoianu, I. (1995), 'Environmental Constraints on Rural Development in the Curvature Subcarpathians of Buzau County', in D. Turnock (ed.), *Rural Change in Romania*, Leicester: Leicester University Press, pp.61–3.

Zoltan, I. (1996), 'Sistemele de alimentare cu apa din Campia Transilvaniei: prezent si perspective', in C. Vert *et al.* (eds.), *Proceedings of the Second Regional Geography Conference: Geographic Researches in the Carpathian-Danube Space, Volume 2*, Timisoara: Universitatea de Vest din Timisoara, pp.173–8.

Bulgaria: Managing the Environment in an Unstable Transition

SUSAN BAKER and BERND BAUMGARTL

Bulgaria is facing an uncertain future. Communist rule has gone and with it the wider political, economic and trade networks that supported the old regime. However, the adoption of new Western-style economic and political models has proved problematic, as has achieving EU membership. Initial optimism surrounding the ability of Bulgaria to adopt Western models was misplaced. Since the end of the Communist regime the country has experienced considerable political and economic instability, and the revolution of 1989 remains incomplete as the processes of democratisation and marketisation falter. This has had a negative impact upon Bulgaria's ability to tackle the severe environmental legacy of Communist rule. Lack of institutional and administrative capacity, corruption, and the failure to implement reforms at the local level add to Bulgaria's inability to manage its environment. Furthermore, the end of Communist rule has brought new environmental threats, particularly with respect to nuclear power and the transport sector. Western environmental aid is restricted by the belief that Bulgaria lacks the capacity to put this aid to effective and efficient use.

Bulgaria is facing an uncertain future. It has overthrown the old Communist regime but finds it difficult to embrace the alternative, Western economic and political models. Many features of the period of state socialism still play a major role in shaping present-day Bulgaria. The same elites still dominate, having, in many cases, converted their previous political monopoly into a new kind of economic hegemony. Their power is strengthened by the relative weakness of Bulgaria's new political actors and of its civil society. Yet, the old networks of political and economic support, built on the Soviet domination of Eastern Europe, have been dismantled as have the political certainties that maintained stability within Bulgaria since the end of the Second World War.

The current uncertainty about Bulgaria's future stands in sharp contrast to the mood of the country in the period following the collapse of the old regime. Then, grievances were attributed to the failures of the former system and their solution seemed well in sight. There was a strong belief that it was only a matter of a few years before the substitution of existing institutions with new, Western-style ones would be complete. This would lead, in turn, to a Western-style democracy, backed up by an economy that would provide the population with the same, or nearly the same, benefits as those enjoyed by the West. The country was not faced by issues of principle, but rather by questions of detail – which Western model to adopt: the American type of individualism, or the Swedish model of strong state institutions combined with a market economy [*Genov, 1994: 7*].

However, eight years into the transition, Bulgarians are confronted by new poverty, periods of hyperinflation, unemployment, crime, and the daily health problems associated with environmental degradation and pollution. The transition has confronted people with the more unpleasant aspects of a market economy: there is no longer any demand for their knowledge, skills or work [*European Training Foundation, 1997*]. Real income figures have decreased considerably [*UNECE, 1993; OECD, 1994; National Observatory Bulgaria, 1997*]. It comes as no surprise to find that increasingly large sectors of society hanker after the former period, when social security was guaranteed even if at a low level. This is illustrated by the continuous support for the Communists' successor party, the Bulgarian Socialist Party (BSP).

The purpose of this article is to examine the impact of the political and economic situation that has developed in Bulgaria since the fall of the Communist regime in 1989, on its environment management policies. The chapter has two specific concerns. First, to examine how the process of democratisation and marketisation are influencing the country's capacity to manage its environment. Second, to trace the fate of the environmental movement, which played an important role in the revolution of 1989, in post-Communist Bulgaria. Developments in Bulgaria, including in the environmental policy arena, have been strongly influenced by the desire of its political elites to join the European Union. The preparations made by Bulgaria to join the EU are also explored in so far as they cast light on the capacity and willingness of the country to begin to manage effectively its environment.

This article begins by examining the political and economic features of post-Communist Bulgaria and the limited nature of its transition to democracy and a market economy. A brief outline is then provided of the environmental legacy of Communist rule. The administration of environmental policy in post-Communist Bulgaria is examined and the institutional capacity of both national and subnational levels of government appraised. The fate of the environmental movement during the transition, including the involvement of environmental groups in party and electoral politics is then examined. Finally, the international dimensions of environmental management are explored, including the significance of the EU's decision to put Bulgaria's membership on hold, at least for the medium term.

Political and Economic Features of the Transition Process

Political Features

In 1947, the Communist Party established control in Bulgaria and in 1956 Todor Zhivkov came to power and ruled the country for over thirty years. Under Zhivkov's highly centralised regime priority was given to industrialisation and agricultural collectivisation. However, from the 1970s onwards, economic growth slowed and by the second half of the 1980s had come to a standstill [*CEC, 1997*]. These economic difficulties did not weaken the hold of the state on the citizens and throughout the regime of Zhivkov, Bulgaria remained a highly repressive totalitarian state. During this period Bulgaria was also regarded as the Soviet Union's most faithful servant.

However, as in other East Central European (ECE) countries, in November 1989 Communist rule in Bulgaria collapsed, Zhivkov was removed from office and an interim government established. In July 1991 Bulgaria adopted a new constitution, marking the transition to parliamentary democracy. However, the collapse of the old Communist regime heralded the beginning of a new period of political instability and economic uncertainty for Bulgaria.

Bulgaria's transition to democracy has been hampered by its lack of experience of democratic rule. The foundation of the Bulgarian state, following more than 500 years of Turkish rule, only occurred in 1878. The monarchy which followed was interrupted only for short periods by republican rule. This was succeeded by Communist rule in the post-war period. The lack of historical experience with democracy and its traditions is mirrored in current political instability, as seen in party formation, party splits, and the high turnover rate of government since the first free elections.

These elections, held in June 1990, were won by the BSP. They were marked by allegations of fraud, intimidation and some violence [*Waller and Millard, 1992: 168*]. Furthermore, the BSP is generally recognised as one of the least reformed of all the former Communist parties in Eastern Europe. Nevertheless, it maintains a strong popular support base and is keen on establishing good contacts with the West, and wishes especially to foster foreign direct investment.

In November 1990, the BSP government was forced to resign due to the economic crisis, to be replaced by a programme government (see Sjöberg and Wyzan [*1991*] for a fuller analysis of the economic problems of this period). The Union of Democratic Forces (UDF), the other main political party, topped the poll in the subsequent election of October 1991, resulting in their leading a new coalition government. During this period, however, the internal divisions within the UDF, which had been formed from an alliance of numerous interests, including environmental ones, began to surface and the party continues to be plagued by disunity. This contributed to its lack of effectiveness during its first period of government and the UDF-led government was replaced by a government of non-party technocrats the following year. The problems experienced by the UDF reflect a tendency seen throughout ECE, namely the political demise of the idealistic, intellectual dissidents who formed the core of the opposition during the Communist era and their replacement by more pragmatic politicians with greater popular support [*Bell, 1993: 92*].

The 1994 elections returned the BSP to power, a victory that owes much to public dissatisfaction with the economic hardships of the transition process. This victory made Western governments and investors reluctant to deepen their involvement with Bulgaria. However, this government was forced to resign in February 1997 due to severe economic difficulties. This led to another interim government and a period of political crisis, which was followed in April 1997 by new elections. These resulted in a majority for the UDF and its allies, who had put priority on tackling corruption and crime, and carrying out the economic reforms previously agreed with the IMF (*The Guardian*, 12 and 28 April 28 1997).

Thus, since the end of the Communist regime, the political climate in Bulgaria has been marked by a high degree of instability, repeated changes of government, economic and political crises, and marked polarisation between Communist and non-Communist parties. Added to this instability is the failure of the transformation process to topple the old elites within Bulgaria. Often the old and new leaders are the same people, particularly at the subnational level, where political activity is often reminiscent of the single-party era. Parties, other than the BSP, remain weak and internally divided. Within this political climate corruption thrives. The BSP has even publicly apologised in 1997 to their people for misrule and corruption while they previously held power (*The Guardian*, 22 Jan. 1997). The democratisation process is also blocked by insufficient control over the secret service, police abuse and serious shortcomings in the dispensing of justice [*CEC, 1997*]. The lack of independent media, including radio and television, is also of concern [*Crawford, 1996: 107*]. Furthermore, ethnic tensions continue to exist between Bulgarians and ethnic Turks, and the rights of gypsies are not respected [*Gradev, 1995*].

Economic Features

During the Communist era Bulgaria experienced significant economic restructuring, shifting from being a predominantly agricultural country with a low degree of urbanisation, to an industrial stronghold of the Council for Mutual Economic Assistance (CMEA). Bulgaria's industrialisation was driven by strategic and ideological concerns, which neglected ecological and geophysical conditions.

Since the end of the old regime, Bulgaria has found it difficult to respond to the economic demands of the transition process. From an economic point of view, the main weakness lies in the failure to introduce structural changes. Privatisation has been slow and amongst the lowest for ECE countries.[1] This can, in part, be explained by the energy-intensive nature of Bulgaria's industry and their weak financial situation, which makes them unlikely candidates for private buyers. It can also be attributed to the fragmentation of responsibility and the lack of administrative coordination among those responsible for privatisation [*CEC, 1997*]. Behind this lies a lack of political will and as a consequence the growth of the private sector has been slow [*CEC, 1997*], with the state continuing to play a major role in the economy.

Bulgaria's precarious economic situation has made it difficult to make the transition to a market economy. It has, for example, experienced declining GDP and agricultural output, the latter arising partly as a result of the slowness of land restitution policy. This has prevented the emergence of a market economy in the agricultural sector. In contrast, GDP's share of the informal black market has grown [*Economist Intelligence Unit, 1996*]. Bulgaria has also the highest level of unemployment in ECE [*Economist Intelligence Unit, 1995; 1996*]. Furthermore, by 1996, many state employees had not been paid for several months (*Der Standard*, 5 Sept. 1996). High inflation is also a serious problem, as is exchange rate instability. In 1997, hyperinflation rates were reached [*National Observatory Bulgaria, 1997: 9*]. Public sector wages have fallen, the value of pensions has eroded, and in 1996 it was estimated that 40 per cent of the population lived below the official poverty line [*CEC, 1997*].

Bulgaria's economic transition is also made difficult by its unstable banking system. The mushrooming of private banks in the early 1990s was followed by a severe banking crisis in 1996, despite which market discipline remains largely absent in the financial sector [*CEC, 1997*]. In particular, there is weak banking supervision and a lack of a proper regulatory framework governing the behaviour of banks.

Bulgaria's position in the international economic system is also weak. It has achieved little foreign direct investment (*Transition*, No.11–12, 1995).

The financial crisis of 1996 further reduced investors' trust in the Bulgarian economy and some foreign firms, which initially invested following the collapse of Communist rule, have abandoned the country. Bulgaria has also inherited a high debt from the Communist regime, which it finds increasingly difficult to service [*National Observatory Bulgaria, 1997: 13*]. While other ECE countries have been able to reschedule their debt repayments, the bulk of Bulgaria's debt is owed to the London Club of Private Creditors, where rescheduling is far more difficult. The low purchasing power of the Bulgarian currency, combined with a lack of foreign currency reserves, led the government in 1990 to temporarily suspend debt payment. Since then Bulgaria has been unable to develop an adequate debt-management strategy [*Pishev, 1991: 109*]. In short, Bulgaria now lacks international creditworthiness.

The economic profile of Bulgaria that emerges is of a country where central planning has been abolished but where the basic institutions of a functioning market economy are not yet in place [*Wyzan, 1991: 96*]. There are a number of reasons why Bulgaria has found it difficult to respond to the economic demands of the transition process. During the Communist era Bulgaria was heavily dependent on the market of the other Communist countries and the breakdown of the CMEA hit Bulgaria badly. These difficulties have been exacerbated by the introduction of the US dollar as the main currency throughout the region. The slowness of reform can also be partly explained by the fact that Bulgaria started its transition to a market economy later and under more unfavourable conditions than most of the other ECE countries. Economic reform had not begun until 1991, by which time the country was undergoing a deep economic crisis [*CEC, 1997*].

However, political instability and lack of commitment to reform are also important explanatory factors [*CEC, 1997*]. The history of post-Communist Bulgaria is marked by an absence of political commitment to economic reform. Often the severe hardship of reform has forced the government to modify, and at times, even halt the process [*Bell, 1993: 95*]. For example, in 1995 a Prices Act was adopted which allowed government to control the price of a large number of food items. The BSP is particularly sensitive to popular demands to modify the economic reform process, even though the party does not want to see a return to the old central-command economy. In contrast, the new government of 1997, led by the UDF, is committed to the continuation of economic reforms. However, in Bulgaria such commitment has the potential to destabilise the country politically. Demonstrations in the capital Sofia in January 1997 have shown how fragile the political situation is in Bulgaria (*The Guardian*, 13 Jan. and 25 Jan. 1997) as does the continuing crisis in the value of Bulgaria's currency.

The Environmental Legacy of Communist Rule in Bulgaria

Intact Nature

Bulgaria still has extensive tracks of intact nature. Although relatively small, its varied climate and landscape support great biological diversity and it has a long history of nature protection. In 1928, for example, the Council for the Protection of the Countryside was founded. This led to the establishment of numerous national parks. Furthermore, specific areas, like the hunting and leisure reserves designed for *nomenklatura* politicians, or the border regions, to which access was denied completely, are thought of as de facto nature reserves.

Under Communist rule environmental legislation also sought to protect Bulgaria's rich ecological heritage. In 1960, the first state decree for the protection of the countryside was passed. This led to an increased momentum for nature protection. Environmental themes were also included in the countries Five-Year Plans, which dealt with pollution control measures as well as measures designed to protect the countryside [*Carter, 1993: 38*]. As late as 1988, a national programme for environmental conservation was adopted and a new Ministry for Land, Forest and Environmental Conservation was set up.

However, despite this legislative and administrative activity, Bulgaria's environment suffered severe degradation during the Communist regime. A failure to implement policy, particularly in the industrial and agricultural sectors, resulted in an increasing gap between the demands of economic development and those of environmental protection.

Environmental Degradation

Bulgaria shares many environmental problems with other ECE countries. Rapid industrialisation after the Second World War changed the face of the countryside and although this brought an improvement in living standards, it caused serious environmental problems. Communist ideology, including the belief that natural resources can be treated as free goods, resulted in an industrialisation process that paid little attention to energy consumption or pollution abatement. Bulgaria's heavy industry has contributed to air pollution in cities and contamination in and around specific industrial sites. There are also problems arising from inadequate disposal of waste, soil erosion and localised water contamination, as well as contamination from agricultural practices.

However, it is difficult to get an accurate picture of the extent of this pollution because of numerous but often conflicting estimates (see, for example, the study for USAID by Wolf [*1991*]; EAP [*1993*]; Georgieva [*1992*]; World Bank [*1994*]; Stanchev [*1992*]; Oschlies [*1987*]; Dimitrova

[*1994*]). There are also other sources available. In 1989, for example, The Ministry for the Environment produced a Green Book on the Environment which detailed the extent of degraded and polluted land [*Ministry of Environment, 1991*]. The Ministry also prepared a report for the Rio UNCED conference which provided evidence as to the extent of contamination of agricultural land. Bulgaria also has a specific problem relating to extremely poor water resources [*Dimitrova, 1994: 96*], and water quality and quantity has become an issue in national elections. This problem is exacerbated by the fact that all the major rivers in Bulgaria are either organically dead or are becoming so in their middle or lower reaches [*Russell, 1991: 18*].

There are also specific ecological hot spots, some of which have received international attention. These include the Kremikovtsi metallurgy plant, the mining region of Maritsa Istok, Burgas on the Black Sea (*Pogled*, 9 Dec. 1991), the lead and zinc production at Plovdiv, Silistra, which suffered transboundary pollution from a Romanian factory[2] and the infamous Vulkan cement plant. Many other examples could be mentioned [*Schaffer 1992; Duma*, 20 Feb. 1992]. Pollution has led to documented health problems, including, for example, high infant and lung cancer mortality in the mining district of Southern Bulgaria.

Of all the environmental problems facing Bulgaria, air pollution is recognised as one of the most serious, especially given its links to health problems [*EAP, 1993*]. For this reason it is one of the main priority areas in the environmental strategies developed since the end of the Communist era. However, air-quality control and pollution abatement is difficult to achieve for a number of reasons. Only half of the country's industrial enterprises are furnished with purifying systems. Furthermore, Bulgaria's industry remains by and large in state hands, suffering large losses, burdened by debts, declining investment and production, and with an overall lack of international competitiveness [*CEC, 1997*]. It is difficult to see how this sector can, at least in the medium term, contribute to a more effective management of Bulgaria's environment. There are also problems at the level of the household, due to the fact that lignite is the main domestic source of energy which emits high levels of pollution [*Dimitrova, 1994*]. Unfortunately, the interest of Western aid agencies in local air pollution is lower than in transboundary air pollution management problems.

Environmental problems relating to Bulgaria's reliance upon nuclear power are also pressing, and are particularly seen so at the international level. Bulgaria has four Soviet pressurised-water reactors, the most infamous of which is that of Kozloduy. Its safety standards are exceptionally lax, radioactive hot spots have been discovered around the plant, it has a history of accidents and technical problems, including a fire in the radioactive-waste storage facility as well as three near misses when Chernobyl-scale catastrophes were narrowly averted [*Carter, 1993: 52; Waller and Millard, 1992*]. The International Atomic Energy Authority has strongly recommended the closure of the Kozloduy reactor.

The problems in Bulgaria's nuclear industry have been made worse by the collapse of Communism. The disintegration of Comecon and of the Soviet Union has increased the risks in the industry. The old networks, including those relating to construction and management, the supply of fuel and the disposal of nuclear waste, have disappeared. There is also a new risk relating to the unregulated sales of nuclear material to foreign countries [*Tellegen, 1996: 86*].

However, the resolution of Bulgaria's nuclear energy problems has not proved easy. The country is highly dependent on nuclear power and has a shortage of energy supply. As a consequence there have been plans to expand Bulgaria's reliance upon nuclear power, plans which have been strenuously opposed by one of Bulgaria's main environmental groups, *Ekoglasnost*. (Although it should be noted that artificially low prices for energy, which lasted until 1996, encouraged waste production: Bulgaria is estimated to use between two and four times more energy per unit of output than the EU economies [*CEC, 1997*].) The Kozloduy plant accounts for around 40 per cent of Bulgaria's entire electricity output [*Carter, 1993: 44*]. The reliance upon the output of the Kozloduy plant has allowed the Bulgarian government to use Kozloduy as a political tool: putting pressure on the EU to fund alternative energy sources in return for its closure. However, despite temporary closure in the past, at present the Bulgarian government has made no plans to permanently close the plant. The failure to timetable the decommissioning of Kozloduy is related to the more general failure to develop a coherent, national energy policy.

The Administration of Environmental Policy in Post-Communist Bulgaria

Legislative Framework

Like many other ECE countries, much new legislation was passed in Bulgaria in the initial period following the collapse of the old regime. This legislation was often hastily constructed and had to be subject to subsequent, and at times frequent, revisions. The main legislative development in the environmental arena has been the passing of the Environmental Protection Act on 18 October 1991 by the first post-Communist parliament [*Kostov, 1993: 177ff.*]. The law introduced environmental impact assessment (EIA) and the polluter pays principle

[*Tóth Nagy et al., 1994: 142–3*]. The introduction of this law is a welcome step, even though it has been subject to some criticism. The Commission of the European Communities, for example, has argued that the legislation, including regulations on EIA, remains inadequate. Standards, including those relating to air and water emission, are seen as too low and are not always enforced. Furthermore, there are areas not covered by legislation, despite their potentially harmful environmental effects. For example, there is no coherent national policy or legislation for waste management in Bulgaria. There is also a lack of regulation governing chemical substances and agriculture pollution.

There are a number of problems with the functioning of the judiciary in Bulgaria that have a bearing on the effectiveness of its laws, including environmental laws. There is a shortage of qualified judges, which, combined with the complexity of legal procedures and the plethora of new rules, has resulted in severe bottlenecks. As a consequence, the system is not always able to deal with particular cases of infringement, including the imposition of penalties and sentencing. This, combined with corruption, undermines the effective implementation of legislation, including environmental legislation, in Bulgaria [*CEC, 1997*]. The lack of well-defined, enforceable property rights is also a problem.

Policy Initiatives

While difficulties within the legislative process hamper the effective implementation of environmental legislation in Bulgaria, the period since the end of the Communist regime is nevertheless marked by a heightened environmental awareness among policy-makers. This is reflected in numerous new policy initiatives. The 1991 Environmental Act, for example, was followed a year later by an environmental strategy, which was updated in 1994. The National Environmental Action Programme of 1994 laid down requirements with respect to the institutional, legal and regulatory frameworks governing environmental management, and identified areas requiring priority actions. This led in turn to the establishment of the National Environmental Protection Fund in 1995, financed from fines and taxes for industrial pollution and taxes on fuels. The Fund is used to provide grants and loans to municipalities for environmental management. However, given that Bulgaria has a persistent problem with tax collection and low capacity for environmental management at the local level, the impact of this fund remains low.

Nevertheless, some political will to deal with Bulgaria's environmental problems remains, even if it is hampered by difficult circumstances. Bulgaria has, for example, developed a Biodiversity Strategy (1995) and an Ecofund (1993). The Biodiversity Strategy aims to prevent further loss of species and habitats by developing a network of protected areas, introducing sustainable resource-management practices, improving legislation, and investing more resources in environmental education. To date 90 per cent of the funds spent on biodiversity measures have come from foreign sources. Bulgaria has also signed a debt-for-nature swap with Switzerland [*OECD, 1996*]. It is also one of three pilot countries involved in the OECD Environmental Reviews, as agreed at the Lucerne Conference [*OECD, 1996*]. A report has been produced by the OECD's Centre for Co-operation with the Economies in Transition which recognises that some important steps have been taken towards environmental improvement during the transition period. Mentioned are the new basic legislation, the national environmental strategy and attempts to enhance institutional capacity [*OECD, 1996*].

Institutional Capacity

In 1990, a Ministry of the Environment was created and in September 1994 an interministerial committee for environmental protection and development was established [*Stec, 1994*]. The position of the Environment Ministry within the government has generally been a weak one. There have also been persistent problems with regard to the effectiveness of government institutions in Bulgaria which are not confined to the environmental arena alone.

To begin with, there are few regulations governing the behaviour of the civil service in Bulgaria. This has made it easy for political parties to gain control of the civil service, as witnessed by the fact that changes of government have been accompanied by changes at all levels of public administration. In effect, the civil service lacks political independence; decision-making remains centralised; there are few if any effective management and training methods; information exchange between ministries is limited; and there are few auditing and financial control mechanisms. Furthermore, considerable discretionary powers, combined with a lack of clarity in allocating responsibilities and power among civil service departments, has resulted in a great deal of corruption [*CEC, 1997*]. The fact that public-sector wages are low does not help, nor that officials are frequently dependent upon secondary sources of income, which often give rise to conflicts of interest. This has reduced the attractiveness to the young of a civil service career. Furthermore, the failure to depoliticise Bulgaria's system of public administration means that this and the rule of law are seen by the public as instruments of political control.

The slow pace at which reforms are implemented, including within the environmental policy arena, is also due to inadequate resources. This is a consequence of the poor performance of the Bulgarian economy. Effective implementation of environmental policy is also hindered by often lengthy administrative procedures and instability at the apex of government, in particular at the ministerial level, making it difficult to ensure policy continuity.

Besides these more general problems, there are specific problems with respect to the country's institutional capacity to implement environmental legislation and policy. The Environment Ministry is relatively small, employing approximately 140 staff. Monitoring is carried out by the National Centre for Environment and Sustainable Development and enforced by the Ministry and 16 regional inspectorates. Staff in the regional inspectorates suffer from low wages and poor career prospects. There is also considerable fragmentation of responsibility, poor lines of communication between responsible agents, and conflicts of interest. For example, civil servants' involvement in the management of public enterprises can create conflicts of interest with respect to their responsibility to implement environmental policy. To take another example, the Commission of the European Communities also found that ministries are unable to exercise control over state-enterprise managers. This has severe implications for environmental policy, given that industrial production is a major source of Bulgaria's environmental degradation.

As well as problems of implementation arising from its ill-resourced and highly politicised public-administration system, Bulgaria has to rely upon a very narrow range of policy tools to achieve implementation. Market-based tools, such as green taxes and pollution and product charges are of only limited use, given the underdeveloped nature of the country's market economy. This forces reliance upon centralised, command-and-control mechanisms, which, as we have seen, are weak.

Local Level

Administratively, Bulgaria is organised around nine decentralised, regional arms of central government, in which a regional governor coordinates action by the state. Below this level there are 255 municipalities. The law of 1991 gives municipalities responsibility for managing local public services. There are plans to introduce administrative reform and to replace the nine regions with between 12 and 21 districts with self-government rights, although to date, these plans have not been fully formulated. In the meantime, local authorities lack any effective autonomy and are dependent upon the state for funding. The lack of adequate staffing at the municipal level as well as inadequate resources and a lack of political will, have combined to hamper the effective implementation of environmental legislation at the local level in Bulgaria. There is also a serious problem with corruption, particularly at the local level [*CEC, 1997*]. It is not surprising then to find that the involvement of local environmental interests in the policy-making process remains very limited.

The Expression of Environmental Interests in Post-Communist Bulgaria

The Role of the Environmental Movement in the Fall of the Old Regime

More so than in any other ECE country, it was concern about the deteriorating environment and its impact upon health that sparked off the protest which led to the collapse of the old regime in Bulgaria. This occurred within the context of Soviet *perestroika*. Environmental protest in Bulgaria began at the local level, with the formation of the Social Committee for Environmental Protection of the Town of Ruse [*Baker,* *1996*]. This was a locally-based environmental protest group formed in the town of Ruse to protest against the health hazards posed by chlorine gas emissions from a Romanian chemical plant across the border. Its significance lies in the fact that the Ruse Committee was subsequently to help spawn the broader, national environmental group *Ekoglasnost.* *Ekoglasnost* played a leading role in the protests that lead to the collapse of the old regime (for the early history of *Ekoglasnost* see Baumgartl [*1992*]; Carter [*1993*]). In December 1989 another environmental group, the Green Party, was formed. At the same time other groups were forming to promote human rights, religious freedom or to revive old political parties [*Bell,* *1993: 35*]. The involvement of environmentalists in the protests that led to the toppling of the old regime was risky: many street demonstrations were violently attacked by the police, and in October 1989 40 *Ekoglasnost* activists were beaten up and arrested.

While primarily an environmental group, *Ekoglasnost* went on to become a key actor on the wider post-Communist political stage in Bulgaria. This is because it was a central component in the opposition forum, the Union of Democratic Forces, which was formed in December 1989 (for a history of this see Crawford [*1996: 66–8*]). This political party now (1997) holds power in Bulgaria. As a consequence of this political engagement, to understand the impact of the transition process on the expression of environmental interest in Bulgaria attention has to be paid to the involvement of environmental groups with party politics and the electoral process.

Involvement with Party and Electoral Politics

Environmental groups have put themselves forward as candidates within the UDF in all elections held in Bulgaria since 1989. However, they have been plagued by internal divisions. During the initial transition period many of *Ekoglasnost's* members joined the Green Party and both groups suffered internal divisions. As a consequence by the second free election of October 1991 environmentalists had split into two separate *Ekoglasnosts* – the Movement Ekoglasnost (*Ekoglasnost dvizhenie*), which continued to take part in the UDF, and the Political Club (*Politicheski Klub*), which later joined the BSP in the Socialist Alliance – and two green parties – the Green Party and the Conservative Ecological Party. In this election, however, many of the green candidates stood under the label of the UDF, which resulted in a coalition government led by the UDF.

Even though this victory allowed the environmental movement to enter parliament with some degree of strength, its potential was weakened by their internal divisions. When Filip Dimitrov, as leader of the UDF, became premier in 1991, for example, he was a member of the splinter group the Conservative Ecological Party. Dimitrov started his political career as a legal advisor and vice-president in the Green Party (for a history of the Green Party, see Baumgartl [*1994*]). However the splinter group which he joined showed a weak commitment to environmental goals. The splits within the environmentalists are mirrored by the wider disunity of the UDF.

Nevertheless, the involvement of environmentalists in party politics in Bulgaria has allowed them to hold a number of key positions at different levels of government. They held two ministerial posts in the coalition government of Popov, which was formed in December 1990. At the beginning of 1991, furthermore, environmentalists held the position of mayor of Sofia as well as president of the UDF. The vice-president of the UDF parliamentary club, Edvin Sugarev, was a member of *Ekoglasnost* as were two past Ministers for Finance and for the Environment, Ivan Kostov and Valentin Vasilev.

However, political instability, internal party feuding and party splits, the high turnover rate of government, combined with economic difficulties, weakened the capacity of environmental parties to effectively utilise these positions. Williams has found that across ECE there are three main reasons for the absence of strong green parties: internal division, Communist infiltration, and difficulties in party formation as other parties integrated environmental issues into their policies [*Williams, 1991: 18*]. In Bulgaria internal divisions are a main contributor to weakened party support and party ineffectiveness. Communist infiltration also played a role in the early transition period, causing party splits, although there is little evidence of a real conspiracy. However, an important factor for Bulgaria is that the centrality of the environment declined in the face of the hardships brought by the transition. Expensive investment in pollution abatement technology or even environmental auditing are seen as having the potential to jeopardise privatisation and foreign investment and are extremely unpopular. The feeling that the economy has to be developed before attention can be turned to environmental management has become widespread [*Baumgartl, 1997*].

The expression of environmental interest has taken other forms than involvement in party politics. In both Bulgaria and across ECE environmental protest has also occurred at the grass-root level, expressing itself as a social movement – as seen in the rise of environmental non-governmental organisations (NGOs).

The Bulgarian Environmental Movement

A major environmental umbrella organisation in Bulgaria is the Union of Bulgarian Foundations (UBF), which was established in 1992. It now represents approximately 63 groups drawn from foundations and associations throughout Bulgaria. One of its main aims is to foster collaboration between NGOs. It is mostly financed and supported by universities and foundations from the USA, but it also has European partners, including the Prince of Wales Business Leaders Forum in Britain and the Phare Civil Society Development Programme of the EU.

NGOs in Bulgaria have also formed into the Green Parliament, which was founded primarily to monitor, from an environmental point of view, proposed laws or amendments to existing laws. The impact of the Green Parliament has been limited because some NGOs see it partly as a party-political organisation and, furthermore, it lacks recognition by the political authorities.

There is also the Danube Forum Experts Group, an umbrella group of Romanian and Bulgarian NGOs, whose members include the Ecologist Youth Club of Romania, the Regional Environmental Centre (REC) in Budapest and *Ekoglasnost*. The Forum has called for increased public participation in decision making on the Danube and wishes to see more funding given to NGOs so as to enable them to act as environmental watchdogs for the Danube.

International support has been very important for the development of environmental NGOs in Bulgaria. The REC in Budapest, for example, has helped with the development of NGO capacity. It has also facilitated access to information on international environmental-management strategies aimed at ECE, including the environmental action plans agreed to at the Lucerne Conference. The production of a Manual by the REC has also proved invaluable, providing much needed guidance on participation [*Tóth Nagy et al., 1994*].

Despite the criticisms that have been made of foreign involvement in the development of NGOs in ECE, including that it has the effect of isolating environmental activists from the grass roots, in Bulgaria all the main environmental groups claim to have close links with the grass roots.[3] Among the main environmental groups, the movement *Ekoglasnost* seems to maintain the most effective network of activists. Several branches exist throughout the country and these are able to carry out local activities without contact with the capital.

However, several former activists have abandoned the movement and are now employed by big firms, have joined political parties or government or have left the country. As a consequence, the environmental movement has been stripped of its political expertise and experience. In a country where dialogue between government and the social partners remains very underdeveloped it comes as no surprise to find that environmental NGOs have not been able to establish an effective working relationship with government. Furthermore, these are serious obstacles to increasing public participation by environmental NGOs in the environmental policy arena.

To begin with, environmental NGOs lack resources. Before the Second World War, there was a tradition of philanthropic donations and sponsorship in Bulgaria. This tradition, however, was broken during the Communist years. Today, there is little sponsorship and a lack of financial support from government. This forces NGOs to rely almost exclusively upon the limited income they receive from membership fees and, when available, grants from international foundations or aid projects.

The development of NGOs in Bulgaria has also been restricted by a 40-year-old law on individuals and families [*Tóth Nagy et al., 1994: 150*]. This law also restricts NGO participation in international environmental projects, as it creates uncertainty as to their legal right to contribute to, or criticise, project proposals [*Paskalev, 1994*]. There is also a lack of clear procedures, such as a freedom of information act, giving NGOs access to relevant information. Lobbying for a change in the law that would make it easier for NGOs to form and operate, has been undertaken by both the Green Parliament and the UBF. However, frequent changes of government coalitions have made it very difficult to pursue this. The chances of changes in the law in the near future is deemed low by experts.[4] Nevertheless, the 1991 Environmental Protection Act does give NGOs a number of rights, including being considered as relevant parties to be informed as to the findings of an EIA. It also allows NGOs or citizens to lodge a claim against offenders to stop damage and eliminate the consequences of pollution. This may seem weak but is nonetheless important.

Changing the law, however, is only one step in removing the obstacles to effective public participation in environmental policy making in Bulgaria. Deeper changes are also needed. The lack of a tradition of participatory democracy has also to be addressed. Similarly, attention needs to be paid to the lack of faith in the responsiveness, and often the integrity, of public officials and the lack of impartiality in the application of the rule of law. Participation is also linked with the development of civil society: it is both an agent for the development of civil society and a precondition of it. In Bulgaria the development of civil society is related to the need to redefine the rights of the individual in relation to the state. This is not easy, because in Bulgaria's political instability, and the failure to politically and economically complete the revolution of 1989 means that political elites fear that further steps towards democratisation may undermine the stability of their regime.

The International Dimensions of Environmental Management

International Environmental Initiatives

How the transition process affects the capacity of Bulgaria to manage its environment is of international significance. This is because the country is a major contributor to transboundary air pollution problems. Bulgaria, for example, is one of Europe's bigger producers of transboundary SO_2 pollution [*Carter, 1993: 43*]. The international community is also interested in the management of transboundary water-borne pollution, some of which originates in Bulgaria.

As a consequence, the transition period has seen the rise of international environmental programmes, such as the Environmental Programme for the Danube River Basin, which was launched in 1991. This Programme is the result of an agreement by international donors and the governments of the Danube countries to coordinate investment aimed at improving the ecological management of the Danube river basin [*CEC, 1992*]. A separate grant from the Global Environmental Facility is aimed at the formulation of a long-term management plan for the Danube Delta [*EAP, 1993: II/12*]. While the flow of aid for this Programme from Western donors is mainly directed towards Hungary and Slovakia, Bulgaria, Romania and Ukraine nonetheless receive financial aid from it to help them manage the Danube in a more environmentally-effective way [*Connolly et al., 1995*]. Another such programme is the Black Sea Environmental Management Programme, which was initiated by the Global Environmental Facility and operates in conjunction with governments within the region, including Bulgaria.

These programmes are extremely important because they provide concrete help in ameliorating environmental pollution in the region and at the same time help develop long-term environmental-management programmes. But they also play another strategic function: they provide the governments of the region with environmental-management models that can be applied elsewhere. At the same time they facilitate the development of expertise and experience in pollution-abatement strategies and technology.

Nevertheless these programmes have been criticised because they often lack adequate resources. In general, Western assistance amounts to less than seven per cent of the environmental funding needed in ECE (see Kolk and van der Weij, this volume). Despite pressure from ECE governments to increase the flow of funds, the Lucerne Conference gave a clear message to ECE governments: they themselves are going to have to provide the bulk of the growing price of environmental protection and management in the region [*Baumgartl, 1993*]. Furthermore, while acknowledging that improving environmental protection will require substantial investment, the EU has pointed out that the sums involved go well beyond what they are capable of financing. Hence, it has urged ECE countries to seek investment from the private sector and international financial institutions. This presents particular difficulties for Bulgaria, given that its unstable political, economic and legal climate continues to discourage foreign investment [*CEC, 1997*].

There are also problems in relation to the lack of appropriate accountability mechanisms for monitoring international aid. For the international community the level of aid is only part of the story: equally important are the existence of institutional, administrative and legal arrangements in the recipient countries that can ensure adequate capacity to absorb the aid.

The EU has played a major role in these international environmental-management programmes, an involvement that is closely linked with its wider, politically more strategic, involvement with the transition process in ECE.

Bulgaria and the EU

Seeking membership: In 1993 the EU and Bulgaria signed a Europe Agreement which came into force in February 1995. The Agreement aimed at achieving convergence between the EU and Bulgaria in a wide range of areas with a view to eventual Bulgarian membership of the EU, as agreed by the Copenhagen Summit in June 1993. The details for the preparation for membership were set out following the European Council meeting in Essen in 1994. This led to the publication in 1995 of the Commission's White Paper on preparation of the so-called Associated Countries for integration into the Union [*CEC, 1995*].

The conditions for membership include the establishment of stable institutions guaranteeing democracy and of a functioning market economy. The applicant also has to show an ability to take on the obligations of membership, including political, economic and monetary union. Achieving these conditions is seen as a gradual process, with initial priority given to the development of a market economy, reform of the administrative system, and the creation of a stable economic and monetary environment [*CEC, 1997*]. This, in turn, involves price liberalisation, structural change and reform of the financial sector.

Despite frequent changes of government, the objective of membership has been held by all governments in Bulgaria since 1990. There is broad consensus among political actors on this goal. When Bulgaria's application for membership was lodged in 1995, a government memorandum accompanying the application stressed the importance of membership in the consolidation of the process of democratisation and as an international acknowledgement of Bulgaria's political maturity. Membership, it was stressed, is also seen as an important aid to further economic development and as making a positive impact on the security and stability of the region [*CEC, 1997*].

Policy initiatives and PHARE: As part of its involvement with the EU, Bulgaria has participated in PHARE. However, the Commission has found that Bulgaria has not been able to take full advantage of this programme, due to a lack of momentum for reform within the country. As a consequence it has found that the assistance it has provided for enterprise restructuring, reform of the financial sector, privatisation and modernisation of agriculture has been less than successful. The Commission hopes that the change of government following the elections of 1997 may improve this situation [*CEC, 1997*].

The Commission has also been critical of Bulgaria's involvement in cross-border projects funded by the EU. For example, implementation of the Cross-Border Co-operation Programme with Greece has been severely delayed, due to what the Commission regards as Bulgaria's 'inability to match its constructive regional role with administrative and managerial measures' [*CEC, 1997: Preface*].

Approximation of environmental legislation: The Europe Agreement signed between Bulgaria and the EU laid down a number of conditions governing the management of Bulgaria's environment. First, it required that economic development be guided by the principle of sustainable development; second, that policies incorporate environmental considerations; and third, that environmental policy be an area for approximation of legislation. This latter condition was recently reinforced by the European Commissioner responsible for the environment, Ritt Bjerregaard, during a meeting in Sofia. Calling on ECE countries to give immediate consideration to the approximation of environmental legislation, she indicated that doing so would help smooth the way in future accession negotiations (*European Union Newsletter for Central Europe*, No.53, 1994, p.10). In return for fulfilling these conditions the environment would become a priority in bilateral programmes.

However, in its 1997 assessment, the Commission found that Bulgaria's serious environmental problems have not been effectively addressed during the transition period [*CEC, 1997*]. In particular, they found that approximation of Bulgarian legislation remains low in most areas, including air and water quality, waste management, chemical substances, radiation protection, and nature protection. Furthermore they see the newly introduced EIA legislation as weak and have found little effective compliance with EU environmental standards [*CEC, 1997*]. As a consequence the Commission concluded that 'effective compliance with a number of pieces of legislation requiring a sustained high level of investment and considerable administrative efforts (for example urban waste water treatment, drinking water, aspects of waste management and air pollution legislation) could be achieved only in the very long term' [*CEC, 1997: 3.6*].

The problems in the environmental policy field are reflected in a wider failure of Bulgaria to adequately respond to the challenge of preparation for membership. Not only in the environmental field, but in all the major policy fields under consideration, the Commission found a very limited transposition and implementation of Community legislation. The country has, as yet, failed to develop a functioning market economy, has a dysfunctional financial system, lacks strong legal institutions, proper regulatory frameworks, and has a weak public administration system [*CEC, 1997*].

Putting membership on hold: The deep economic problems facing Bulgaria, combined with institutional and political instability and administrative incapacity, has effectively ruled out Bulgarian's membership of the EU in the medium term. In this context, the large volume of new legislation that relates to membership, being drafted or awaiting adoption by the national parliaments has overloaded the system; and subsequently, the legislative progress has slowed. The administrative machinery of state is also lagging, which in turn impedes implementation. At the root of this lies the failure of Bulgaria to effectively complete its 1989 revolution.

Nevertheless, the failure to join the EU in its next enlargement is not viewed negatively by all Bulgarians. In 1996 only 27 per cent of the population believed that their future lies in closer ties with European Union (*Central and Eastern Eurobarometer*, No.6, 1996). A further 23 per cent would like to see their future lie with closer links with Russia.

Conclusion

In the initial period following the collapse of the old regime a great deal of optimism existed in Bulgaria: the solution to its economic, political and indeed environmental problems were seen as lying with the adoption of Western economic and political models. However, Bulgaria has found it difficult to embrace these models. Both politically and economically its revolution remains incomplete. Bulgaria's transition to democracy is hindered by the lack of democratic traditions and the weak nature of its civil society. This has allowed the old elites to retain their powers, and has hampered the reform of the system of public administration and of national and subnational levels of government. The adoption of Western economic models, in particular marketisation, is also hindered. Quite simply, Bulgaria's fragile economic position makes it difficult to introduce effective economic reform.

Western models have proved unhelpful to post-Communist Bulgaria. The ease with which the country could adopt these models and their ability to help the completion of the 1989 revolution may well have been exaggerated. Furthermore, restricted Western support has forced the country to rely on its own limited capacities and resources. At the same time, its involvement with the West has locked Bulgaria into a very dependent position on the international stage. This is evident by the reluctance of the EU to fully integrate Bulgaria into its fold, while at the same time imposing its own notions of good governance and economic practice on the country.

In the meantime, the likelihood of an environmentally-sustainable future in Bulgaria remains depressingly low. In all policy fields, not just the environmental arena, policy makers have to act under severe financial, institutional and political constraints. Eight years after the overthrow of the old Communist regime, Bulgaria has still a number of environmental problems that require urgent attention and has failed to introduce proactive strategic programmes to enable it to effectively manage its environment.

It is difficult to see how Bulgaria's environmental problems can be addressed in the short, or indeed, even the medium term. Bulgaria's environmental problems will not disappear with further attempts at democratisation and marketisation, as even a cursory examination of the environmental problems of Western Europe will show. More stringent environmental management may give rise to further factory closures and job losses which will increase social dislocation and undermine the already fragile transition process. Indeed, the transition to democracy and a market economy may even exacerbate Bulgaria's environmental problems, and the difficulty it faces in trying to resolve them.

NOTES

1. It is too early to assess the success of the mass voucher privatisation (shares in 1,300 state enterprises totalling US$2.8 billion), started in January 1996.
2. Interview with Aleksander Aleksandrov, the then secretary of the environmental movement *Ekoglasnost*, Ruse, 4 Nov.1994.
3. Interviews with Edvin Sugarev (then leader of the anti-Communist Movement Ekoglasnost), Stefan Gajtandziev (one of the founders of *Ekoglasnost* and joined the Political Club after the split), and Ljobomir Ivanov (a biologist and former member of the Green Party) respectively, 18 Nov. 1991.
4. Interviews with Tzevatana Dimitrova (a member of the NGO Green Future Alliance), Plamen Peykov (a member of the UBF), and Margrita Maleeva (director of the Sofia office of the REC), Nov. 1994.

REFERENCES

Baker, S. (1996), 'The Scope for East–West Co-operation', in A. Blowers and P. Glasbergen (eds.), *Environmental Policy in an International Context: Prospects, Vol. 3*, London: Arnold, pp.135–65.

Baumgartl, B. (1992), 'Environmental Protest as a Vehicle for Transition. The Case of Ekoglasnost in Bulgaria', in A. Vari and T. Pal (eds.), *Environment and Democratic Transition: Politics and Policy in Central Eastern and Eastern Europe*, New York: Kluwer Academic Publishers, pp.157–75.

Baumgartl, B. (1993), '"Realism" and No Fresh Money for the Environment', *Radio Free Europe/Radio Liberty Research Report*, Vol.2, No.3, pp.41–8.

Baumgartl, B. (1994), 'Green Protest against Red Politics: Environmentalsis' Contribution to Bulgaria's Transition', in W. Rüdig (ed.), *Green Politics Three*, Edinburgh: Edinburgh University Press, pp.154–91.

Baumgartl, B. (1997), *Transition and Sustainability: Interest and Actors in Eastern European Environmental Policy*, The Hague: Kluwer Law International.

Bell, J.D. (1993), 'Bulgaria', in S. White, J. Batt and P.G. Lewis (eds.), *Developments in Eastern European Politics*, Basingstoke: Macmillan, pp.83–97.

Carter, F.W. (1993), 'Bulgaria', in F.W. Carter and D. Turnock (eds.), *Environmental Problems in Eastern Europe*, London: Routledge, pp.38–62.

CEC (Commission of the European Communities) (1992), *Environmental Programme for the Danube River Basin*, proposed Programme Work Plan, Brussels: CEC–DG XI.

CEC (1995), *White Paper on the Preparation of the Associate Countries of Central and Eastern Europe for Integration into the Internal Market of the Union*, Brussels: Commission.

CEC (1997), *Commission Opinion on Bulgaria's Application for Membership of the European Union*, COM(97)2008 final, Luxembourg: Office for Official Publications of the European Communities.

Commission Spokesman Service (1996), 'Address at the Informal Meeting between the Commission and Environment Ministers from Central and Eastern European Countries by Hans Van Den Broek – Brussels, 16 Sept. 1996 – Centre Borschette', *Speech*, No.212 (16 Sept. 1996).

Connolly, B., Gutner, T. and H. Bedarff (1995), 'Organisational Inertia and Environmental Assistance to Eastern Europe', in R. Keohane (ed.), *Institutions for Environmental Aid. Pitfalls and Promise*, Cambridge, MA: Harvard University, pp.12–29.

Crawford, K. (1996), *East Central European Politics Today*, Manchester: Manchester University Press.

Dimitrova, T. (1994), *Opportunities for Environmentally-Friendly Development for Bulgarian Industry*, Sofia: Boris Hranov.

EAP (Environmental Action Programme) (1993), *Immediate Environmental Action Programme for Central and Eastern Europe*, document for the Ministerial Conference Environment-for-Europe, Lucerne, 28–30 April.

Economist Intelligence Unit (1995), *Country Report Bulgaria*, London: Economist Intelligence Unit.

Economist Intelligence Unit (1996), *Country Report Bulgaria*, London: Economist Intelligence Unit.

European Training Foundation (1997), *Vocational Education and Training in Bulgaria. Country Report*, Turin: European Training Foundation.

Genov, N. (ed.) (1994), *Riskove na Prexodu. Natsionalno i Globalno Razvitie*, Sofija: Jusautor.

Georgieva, K. (1992), 'Environmental Policy in Southeastern Europe: Green Desires, Gray Realities', *Environmental Impact Assessment Review*, Vol.12, No.3, pp.239–44.

Gradev, V. (1995), 'The Rediscovery of the Balkans', in B. Baumgartl and A. Favell (eds), *New Xenophobia in Europe*, The Hague: Kluwer Law International, pp.56–67.

Kostov, D. (1993), *Gorsko i Prirodozstitno Pravo. Cbornik Normativni Aktove*, Sofija: Universitetsko Izdatelstvo.

Ministry of the Environment (1991), *Green Book of the Environment for 1989*, Sofia: Ministry of the Environment.

National Observatory Bulgaria (1997), *Report on Vocational Education and Training*, Sofia: PMU–Education.

OECD (Organisation for Economic Co-operation and Development) (1994), *Employment and Unemployment in Economies in Transition – Employment and Labour Market Statistics*, Paris: OECD.

OECD (1996), *Environmental Performance Reviews – Bulgaria*, Centre for Co-operation with the Economies in Transition, Paris: OECD.

Oschlies, W. (1987), *Schwebelstaub auf Rosenblüten. Umweltsorgen in Bulgarien*, Köln and Wien: Böhlau Verlag.

Paskalev, A. (1994), 'A Short Review of the NGO Danube Forum, International Activities and Some Problems in Bulgaria', unpublished paper, Sofia: Ekoglasnost.

Pishev, O. (1991), 'The Bulgarian Economy: Transition or Turmoil', in O. Sjöberg and M.L. Wyzan (eds), *Economic Changes in the Balkan States: Albania, Bulgaria, Romania and Yugoslavia*, London: Pinter, pp.101–14.

Russell, J. (1991), *Environmental Issues in Eastern Europe: Setting and Agenda*, London: Royal Institute of International Affairs.

Schaffer, J. (1992), 'Bulgariens Umwelt in Gefahr?', manuscript, Bologna: The Johns Hopkins University.

Sjöberg, O. and M.L. Wyzan (1991), 'The Balkan States: Struggling along the Road to the Market from Europe's Periphery', in O. Sjöberg and M.L. Wyzan (eds.), *Economic Changes in the Balkan States: Albania, Bulgaria, Romania and Yugoslavia*, London: Pinter, pp.1–15.

Stanchev, K. (1992), 'Environmental Protection Policy in Bulgaria: Background, Inherited State of Affairs and Possible Ways Out', unpublished paper, Sofia.

Stec, Stephen (ed.) (1994), 'CEELI Law Report', *The REC Bulletin*, Vol.4, No.3, p.22.

Tellegen, E. (1996), 'Environmental Conflicts in Transforming Economies: Central and Eastern Europe', in P. Sloep and A. Blowers (eds.), *Environmental Policy in an International Context, Vol. 2*, London: Arnold, pp.67–96.

Tóth Nagy, Magdolna, Bowman, Margaret, Dusik, Jiri, Jendroska, Jerzy, Stec, Stephen, van der Ziep, Karel and János Zlinszky (eds.) (1994), *Manual on Public Participation in Environmental Decisionmaking: Current Practice and Future Possibilities in Central and Eastern Europe*, Budapest: Regional Environmental Center for Central and Eastern Europe.

UNECE (United Nations Economic Commission for Europe) (1993), *Economic Survey of Europe in 1992–1993*, New York: United Nations.

Waller, Michael and Frances Millard (1992), 'Environmental Politics in Eastern Europe', *Environmental Politics*, Vol.1, No.2, pp.159–85.

Williams, C. (1991), 'From Iron into Green Curtain: The Environmental Crisis in Central and Eastern Europe and the Emerging Green Movement/Parties 1989–91', paper prepared for the Conference on New Perspectives for Social Democracy in Central and Eastern Europe, Vrije Universiteit Brussel, Brussels, Oct.

Wolf, J.M. (1991), 'Bulgaria – Agriculture and Natural Resources: Environmental Concerns', study for the US Agency for International Development, Bethseda, MD: Development Aid International.

World Bank (1994), 'Bulgaria. Environmental Strategy Study – Update and Folow-up', confidential draft, Report No.13493BUL, Washington, DC: World Bank.

Wyzan, M.L. (1991), 'The Bulgarian Economy in the Immediate Post-Zhivkov Era', in O. Sjöberg and M.L. Wyzan (eds.), *Economic Changes in the Balkan States: Albania, Bulgaria, Romania and Yugoslavia*, London: Pinter, pp.83–100.

Notes on Contributors

Susan Baker is Senior Lecturer in European Social Research in the School of Social and Administrative Studies at University of Wales Cardiff. Previously she was Associate Professor in Public Administration at the Erasmus University Rotterdam. Her most recent relevant publications include *Sustainable Development: Theory, Policy and Practice within the European Union* (edited with M. Kousis, D. Richardson and S.C. Young, London: Routledge, 1997); 'Environmental Policy in East and Central Europe: The Role of the EU', in P. Glasbergen (ed.), *Enviromental Policy in an International Context* (London: Arnold, 1995).

Bernd Baumgartl is currently working at the European Training Foundation, Turin, the EU agency responsible for reform in education and training in the countries eligible for the PHARE, Tacis and Meda programmes. He is also part-teaching at the University of Turin. He received his Ph.D. in Social and Political Sciences from the European University Institute, Florence. His publications include *Transition and Sustainablility — Actors and Interests in Eastern European Environmental Policy* (1997), and he has co-edited *New Xenophobia in Europe* (with Arian Favell, 1995).

Simina Dragomirescu, Institute of Management, Bucharest, was formerly an engineer working on hydropower projects. She is now concerned with the training of managers to operate effectively in the market economy. She has travelled widely to conferences in various parts of Europe to discuss such matters as business incubation, privatisation and management training programmes. Her interest in the environment arises largely through her work with research and development organisations.

Adam Fagin is Lecturer in Eastern European Politics at the University of Portsmouth. He has published 'Environment and Transition in the Czech Republic', *Environmental Politics*, Vol.3, No.3 (1994), and 'Incorporating Community: Complications to Theories of Democratic Transition in East and Central Europe', in R. Lenke (ed.), *The State of the Academy – New Reflections on Political Studies* (London: Network, 1995).

Kenneth Hanf is Senior Lecturer in the Department of Public Administration of the Erasmus University Rotterdam, the Netherlands. His research has dealt primarily with the implementation of environmental policy. Most recently this work has focused on the relationships between national policy processes and international cooperation in dealing with transboundary environmental problems.

Petr Jehlička is Lecturer in Political Geography at the Charles University, Prague, Czech Republic and a Ph.D. student at the University of Cambridge Global Security Programme. His publications include 'Czechoslovak Parliamentary Elections 1990', with T. Kostelecky and L. Sykora, in J. O'Loughlin and H. v.d. Wusten (eds.), *The New Political Geography of Eastern Europe* (London: Belhaven Press, 1993); 'Environmentalism in Europe: An East–West Comparison', in C. Rootes and H. Davies (eds.), *A New Europe: Social Change and Political Transformation* (London: UCL Press, 1994).

Ans Kolk is Senior Research Fellow at the Institute for Environmental Management, University of Amsterdam, the Netherlands. Her areas of research and publications are international environmental politics and international political economy. Recent publications in English include *Forests in International Environmental Politics: International Organisations, NGOs and the Brazilian Amazon* (International Books, 1996), and articles on Dutch environmental policy (in *International Environmental Affairs*, 1996) and environmental regulation (in *The International Journal of Environment and Pollution*, forthcoming).

Frances Millard is Senior Lecturer in the Politics of the Visegrad States at the University of Essex. Her main research interests lie in the politics of social policy in Eastern Europe and post-Communist political developments, particularly in regards to Poland. She has written numerous articles dealing with health, welfare, environmental issues, political parties and elections. Her most recent book is *The Anatomy of the New Poland* (Aldershot: Edward Elgar, 1994).

Cristina Muica is a researcher in the Romanian Academy's Geography Institute in Bucharest. As a plant specialist she is keenly aware of the consequences of agricultural mismanagement and high atmospheric pollution levels. She had made several studies of the way in which the privatisation and land restitution processes have impacted on the vegetation and sees dangers in the return to small-scale family farming through overgrazing on low quality pastures and a restoration of cropping on unstable hill slopes.

Laurence J. O'Toole, Jr. is Professor in the Department of Political Science and Senior Research Associate in the Institute of Community and Area Development of the University of Georgia (USA). Much of his research focuses on implementation and institutional arrangements for environmental policy. He is author of a forthcoming book on acidification policy in Hungary.

Juraj Podoba is a researcher in the Institute of Ethnology of the Slovak Academy of Sciences, Bratislava, where he obtained his doctorate. He was Visiting Lecturer at the Zürich University, Switzerland and Comenius University, Bratislava and a Visiting Fellow at the University of Cambridge, UK. His academic interests include, first, historical issues, including cultural diversity and development in the Carpathians; social, cultural and axiological changes connected with the process of industrialisation in Central Europe; and social processes in agriculture during the period of communist regime. Second, he is interested in issues related to the current period of transition. In this area he focuses on inter-ethnic relations in Eastern Europe and the link between environmental issues and nationalism.

David Turnock is a Reader in Geography at the University of Leicester, specialising in the regional geography of Eastern Europe. He has written extensively on Romania, particularly about the growth of the economy and the associated environmental problems. Along with Frank Carter he has edited a book on *Environmental Problems in Eastern Europe* (London: Routledge, 1993) and is currently preparing a new edition of this work.

Ewout van der Weij (M.A. in Political Science and East European Studies) was project co-ordinator on environmental policy-making with Stichting Milieukontakt Oost-Europa, a Dutch NGO which serves environmental citizens' organisations in Central and Eastern Europe, and the former Soviet Union. Currently he works as policy adviser to the parliamentarians in the Dutch Labour Party in the areas of transport, public works and environment.

Michael Waller is Professor of Politics and Director of European Studies at Keele University, UK.

Index

TITLES OF RELATED INTEREST

Sustainable Development in Western Europe
Coming to Terms with Agenda 21

Tim O'Riordan *and* Heather Voisey, *University of East Anglia (Eds)*

The transition to sustainable development will test government and democracy in a fundamentally radical way. There is probably no such end state as truly sustainable development so the pathways towards it are endless.

This series of essays looks at three elements of sustainable development in terms of the institutional challenge they pose, and from the viewpoint of five European Union Member States.

Contributors: Liv Astrid Sverdrup, Christiane Beuermann, Bernhard Burdick, Teresa G Ribeiro, Valdemar J Rodrigues, Panos Fousekis, Josheph N Lekakis, and David Wilkinson.

184 pages   1997
0 7146 4830 2   cloth   0 7146 4376 9 paper
A special issue of the journal Environmental Politics

Ecology and Democracy

Freya Mathews, *La Trobe University, Australia (Ed)*

What is the optimal political framework for environmental reform – reform on a scale commensurate with the global ecological crisis? In particular, how adequate are liberal forms of parliamentary democracy to the challenge posed by this crisis? These are the questions pondered by the contributors to this volume. Exploration of the possibilities of democracy gives rise to certain common themes. These are the relation between ecological morality and political structures or procedures and the question of the structure of decision-making and distribution of information in political systems. The idea of 'democracy without traditional boundaries' is discussed as a key both to environmentalism in an age of global ecology and to the revitalisation of democracy itself in a world of increasingly protean constituencies and mutable boundaries.

280 pages   1996
0 7146 4252 5 paper
A special issue of the journal Environmental Politics

FRANK CASS PUBLISHERS
Newbury House, 900 Eastern Avenue, Newbury Park, Ilford, Essex IG2 7HH
Tel: +44 (0)181 599 8866 Fax: +44 (0)181 599 0984 E-mail: info@frankcass.com
NORTH AMERICA
c/o ISBS, 5804 NE Hassalo Street, Portland, OR 97213 3644, USA
Tel: 1 800 944 6190 Fax: 503 280 8832 E-mail cass@isbs.com
Website: http://www.frankcass.com

Rio: Unravelling the Consequences

Caroline Thomas, *Southampton University (Ed)*

The interdisciplinary collection of essays investigates whether UNCED and its output were appropriate for averting global environmental and developmental catastrophe. The intellectual debate inside and outside UNCED has been dominated by powerful entrenched interests which marginalise rival interpretations of the crisis and block possible alternative ways forward. The crisis is therefore being tackled by a continuation of the very policies that largely caused it in the first place.

244 pages   1994; repr.   1996
0 7146 4110 3 paper
A special issue of the journal Environmental Politics

Networks for Water Policy
A Comparative Perspective

H Bressers, *University of Twente*, L J O'Toole, Jr., *University of Georgia* and J Richardson, *University of Warwick (Eds)*

Networks models for analysing public policy have become widely used in recent years. This volume assesses the network idea by applying a common perspective on network analysis to the constellations involved in water policy formation and implementation in several countries – England and Wales, Germany, Hungary, the Netherlands and the United States – and at the level of the European Union. In addition to offering lively studies of such contemporary developments as the privatization of water in England, the dynamics of transformation in the changing setting of Central Europe and the emergent policy influence of the European Union, this book is an important addition to the literature on policy networks, comparative policy and environmental policy.

273 pages   1995
0 7146 4642 3 cloth
A special issue of the journal Environmental Politics

FRANK CASS PUBLISHERS
Newbury House, 900 Eastern Avenue, Newbury Park, Ilford, Essex IG2 7HH
Tel: +44 (0)181 599 8866 Fax: +44 (0)181 599 0984 E-mail: info@frankcass.com
NORTH AMERICA
c/o ISBS, 5804 NE Hassalo Street, Portland, OR 97213 3644, USA
Tel: 1 800 944 6190 Fax: 503 280 8832 E-mail cass@isbs.com
Website: http://www.frankcass.com